THACKERAY
Prodigal Genius

BY JOHN CAREY

The Violent Effigy: *A Study of Dickens' Imagination*

THACKERAY

Prodigal Genius

JOHN CAREY

Faber & Faber
3 Queen Square London

First published in 1977
by Faber and Faber Limited
3 Queen Square London WC1

Printed in Great Britain by
Western Printing Services Ltd, Avonmouth

British Library Cataloguing
in Publication Data
Carey, John   Thackeray
1. Thackeray, William Makepeace
–Criticism and interpretation
823′.8   PR5638
ISBN 0–571–11126–2

Contents

	Introduction	9
1.	Life	11
2.	Light and Colour	34
3.	Commodities	58
4.	Food and Drink	79
5.	Theatre	103
6.	Time	125
7.	What Went Wrong	150
8.	*Vanity Fair*	177
	Postscript	202
	Index	204

Introduction

Thackeray was a prodigal himself, and intrigued by prodigals: the Prodigal Son is, in one guise or another, an almost permanent inhabitant of his fiction. Perhaps his prodigality was rooted in his self-doubt – a way of asserting that life in Vanity Fair should not, after all, be taken very seriously. Anyway, it had a decisive effect on his career. He squandered his fortune; he was an incorrigible gambler; he ate and drank with ultimately fatal abandon; he refused to husband his gifts. He threw away brilliant impromptu things in conversation, and did not bother – as critics have endlessly complained – to remove the marks of carelessness from his writing.

Nevertheless, the case for his imaginative vitality must largely rest, nowadays, on the products of what such critics might regard as his most prodigal period – the years before 1848, when he was lavishing his creative energies on satirical articles and picture-gallery gossip and suchlike literary journalism. Because the Victorians preferred his later and staider works, they have come to be regarded, in critical tradition, as the major achievements. Consequently they, apart from *Vanity Fair*, are all of Thackeray that is kept in print today – and today's readers, having tried them, mostly hasten to try something else.

As far back as 1944 George Orwell – in a paper called 'Oysters and Brown Stout' – observed that several of the 'major' works such as *Henry Esmond* and *The Virginians* were scarcely readable, and that if one wanted to choose something representative of Thackeray it would have to be *The Book of Snobs* or the burlesques or a collection of his contributions to *Punch*. Orwell himself particularly admired *Memorials of Gormandizing*, *The Fatal Boots* and *A Little Dinner at Timmins's* ('one of the best comic short stories ever written') – titles which generally meet with a blank look nowadays, even from students of English literature.

To read Thackeray from start to finish is to appreciate the accuracy of Orwell's emphasis. Yet not a single critic has followed his lead, perhaps because the full-length novels, coming in solid lumps, seem manageable, whereas the early things are diffuse – spreading through ten volumes of Saintsbury's Oxford edition – and fragmentary.

Geoffrey Tillotson's remark that Thackeray is a writer of 'a thousand brilliant spurts' is particularly true of the early work – even if it does make him sound a little like a fire-appliance – and spurts are hard things to catch and assemble critically. Still, the attempt must be made, for any account of Thackeray which confines itself to the 'major novels' immeasurably diminishes him.

To give an instance of a spurt, before getting down to Thackeray's life and imaginative realms, one might take this piece of travel-chat from the *Memorials of Gormandizing*:

They have clapped a huge fountain in the very midst of the Champs Élysées – a great, glittering, frothing fountain, that to the poetic eye looks like an enormous shaving brush.

Being about light, about Paris, about a changing townscape, and about a toilet article, it is, on several counts, highly Thackerayan, as later chapters will show. But what makes it unmistakably early Thackeray is the mixture of buffoonery and vividness – scoffing at 'poetic' aspirations, but grabbing exactly the image (quick and unexpected enough for an Imagist poem) that will bring the frothing spectacle before us. Later, the tone sobered and the eye dulled.

One debt I must record at the outset: to Gordon N. Ray, whose edition of the *Letters and Private Papers*, together with his masterly biography of Thackeray, have afforded me boundless pleasure and, I hope, profit.

1

Life

Thackeray's life was punctuated by wild ups-and-downs of fortune. It reads like a fiction. More accurately, it reads like one of his own fictions, for, try as he might to invent some other topic, he kept writing half-disguised versions of it, and most of his main characters are based on his acquaintances or himself. That is one reason why the critic needs to know about the biography. The other reason is that the disastrous collapse of Thackeray's art, after *Vanity Fair*, into gentle-manliness and cordiality, can partly be traced to the upsurge in his fortunes, and the corresponding social eminence, which that work's publication brought. He was destroyed by success.

The ups-and-downs began early. He was born in India in 1811 into a glittering, luxurious world. 'I have far off visions', he later recalled, 'of great saloons and people dancing in them, enormous idols and fire-works, rides on elephants or in gigs, and fogs clearing away and pagodas appearing over the trees.' His father, Richmond Makepeace Thackeray, was a highly-placed East India Company official, Collector of the Twenty-four Pergunnahs, with a resplendent mansion near the Esplanade in Calcutta, scores of servants and a Eurasian mistress, as well as a beautiful eighteen-year-old English wife, Thackeray's mother.

One day, a year after Thackeray's birth, an officer in the Bengal Engineers, Henry Carmichael-Smyth, turned up for dinner at the Thackeray residence, invited by Thackeray's father. For Mrs. Thackeray his arrival was a bombshell, for she had been desperately in love with him, and he with her, back in England before her marriage, and had been solemnly assured that he was dead. Her unscrupulous old grandmother, with whom she lived, had made up this tale, and bundled the girl off to India immediately afterwards, so shocked was she at the prospect of her grand-daughter marrying an impecunious subaltern. The lovers, once reunited, could not keep their joy, or their indignation, to themselves: they revealed all to Richmond Thackeray. With what seems, in retrospect, extremely generous celerity, he died three years later of fever, leaving the way clear for his widow to marry her first love. This, after a decent interval of mourning, she did. But mean-while Master Thackeray, aged five, was sent away to England in the care of a black servant. He never saw India again. It figures in his fiction as a source of private incomes, inconveniently situated at the end of a long sea route. Gifts of cashmere shawls frequently arrive from it, as do East India Directors and retired military men with many lakhs of rupees and names like Goldmore. That India was also a vast sub-continent with its own multifarious cultures and populations, Thackeray did not allow to concern him.

The ship that brought him to England put in at St. Helena, and his black servant took him to see a man walking in a garden. 'That', he said, 'is Bonaparte! He eats three sheep every day, and all the little children he can lay hands on.' This was the only personal contact the author of *Vanity Fair* had with the titan around whose fall the novel's action revolves.

Back in England, his mother's absence was a bitter grief to the boy. To make matters worse, he was sent to a private school in Southampton which seems, even by English standards, to have been a hideous place. Almost half a century later he still remembered the cold, the chilblains, the bad food, and the canings, and the queer ritual, somehow directed towards the discovery of a thief, whereby the children had to line up and plunge their hands into a bag of soot in a dark shed. Each night he would offer up the same plea: 'Pray God I may dream of my mother.' In his loneliness he transformed his mother into something almost divine; and he would often, later in life, speak of her as an angel. Mother-worship is a recurrent lubricant in the novels of his declining years like *Pendennis* and *Henry Esmond*, though the work up to and including *Vanity Fair* is quite clean of it.

Eventually, after three and a half years, Mrs. Thackeray rejoined her son. She was now married to Carmichael-Smyth, an attachment which the boy felt to be sullying to one so pure. Visiting his step-father's house, he recognized his mother's bed, and it made him feel, he recollects, 'very queer'. It disgusted him to hear Carmichael-Smyth 'snoring in my mother's room'.

Carmichael-Smyth had been to Charterhouse, so it was to that school that Thackeray went. It was not an ideal choice. Fagging and flogging formed the basis of its system, the small boys being called on to perform all kinds of service for the larger ones. Among the first orders Thackeray received was 'Come and frig me'. Fighting was a popular entertainment. In order to amuse his seniors Thackeray, though short-sighted and unused to sport, had to fight another boy called George Venables who, with a well-directed punch, broke his nose. Thackeray used to recall the 'scrunch' it made. The accident disfigured him for life.

The headmaster at Charterhouse, Dr. Russell, was not conspicuous for self control. If riled he would smash a child's head between two books until his nose bled. He was, however, careful to allow boys of noble family every indulgence. To some extent Charterhouse converted Thackeray to its ethos. In later years he would speak of its brutality as if it were somehow manly and laudable. He remained firm friends with Venables, alluding to him as 'my old schoolfellow, you know, who spoiled my profile'. By such means he associated himself with the robust, gentlemanly classes rather than with artists and writers.

From Charterhouse Thackeray proceeded to Trinity College, Cambridge, in 1829. His mother, who thought him 'the divinest creature in the world', longed for him to succeed, and he had no doubt that he would. Finding himself lodged near Sir Isaac Newton's old room, he wrote home exultantly 'Men will say, some day, that Newton and Thackeray kept near one another'. It seemed unlikely they would say so very soon. The letters are full of stern plans for work, each as quickly abandoned as the last. The one aspect of Cambridge that genuinely captured his enthusiasm was the food, especially the lobster suppers served in examination week. In the exam itself he did poorly. Undaunted, he went off to Paris for the summer, and devoted himself to the city's delights. He was enraptured by Marie Taglioni, the ballerina, and by Mlle Mars and Leontine Fay – 'such a pair of lips!' – at the Théâtre de Madame. It was the start of a lifelong passion: theatre, ballet, the shimmering realm beyond the darkly seething orchestra, where lightly-clad girls jumped about and showed their legs, became a familiar haunt of Thackeray's imagination.

Another momentous event on the Paris trip was his first evening at Frascati's. 'The interest in the game of Rouge et Noir is so powerful', he wrote, 'that I could not tear myself away until I had lost my last piece – I dreamed of it all night.' By the time he left Paris he was a compulsive gambler. The allure of the city drew him back at Easter, 1830, accompanied by Edward Fitzgerald, later the *Rubàiyàt* translator. It was on this holiday (of which his mother knew nothing) that he met, at a masked ball, the ex-governess Mlle Pauline, who became his mistress, and who was to some degree the model for Becky Sharp. By now he had given up hope of academic success at Cambridge. The men who gained first classes were, he explained to his mother, 'very nice fellows, only they smell a little of the shop'. Instead he developed his taste in wine, jewellery and cigars, and mixed with fast youths like John Bowes Bowes, later one of the first members of the Jockey Club who was to win the Derby four times, and Saville Morton, a notorious rake, eventually stabbed to death by the husband of one of his conquests. Before long, young Thackeray's easy way with money attracted the attention of a group of professional gamblers. They took lodgings opposite Trinity, and invited him to dinner and écarté. By the end of the evening he had lost £1,500. Though it didn't cure him of his zest for gaming, this experience deeply impressed Thackeray. He keeps returning to it in his fiction, and it is not the fate of the innocent victim that he is stirred by so much as the shady glamour of the professional card-sharper, stalking his prey through the *estaminets* and casinos of Europe.

After a second dismal performance in the university examinations, Thackeray left Cambridge without a degree. Despite his losses, he could still consider himself a wealthy young man, heir to his father's fortune, and he showed no inclination to earn his living. He idled around Europe for a while, sampling the students' drinking and duelling clubs in Germany, and spending six idyllic months in Weimar, where he flirted with the maids of honour and paraded at dinners and balls in pink and blue military uniform, having persuaded his stepfather to secure him a cornetcy in the Devon Yeomanry. He had an interview with Goethe, and bought and wore a sword that had been Schiller's. Weimar, with its tiny, autocratic court and its salons, was like a fragment of eighteenth-century culture, miraculously preserved. On winter nights you could still charter sedan chairs to carry you through the snow to court entertainments. Thackeray's imagination kept harking back to it throughout his life and, under playful, stodgy names like Kalbsbraten-Pumpernickel, it figures repeatedly in his writing. So does Paris, his other dreamland, where he loved to saunter in these moneyed years, eyeing the beautiful things in their gigot sleeves and tea-tray hats under the golden chestnuts of the Tuileries, and dining at the Trois Frères Provençaux or the Rocher de Cancale.

Ostensibly he was learning to be a painter. He had always had a talent for comic sketches, and he decided to cultivate it. But what really attracted him were the incidentals of an art student's life, the cigars and the absinthe, the feeling of being Bohemian, and the 'lovely gimcracks' of art as he calls them in *The Newcomes* – the smooth mill-boards and the glistening rows of colour tubes. 'He had not', pronounced George Cruikshank, who was his teacher for a while, 'the patience to be an artist.' Increasingly he lapsed into dissipation – cards, dice, women – filling his journal meanwhile with cries of contrition and vows of amendment, soon broken. 'One of the most disgraceful days I ever spent – playing from after breakfast till 4 o'clock at chicken hazard. . . . Maginn took me to a common brothel where I left him, very much disgusted and sickened.' In London he frequented the gambling saloons along Regent's Quadrant, with their elegant decorations and powdered footmen, and their ingeniously rigged roulette tables. His account book for 1833 shows him losing £668 in one encounter alone. In Paris he squandered his money at Frascati's, attended the Opera and the Variétés, bought and then remorsefully burned pornographic books, and whored. The time left over from these pursuits he occupied in fencing, in going with other dandies to watch the animals slaughtered at the abattoir, or merely, as his diary records, in 'flânerie on the boulevard'.

The event that put an end to Thackeray's career as a wastrel, and drove him to write, was the loss of his fortune. Suddenly, at the end of 1833, he was poor. It seems to have been his stepfather's fault: he had placed Richmond Thackeray's money in Indian banking houses that failed in the 1833 financial crisis. That, anyway, was Thackeray's version of the matter. He later described Major Carmichael-Smyth as 'a simple, honest old bore who ruined them all by his foolish investments'. But he had probably gambled away a quarter of his father's estate himself in the five years since leaving school.

For a while after this disaster he clung to the idea of trying to be a painter, but he gradually came to see that he would never be any good, and from 1837 on he worked as a freelance journalist. He wrote with immense, if spasmodic, energy, turning out book reviews and art criticism and comic sketches and burlesques for *Fraser's* and *Punch* and *The Times* and the *Morning Chronicle* and any other paper that would take his stuff. *Bentley's Miscellany* printed his first story, *The Professor*, in 1837, and that was followed by *The Tremendous Adventures of Major Gahagan* for the *New Monthly* and *Catherine* (which began by deriding novels about engaging criminal types, like Nancy in *Oliver Twist*, but ended up with a 'sneaking kindness' for its husband-slaying heroine), the *Shabby Genteel Story* and *The Great Hoggarty Diamond*, and *The Luck of Barry Lyndon*, the autobiography of an unscrupulous but, again, quite winning Irish adventurer. Then there were topical pieces like *The Second Funeral of Napoleon* and below-stairs pieces like the *Yellowplush Papers* (the memoirs of a retired footman), and social satire like *The Book of Snobs*, originally written for *Punch*, and impressions of foreign parts like *The Paris Sketch-Book* and *The Irish Sketch-Book* and the *Journey from Cornhill to Grand Cairo*, this last sponsored by the Peninsular and Oriental Steam Navigation Company, who gave him a free cruise round the Mediterranean to collect material. Thackeray adopted the perky, self-slighting pseudonym Michael Angelo Titmarsh (Michaelangelo because of the broken nose), and his stance was always sharp, questioning, irreverent, suspicious of anything elevated or distinguished. He loved puncturing. His stories followed the fortunes of down-at-heel types – cockneys, small shopkeepers, failed merchants. There is James Gann, for instance, in *A Shabby Genteel Story*, once heir to an oil firm (Gann, Blubbery & Gann), but ruined by the advent of gas-lighting, who now conducts from his wife's Margate boarding-house an agency for the London and Jamaica Ginger Beer Company and Gaster's Infants' Farinacio or Mothers' Invigorating Substitute (of which a mouldy half-pound packet occupies the 'office' mantelpiece), and who carries a telescope on his walks in order to scrutinize, from the esplanade, the bathing machines and perambulating girls' schools. Or there are clerks like Samuel Titmarsh in *The Great Hoggarty Diamond*, whose boss, Mr. Brough, of Brough and Hoff, Turkey Merchants, does a tremendous business in the fig and sponge way and the Zante currant line, and whose friend Bob Swinney, after a brush with Brough, goes off happily to be a traveller in oil and spermaceti in the Western counties. They remind one of the figures Wells was to write endearingly about in *Mr. Polly*. Thackeray exposes their pretentiousness and ignorance, but he allows them a good deal of chirpiness and bravado as well, and he touches in their life-styles with swift, brilliant strokes.

He composed under tremendous pressure, 'ceaseless whirl and whizz from morning to night', but it suited him, as he realized. 'I love to hear the press thumping, clattering and banging in my rear; it creates the necessity which always makes me work best.' Of course, he found it galling as well. He hated touting for employment from 'low literary men' like James Fraser; would get drunk and abuse them and have to apologize next day. He ranted about the 'odious magazine work', guaranteed to 'kill any writer in six years'; and because he was poor the publishers could impose humiliating conditions on him. Chapman and Hall, for instance, wanted £100 security in case he died before finishing *The Irish Sketch-Book*, and he had to send his chest of domestic plate to them as 'a kind of genteel pawn'. But despite the hurry and hardship, this was Thackeray's golden age. In the years up to *Vanity Fair* he wrote with more wit, more trenchancy, more vividness than he ever managed afterwards. The capacious novels that he put together after 1848, beginning with *Pendennis*, are mixtures of dough and treacle for much of the time, though they come to life intermittently. But in *Vanity Fair* and the ten years before it, his hard, bright genius was wonderfully at work.

The loss of his money was not the only catastrophe that overtook Thackeray in the years before *Vanity Fair*. There was also his marriage. Not that it began catastrophically. He fell in love with Isabella Shawe, a pretty, feather-brained Irish girl, who lived with her mother in a boarding-house near the Champs Elysées. He did not get on with Mrs. Shawe: experience of her converted him to the view that 'every man will, must and should dislike his mother-in-law'. But Isabella was irresistible, and they married in the summer of 1836. They were ecstatically happy, and spent eleven hours of each day in bed. At first they had a little apartment in Paris, but later moved to London, near Brunswick Square. Their first daughter, Anne, was born in 1837; Jane, the second, in 1838, but she died after eight months; and Harriet, the third, in 1840.

Thackeray did not treat his wife entirely as an adult. He called her 'dear Puss' and 'little Trot', and was apt to tease her about the pickling and pie-crust and 'mysteries of stocking mending' which he considered woman's rightful sphere. He encouraged her to take no interest in his work, and she took none. Increasingly he left her alone, dined in clubs, took up with his bachelor friends, and went off for jaunts to the continent, whence he would write to her about the good time he was having. 'Without my favourite talk about pictures or books I am good for nothing', he explained excusingly. Isabella's diversions, by contrast, were few. 'She doesn't put me to much expense in way of amusements', he told his mother.

Three months after the third child was born, Thackeray left for Belgium to see the picture galleries. 'I tried to persuade him not to go', his wife confessed to Mrs. Carmichael-Smyth, 'but it seems as if I was always to damp him.' He was not to be damped. In Belgium he occupied himself with 'having good dinners and sleeping on benches of afternoons and writing between times: a delightful trip, pleasure and sunshine the whole way'. When he got back Isabella appeared listless and depressed. He took her to Margate, then to her mother at Cork, to try to cheer her up. But it became clear that something was deeply wrong. On the way to Cork she tried to commit suicide, jumping from the boat, and floating around for twenty minutes before she was spotted and rescued. From then on she had to be watched night and day to stop her making away with herself. She alternately raved and brooded. It was not safe to leave the children with her, and they were packed off to Thackeray's mother, while he took his wife to various clinics on the continent – at Ivry, at Marienburg, at Chaillot – in search of a remedy. None was found. Sometimes Thackeray put a brave face on it: he wrote amusingly about the water-cure at Marienburg, and about the figure he cut as he stood naked under the sluice with his wife and his 'immense posterior protuberance'. Sometimes he admitted, with his usual honesty, that he was sick and tired of Isabella and her illness. Gradually he reconciled himself to the fact that she was incurably insane. She was taken to England and put in the care of a Mrs. Bakewell, 'an excellent worthy woman', in Camberwell. Thackeray visited her less and less often, and decided at last 'I think it is best not to see her'. She lived on for thirty years after his death, never regaining her reason.

Isabella's loss helped to impress on Thackeray the terrible transience of love and beauty. It also occasioned qualms of conscience. Clearly he had been to blame: had he not deserted her and gone to Belgium, her post-natal depression might never have developed into insanity. He began writing *Vanity Fair* in 1845, the year Isabella was finally shut away, and when in that novel George Osborne abandons his wife on the night before Waterloo and goes panting after Becky Sharp, Thackeray is near to self-portraiture – very near, perhaps, for it is possible that the delights of his ill-timed continental holiday included a reunion with the ex-governess Mlle Pauline, Becky's real-life prototype.

George, of course, has no monopoly of faultiness in *Vanity Fair*. Thackeray pointed out that he had tried to make all the characters 'odious', except Dobbin; and he, though no rogue, was a 'fool', for loving a parasitical little 'milksop' like Amelia. The book made Thackeray's name, but it did not sell well. The Victorians found its cynicism chilling. Mrs. Browning pronounced it 'cruel to human nature'; Forster lamented that he could find in it no 'simple un-contaminated human affection' or 'large cordiality'. With its scathing treatment of the upper classes it was regarded, too, as a perilous instance of the levelling spirit of the times. At this crucial point in his career, with his first masterpiece completed, Thackeray suddenly decided that he must change his style and manner. 'The world is a much kinder and better world than some bilious-covered satirists have painted it', he wrote to Lady Blessington in 1848, alluding to the yellow-paper bindings of *Vanity Fair*'s monthly parts, 'I must give up the yellow cover, I think, and come out in a fresher tone.'

This fatal resolve, which destroyed him as a writer, was partly a bid for popularity. He wanted the great public to take him to its heart, as it had taken Dickens. But it was also a result of a change in his circumstances. Suddenly he found himself a celebrity, fêted by the great: 'I reel from dinner party to dinner party – I wallow in turtle and swim in claret and Shampang', he chaffed jubilantly. Gratification softened his heart and his head, and he began to grow 'ashamed' of his 'former misanthropical turn'. His new friends included the prodigiously wealthy Lord Douglas ('very good natured', Thackeray reported), and *Punch*'s old butt Lord Brougham ('enormously good fun'; 'the best and wickedest old fellow I've met'), and superannuated dandies like Lord Howden and Poodle Byng, and gilded drones like Lord Castlereagh and the Hon. Charles Spencer Cowper. He enjoyed the hospitality of the Palmerstons, the Russells, the Mintos, Lord Brough-ton and other Whig magnificoes, and he was sought after by the society hostesses – Lady Waldegrave, Lady Molesworth, Lady Louisa de Rothschild, Lady Stanley of Alderley.

Life in the great houses profoundly appealed to him – the 'flowers piled up as high as haystacks', the sumptuous food, the fine wines. He loved to recount what a 'power of Lords' he knew, and to describe the glittering social occasions he attended – the 'beautiful dresses and daring gaiety' at the balls, or the swells at the race-meetings, looking 'very languid and handsome, drinking champagne and eating venison pie' as they reclined in their barouches. He had won his way back, he felt, to the luxury and refinement that had been his until the loss of his fortune.

Besides, the sudden end to his marriage had left him with a need for sensual gratification. He had strong bodily desires (we find him praying, in his diary, 'not to yield to lust'), and with his wife still alive he could not remarry. To make matters worse he had fallen in love with the wife of a friend, Jane Brookfield, who, though quite prepared to flirt with this latest lion, had no intention of going to bed with him. He transposed his passion, accordingly, to a high spiritual plane, assuring Jane's husband, who was in the know throughout, that his 'raptures' were 'not in the least dangerous', and expounding his powerful yet pure ardour in long letters to Jane and to mutual women friends, in whose company he evidently found the role of stricken swain rather appealing. Should his mother and Mrs. Brookfield predecease him, he comforted himself, they would enter 'spotless and angelical' into 'God's futurity', and provide him with two useful advocates at the Mercy Seat. Meanwhile, however, he had more earthly requirements to consider. 'It's *a* woman I want more than any particular one', he notified his mother, with accustomed openness. 'The want of this natural outlet plays the deuce with me.' Mrs. Carmichael-Smyth was hardly in a position to help; indeed, she proved thoroughly uncooperative, intervening suspiciously whenever Thackeray hired a governess to look after his daughters. Filling himself with wine and food every evening, and pursuing brilliant society, were ways of making up for poor Isabella's absence, and it would be obtuse to blame Thackeray for devoting himself to these tasks. Old literary friends like Fitzgerald, however, found themselves neglected, as did his colleagues on *Punch*. At Drury Lane he offended Mark Lemon and John Leech by deserting them and going to sit in a stage box with Count d'Orsay and the Earls of Chesterfield and Granville. *Punch's* criticism of the rich, and its zeal for social justice, impressed him as less healthy now than they had done formerly, and he declared that he could no longer collaborate with a 'savage little Robespierre' like Douglas Jerrold.

His defection was widely noted. Harriet Martineau commented tartly on his 'frittered life, and his obedience to the call of the great', and Carlyle observed that his 'dinner-eating in fashionable houses' had made him cover 'his native disposition with a varnish of smooth smiling complacency, not at all pleasant to contemplate'. Charlotte Brontë reported that Thackeray had left her company 'very early in the evening, in order that he might visit respectively the Duchess of Norfolk, the Marchioness of Londonderry, Ladies Chesterfield and Clanricarde, and see them all in their fancy costumes of the reign of Charles II, before they set out for the Palace'. No doubt envy and mean-mindedness intensified, in some cases, the virtuous reproofs of the literati. Thackeray defended himself with galling honesty, explaining that he preferred the society of the great – 'the air is freer than it is in small drawing rooms' – and that inherited wealth was no more unjust an advantage than the possession of literary gifts: 'One has as good a right to be angry with a man for writing a good poem, as for having a good estate.'

He settled comfortably into this line of thought, and applied himself to sweetening the acerbity that had produced his finest work. He resolved to be good natured from now on, a 'kind wag'. 'Love', he announced, 'is a higher intellectual exercise than hatred.' There were prudent reasons, besides his new social elevation, for taking such a view. The democratic revolutions that spread through Europe in 1848 alarmed conservatives. Thackeray began to see that, as a satirist, he had been playing with fire. He came to hate *The Book of Snobs*, and declared that he 'could not read a word of it'. Satire now rather shocked him. French writers, especially, seemed not to know where to draw the line. He went to see the vaudeville *Les Caméléons* at the Variétés and complained that it mocked all the political manoeuvring of the last half century: it was 'awful, immodest'. His interest in the seamy side of life, which several reviewers of *Vanity Fair* had deplored, and the scathing laughter which his observation of human affairs had prompted, struck him as indecorous when he surveyed his improved circumstances. To be 'comic and grinning' seemed 'somehow below my rank in the world'. 'I want to go in a higher class', he informed Mark Lemon.

The novels after *Vanity Fair* are full of people not only of a higher class but nicer – noble fellows, angelic ladies. It is a condition of their insipidity. *Pendennis*, the first of them, is also the first of Thackeray's stories to take a public-school and university man as its central figure. Thereafter, this social level becomes the norm, and unpleasantness is minimized. Thackeray planned *Henry Esmond* as a novel' without any villain', tacitly repudiating the 'Novel without a Hero', *Vanity Fair*. His appreciation of the literary masterpieces of other men also suffered. When he read *Madame Bovary*, it repelled him. 'The book is bad', he announced. 'It is a heartless, cold-blooded study of the downfall and degradation of a woman.' It was, in other words, rather nearer to the sort of book the author of *Vanity Fair* might have hoped to write than is *Pendennis* or *The Newcomes*.

The emasculation of his art was covertly defended in his lectures on *The English Humourists of the Eighteenth Century*, in which he pleaded that love and kindness should be the true ingredients of humour. He peopled his soggy, maudlin version of the eighteenth century with good-hearted types – 'stout old Johnson', Noll Goldsmith, Harry

Fielding – and recoiled in horror from Swift, 'a monster gibbering shrieks', whose plan for eating children in the *Modest Proposal* was sadly unlike Dick Steele's fondness for kiddies. As the acme of literary achievement in the period he came up with the tepid Joseph Addison, an 'ideal Christian gentleman', who 'could scarcely ever have had a degrading thought' (he was also an old Charterhouse man, which naturally recommended him). These discourses were attended by the cream of London society. Thackeray gave them at Willis's Rooms, St. James, in the splendid saloon, with its gilding and blue damask sofas, where the great balls of Almack's were held. A long line of carriages waited outside during the lectures, and the third of them was deferred for a week ('at the earnest petition of the duchesses and marchionesses', said Charlotte Brontë) because it clashed with Ascot.

At heart Thackeray knew the lectures were trash. 'What humbug!' he exclaimed, at the thought of touring the English cities with them. 'My conscience revolts at the quackery.' The tour went forward, nevertheless, and was highly profitable. Increasingly he wrote just for the money. Having wilfully stifled his true gifts – irony, finely poised anatomy of social shams, malicious insight – he found writing a horrible grind. He groaned over *Pendennis*, fully conscious that it was 'stupid, ricketty and of feeble intellect', and he could hardly bear to continue with *The Newcomes*: 'It haunts me like a great stupid ghost. I think it says, why do you go on writing this rubbish? You are old, you have no more invention.' But he kept at it, in the hope of providing for his daughters after his death. He knew that he could manufacture the high-souled confection that his readers wanted, and he resolved to do so. 'I shall write very badly', he acknowledged, 'but the public won't find me out.' This was the way he thought about *Henry Esmond*, too. He confessed it 'dreary', but foresaw that his 'grand and melancholy' hero would do him credit, 'bore as he is'.

The strain told. Soon the whole 'novelist business' sickened him. He felt it 'indecent and despicable'. His imagination would not work any more, and the 'eager observation' that had invigorated his writing up to 1848 had, he realized, deserted him. From 1849 on he complains endlessly in his letters that he is played out – an 'exploded squib'. 'What is it makes one so blasé and tired I wonder at 38?' he demanded. It was ill health, partly. He ate and drank excessively, and almost died in October 1849 from a complaint variously diagnosed as gastric fever, cholera and typhoid. But illness was nothing new to him. For many years he had suffered from a urethral stricture, the result, it seems, of a venereal infection contracted in his festive youth, and it required frequent painful instrumentation. What filled him with dismay and disgust when he contemplated his work in later years was not a physical cause, but the knowledge that social and financial pressures, that he was too weak to withstand, had betrayed him into abandoning his true creative bent.

He returned to it, briefly, in his lectures on *The Four Georges* in 1855. He had planned to write on this subject earlier, but dismissed the idea, knowing that he could only treat it satirically, and that this would alienate his grand friends: 'If I hope for a police magistrateship or what not I had best keep a civil tongue in my head', he calculated. What changed his mind was the Crimean War. The reports of mismanagement and suffering reaching England caused an outcry against the governing classes in which, for a time, he joined. He became a member of the Administrative Reform Association, and stood for Parliament (unsuccessfully) as a representative of the 'educated middle classes' intent on wresting power from the aristocratic families. In *The Four Georges* he attacked aristocracy and monarchy, deriding, in particular, George IV, who had been, he argued, not a man but an assemblage of stays, padding and silk stockings, combined with a high-quality nutty-brown wig. The 'Bo Monde' was furious, he told his mother, and he was barred from the 'halls of splendour'. However, within a year or two the great folks relented. Thackeray, for his part, gave up his radical position. He did not resume it. His work continued its decline – until an Indian summer, shortly before his death, produced the brilliantly original *Lovel the Widower* and, less impressively, *Philip*.

Seen as a whole, then, Thackeray's career is the history of a capitulation. He was touchy, of course, about having this pointed out, as the famous Garrick Club row of 1858 illustrates. Edmund Yates, a young journalist, began this by writing a fairly inoffensive piece for *Town Talk*, which observed that Thackeray had adapted his art to his audience, and knowingly flattered the aristocrats in his *English Humourists*. Stung, Thackeray reported Yates to the committee of the Garrick Club, of which they were both members, claiming that since they had met only on the Club's premises, Yates had dishonoured the privacy of the place by publishing his article. Dickens, also a member, sprang to Yates's defence, and Thackeray reacted with a cold fury that had behind it all the hatred he felt for his more successful rival. Eventually Yates was expelled, and the thing blew over; but Thackeray and Dickens were never on speaking terms again.

The incident shows up the pompous gentility of the later Thackeray. It also reveals how far he had travelled from his vivacious, creative days. Back in 1838 he had written to Blackwood, offering to contribute 'criticism of a spicy nature and general gossip' to his magazine, and adding that, as he belonged to 'a couple of clubs', he would have no trouble gathering material. Yates's ways had been his own.

Changes of front like this come to light whenever Thackeray's early and late views are compared. His thoughts about lords (and he thought about them a great deal) are particularly instructive. In the years before he was taken in tow by fashionable society he was an indefatigable foe of flunkeyism, pathologically concerned with toad-eaters and tuft-hunters and 'lickspittle awe of rank', and always castigating middle class folk who aped aristocrats – saying they were like jays pretending to be peacocks, or potatoes passing themselves off as tulips. When things were going worse than usual, as at the time of his wife's madness, his virulence redoubled. 'When are we to get rid of this insolent scum of lords altogether?' he fulminated; 'I would like to see all men equal, and this bloated aristocracy blasted to the wings of all the winds.' His *Punch* pieces teem with denunciations of nobles, and *The Book of Snobs* ends up by insisting that class-distinction must be abolished forthwith:

It seems to me that all English society is cursed by this mammonical superstition; and that we are sneaking and bowing and cringing on the one hand, or bullying and scorning on the other, from the lowest to the highest.

Rank, precedence, and the 'diabolical invention of gentility' should be done away with. The commons must say to the nobility 'We are as good as you'.

And yet he was never quite sure they were. When he compared the aristocrats he had come across with the vulgar people he had to earn his bread among, there did seem to be a difference in kind (as his favourite peacock and tulip similes concede). Cool reason stood aloof from the popular passions, and he enjoyed giving it its say, especially when he knew that it would rile people. In *The Second Funeral of Napoleon*, for instance (perhaps the finest of his short early things), he scoffs at the democratic notion of 'Nature's gentlemen', and asserts the superiority of the hereditary aristocrat, pointing out that well-formed fathers and mothers, cleanly nursery maids, good meals and good physicians are real advantages which the lower classes cannot lay claim to, and that 'a course of these going on for a few generations are the best gentleman-makers in the world, and beat Nature hollow'.

The firm, annoying rationality is typical of Thackeray at his most successful. He is an unpleasantly acute social critic, fond of drawing attention, for instance, to the importance of apparently trivial failings like dropping aitches or eating peas with a knife. To pretend such things don't matter, he maintains, is humbug. Observation confirms that they are universally accepted as the criteria that make one class of people unfit for the society of another. It is not disrespectful, but simply a fact, he adds in *Mr. Brown's Letters to his Nephew*, to say that someone who exhibits these deficiencies is not well bred.

Thackeray's clear-sightedness reinforces his prejudices in this instance, of course. He was profoundly moved by gastronomic niceties, and people who ate peas with their knives genuinely revolted him. He quarrelled fiercely with Douglas Jerrold for doing so. But he also used his objective, intellectual approach to defend those whose interests clashed with his own. In a late essay, *On a Chalk Mark on the Door*, he observes that it is right and natural for domestic servants to cover up for one another by telling lies: 'This is not lying; this is voting with your party.' It would be intolerable if they told the truth, he explains, since what they are really thinking must nearly always be extremely disrespectful to their masters. It will be the aim of any sensible employer, therefore, to secure the services of 'a worthy, clean, agreeable and conscientious male or female hypocrite'.

Coolness and honesty of this type are particularly likely to give offence when applied to topics, such as Negro slavery, which arouse automatic indignation and prejudice among the liberal-minded. Before Thackeray knew anything about slavery, he held it in decent abhorrence – calling it an 'odious crime' in his review of Frédéric Soulié's pro-slavery novel *Le Bananier* in 1843. When, a year later, he actually came across some slaves, in the market at Cairo, he was surprised to find that they did not stir his humanitarian zeal. They were healthy, happy and physically revolting – even the female ones, with their lips 'the size of sausages' and their great show of 'shuddering modesty' when the dealer stripped off their blankets. He observed, too, that they looked forward to being bought, 'as many a spinster looks to an establishment in England', since once in a family they were kindly treated and well clothed –'the merriest people of the whole community'. His visit to the Southern states of America in 1852 reinforced this view. *Uncle Tom's Cabin* had recently appeared, and controversy raged. Thackeray drew attention to the ignorance prevalent among high-minded agitators in England, and he remained faithful – disgracefully faithful, some will feel – to his own first-hand experience. 'They are not', he wrote to his mother:

my men and brethren, these strange people with retreating foreheads, with great obtruding lips and jaws: with capacities for thought, pleasure, endurance, quite different to mine. They are not suffering as you are impassioning yourself for their wrongs as you read Mrs. Stowe, they are grinning and joking in the sun.

Negroes, he concluded, were not the same as white men, 'any more than asses are the same as horses'. Not that the white man had a right, on this account, to hold them in bondage: he denied this absolutely. But he insisted on recording the facts of slavery as he saw them, and these were that slaves were well-fed and happy; that on average they did less than a quarter of a white man's work; that the more industrious of them could save £30 a year, and so were considerably better off than a labouring man in England; that they were prodigiously expensive to their masters, who supplied them with good medical care and looked after them in old age; and that they were infinitely less brutal, dirty and degraded than the free Negroes he encountered.

Doubtless some of Thackeray's statistics were supplied by the Southern gentry, along with the hospitality and mint juleps which he much appreciated. But it is worth noting that his account of the material well-being of slaves is borne out by the most authoritative modern treatment of the subject, R. W. Fogel and S. L. Engerman's massively documented *Time on the Cross*. This study demonstrates, for instance, that the diet and housing of slaves were superior to those of free workers; that the typical slave received about 90 per cent of the income he produced; and that the masters' concern for the health of their slaves resulted in a slave mortality rate in child-bearing lower than that experienced by Southern white women, and a slave life-expectation much longer than that of urban industrial workers in both the United States and Europe. Thackeray's inclination to record what he saw, and his distrust of reach-me-down philanthropy, make something of a contrast with Dickens, whose own attack on slavery in *American Notes* was largely composed of extracts from W. W. Weld's *American Slavery as it Is*, and newspaper cuttings which Edward Chapman collected for him after he had returned to England.

Thackeray was equally reasonable when justifying his own taste for moneyed society. It was, he argued, natural to like the company of people who possessed fine books and pictures, parks, town and country houses, good cooks and good cellars. 'If So-and-So is as good as you and possesses these things, he, in so far, is better than you who do not possess them: therefore I had rather go to his house in Belgravia than to your lodging in Kentish Town.' Most people find it hard to admit they aren't worth mixing with, and feel inclined to resist the force of Thackeray's bland logicality. As usual, however, he has been careful to put it in a form that is irrefutable.

Being rational, he had no illusions about his motives when he became an appendage of the lordly classes. Though a snob, he was a conscious snob. He remarks in his letters on the 'parasitical air' he finds himself assuming in the company of the great, and acknowledges that he likes Lord Castlereagh, for instance, simply 'because he is a Lord'. He realized that the circles he moved in were those he had satirized in *Vanity Fair*; indeed, he took pains to point this out. In accounts of the grand dinner parties he has attended, he will remark that he has been sitting next to 'Lord Steyne', or has seen, as he left at midnight, his host's carriage lamps blazing in the courtyard, 'for a visit to some Becky, no doubt'. When a friend suggested that he should call the splendid residence he built for himself at Palace Green, Kensington, 'Vanity Fair', he admitted the justice of the crack.

Thackeray's swing to the right, then, though extreme, wasn't simple. Part of him saw through his hobnobbing with the nobs, as part of him had seen through the 'Radical spouters' in his Radical spouting days. The attitude he eventually took up towards another of his pre-possessions, the English Public School, was more self-deceiving.

For Thackeray public school meant primarily Charterhouse (re-named, in his fiction, Slaughter House, Grey Friars etc.). He felt no affection for it when he was there. 'I cannot think that school to be a good one', he wrote to his mother, on leaving, 'when as a child I was lulled into indolence, and when I grew older and could think for myself was abused into sulkiness and bullied into despair'. *A Shabby Genteel Story* refers scathingly to the 'accursed system' called 'the education of a gentleman': public school and university, Thackeray there asserts, teach nothing but selfishness and social pretension. *The Irish Sketch-Book* develops the attack:

There are at this present writing five hundred boys at Eton, kicked, and licked, and bullied, by another hundred – scrubbing shoes, running errands, making false concords, and (as if that were a natural con-sequence!) putting their posteriors on a block for Dr. Hawtrey to lash at; and still calling it education. They are proud of it – good heavens! – absolutely vain of it; as what dull barbarians are not proud of their dulness and barbarism? They call it the good old English system.

The time spent learning the ancient languages is wasted, he adds, since the Etonians, Harrovians and Carthusians he comes across retain no knowledge of them, and it would be of no service if they did. As for torture ('Torture in a public school is as much licensed as the knout in Russia', he remarks in *Vanity Fair*), the notion that it is good for children and 'hardens' them is, *The Irish Sketch-Book* avers, one that could find a footing only in the brains of addle-pated old soaks and club bores, such as public-school men regularly become. Thackeray depicts a representative of this species in *A Night's Pleasure*: a purple-faced, whisky-sodden wreck, who once got the silver medal for Latin Sapphics at school, and who now despises anyone without a classical education, quite unaware that the very waiters are more 'useful, honourable and worthy' than he.

Far from encouraging his appreciation of Greek literature, the 'brutal tyranny' at Charterhouse quenched any pleasure Thackeray might have taken in it. Even at school he had doubts, he said, about the genuineness of an article that was recommended by a 'coarse-grained' schoolmaster who terrorized cowering little boys. And when he finally got to Athens and found it was a let-down – that the temple of Theseus was 'built of Pentelic marble of the exact colour and mouldiness of a ripe Stilton cheese', and the Royal Palace resembled 'Newgate, white-washed' – he hailed the fact with 'gloomy joy'.

Yet alongside these bitter perceptions about contemporary education there may be found in Thackeray's work another kind of allusion to school, which gradually predominates, and which precisely echoes the opinions of the bluff dullards he portrays in *The Irish Sketch-Book*. This side of Thackeray regards flogging and fisticuffs as salubrious and gentlemanlike practices. 'A good thrashing now and then, with a hearty shake afterwards of the hand which administered the beating', as he puts it in *The Virginians*, is, it now appears, the ideal regimen for youth. Colonel Newcome's boyhood illustrates this. Though he disdains to be flogged by the butler or the black footman, he allows his father to horse-whip him, and 'trembling and quivering' holds out his 'little bleeding hand' afterwards, remarking 'I can take it from you, sir'. The improving effect of physical assault is endlessly stressed in the later books, either by Thackeray himself or by sterling figures like Warrington in *Pendennis*, who observes, of the Hon. Percy Popjoy, 'He was my fag at Eton. I ought to have licked him a little more'. Nor is this symptomatic only of the late Thackeray. In *Men's Wives* (1843) the great pugilistic encounter between Frank Berry and the bullying Biggs at Slaughter House School is recounted with patent relish (as is the Dobbin v. Cuff contest in *Vanity Fair*, of which it is an early version). The gallant Berry is coached beforehand by the cock of the school, and his doughty blows make the 'claret spurt out' from Biggs's nose, and so forth. The whole thing, in fact, is exactly at the level of the schoolboy reminiscences ('how Tibbs and Miller fought for an hour and twenty minutes "like good uns"' etc.) which Thackeray scathingly attributes to his old fools in *The Irish Sketch-Book* (also 1843). Yet in *Men's Wives* he puts it across with approval, and goes on to record that he later became Berry's fag, in which capacity, though beaten daily, he 'got no more thrashing than was good for' him (a phrase that became endemic as time went on: Little Rawdon in *Vanity Fair* 'only got that degree of beating which was, no doubt, good for him'; Foker, in *The Virginians*, received 'no more beating than was good for him' at Charterhouse, and so on).

The view of public school in *Men's Wives* differs so markedly from *The Irish Sketch-Book*'s partly because *Men's Wives* was written for *Fraser's Magazine*. Thackeray was buttering up his well-heeled readership. But there was always a part of him that aspired towards hearty mindlessness, and writing school stories brought this out. *Dr. Birch and his Young Friends* (1849) contains a portrait of his ideal schoolboy, George Champion – not over-brainy, but straight as a die, and destined to become 'the bravest of soldiers' or 'the best of country parsons':

He does not play at cricket, except when the school plays the county, or at Lord's in the holidays. The boys can't stand his bowling, and when he hits, it is like trying to catch a cannon-ball. I have seen him at tennis. It is a splendid sight to behold the young fellow bounding over the court with streaming yellow hair, like young Apollo in a flannel jacket.

Such stuff was, for Thackeray, a way of pretending that he was athletic at heart, and did not mind having his nose squashed flat at Charter-house. It became part of his gentlemanly code. A line could no doubt be traced from this section of his work, through Gunby Hadath, Desmond Coke and other spinners of school yarns, to the *Magnet* and the *Gem*. 'Greyfriars' is a Thackerayan name, and Frank Richards, with his insistence that 'foreigners *are* funny' and that 'noblemen generally are better fellows than commoners', is a kind of fearful parody of Thackeray at his worst.

In the end he persuaded himself that he hadn't been wretched at Charterhouse at all – indeed, had loved the place. He enjoyed re-visiting it, and kept Founder's Day 'sacred' each year. *The Newcomes* reaches its warm-hearted climax with the Colonel retiring to Charter-house to live in dignified penury in one of the school almshouses, and he dies with a 'peculiar sweet smile', calling 'Adsum!':

It was the word we used at school, when names were called; and lo, he, whose heart was as that of a little child, had answered to his name, and stood in the presence of The Master.

Heaven was a public school.

One thing that drew Thackeray back to Charterhouse was his interest in flagellation, a subject which his fancy increasingly lingered over. Henry Silver remembers his chattering about how he had seen 'a little fellow with his hands behind him', on a visit to the school, and about 'how they'd take him to the bog and make him show his cuts'. He liked discussing the topic with friends: a letter to C. R. Dicken survives, which contains a sketch of a whipping block with a boy being led to it and a prefect carrying birch rods. Corporal chastisement is dragged into Thackeray's essays and journalism under the strangest pretexts. A discussion of contemporary painting or English Literature will suddenly turn into a classroom scene, with a whipping in progress, and the speeches of victim and punisher lovingly imagined ('Choose me a nice long, swishing, buddy one, light and well poised in the handle' etc.). One of Thackeray's favourite stories, turning up in two of the essays and *Vanity Fair*, concerns an elderly acquaintance who dreamed he was at Charterhouse again, being flogged by Dr. Raine. Foker and Pen both dream of being flogged at Grey Friars in *Pendennis*, and in *Philip* Pen recalls dining with three friends who 'laughed, prattled and rejoiced' as they described being flogged by Dr. Keate. 'Their talk greatly amused and diverted me', reports Pen. Pretending that sexual deviations are a joke is, of course, even nowadays, a common expedient for keeping them socially inoffensive (witness the small ads for 'amusing' rubber underwear, and suchlike). In *Miss Tickletoby's Lectures on English History* Thackeray introduces a school-mistress who inflicts corporal punishment on her male pupils. She makes sly references to 'something hanging up in the cupboard', and carries on a suggestive dialogue with one boy about the last occasion on which she whipped him ('How did I punish you, my dear? – tell the company'). Plainly we are not far away, here, from the stern governess of Victorian pornographic fiction, though, as usual, a humorous front is maintained. Miss Tickletoby illustrates Thackeray's growing tendency to spice up the flagellation by making it heterosexual. The scene in *The Virginians* where Madam Esmond orders George to be caned was meant, presumably, to have a similar appeal, as was the figurative account of old Lord Ringwood whipping the Twysden girls in *Philip*. Ringwood, we are told, 'always brought a cat-o'-nine-tails in his pocket', and the young ladies 'knelt and took their whipping with the most exemplary fortitude' – 'now the lash stung Agnes, and now it lighted on Blanche's pretty shoulders'. Thackeray seems to have got a surreptitious thrill, too, from writing to women acquaint-ances about being beaten like a school-boy when he was actually referring to adverse reviews of his books. 'The *Spectator* has taken down my breeches and whipped me soundly', is a typical instance of this kind of queasy sex-play. What one regrets about the whole fixation is not so much that Thackeray suffered from it, as that he could never raise it into the light and apply his satirical intelligence to it, as he could, in his early period, to other unwelcome results of public school education. He seems to have been content merely to indulge it in a furtive, half-hearted sort of way.

As a result it could never contribute any sharpness to his work. To write well he had to be fully conscious – either of his own absurdity, or of other people's, or both. In the early comic journalism his own demeanour in his young doggy days is frequently ridiculed. The cowardly, boastful militia officers who populate it, with their gaudy uniforms (C. Jeames de la Pluche's in *Yellowplush*, for instance, in-corporating gold-embroidered scarlet tights, yellow morocco Hessian boots, and a huzzar pelisse of purple velvet trimmed with sable), reflect the shame and contempt that Thackeray felt when he thought of himself prancing around the court at Weimar in the pink and sky-blue uniform of Sir John Kennaway's Devon Yeomanry. Jeames's reason for assuming military dress is that the court-suits civilians wear make them look like footmen – and this was, in fact, just the reason

Thackeray had given when he wrote to his mother from Weimar asking that a cornetcy in Kennaway's might be purchased for him. The line of polychrome bogus militarists culminates in Jos Sedley, who sports a frogged frock coat and a foraging cap ornamented with a smart gold band, until rumours of a French victory reach Brussels, whereupon he gives them away in terror to his manservant.

Jos, it will be recalled, had leanings towards martial garb even at school. Little George Osborne was severely punished, on one occasion, for cutting the tassels off his Hessian boots. Bob Stubbs, the craven anti-hero of *The Fatal Boots*, also favoured, as a schoolboy, this fashionable footwear (called after the Hessian troops who originally wore it). Again, Thackeray is contemptuously reviewing, through these figures, a bit of his own past. At Charterhouse he had passionately longed for Hessian boots, and had ordered a pair to be sent home, but they were sternly returned to the shop as unbefitting his years. 'It was a dreadful moment', he confided, years afterwards, to his daughter, 'and one which he could never forget.'

In his later work, however, his attitude towards his own past changes. It becomes more respectful and indulgent. Pendennis and Clive Newcome (both acknowledged self-portraits) may get into scrapes now and then, but we are never allowed to forget that they are well-bred English lads, who merit our esteem. It would be a strain to imagine either of them masquerading in garish regimentals and tasselled boots. Decorousness had supervened.

Sentimentality, too: as we can see if we compare the fictional portraits of acquaintances which Thackeray produced during his vital, journalistic days, with those he turned out in his decline. Take the cockney painter Andrea Fitch from *A Shabby Genteel Story* – one of those scintillatingly documented Thackerayan characters (or neo-Balzacian characters, for Thackeray read Balzac early and critically), who burst in on the reader with a mass of realistic credentials – their family connections, their means of livelihood, their holiday haunts, their clubs, outfitters, legal advisers, and laundry lists. Fitch was:

a fantastic youth, who lived but for his art; to whom the world was like the Coburg Theatre, and he in a magnificent costume acting a principal part. His art, and his beard and whiskers, were the darlings of his heart. His long pale hair fell over a high polished brow, which looked wonderfully thoughtful; and yet no man was more guiltless of thinking. He was always putting himself into attitudes; he never spoke the truth; and was so entirely affected and absurd, as to be quite honest at last: for it is my belief that the man did not know truth from falsehood any longer, and when he was alone, when he was in company, nay, when he was unconscious and sound asleep snoring in bed, was one complete lump of affectation. When his apartments on the second floor were arranged according to his fancy, they made a tremendous show. He had a large Gothic chest, in which he put his wardrobe (namely, two velvet waistcoats, four varied satin under ditto, two pairs braided trousers, two shirts, half-a-dozen false collars, and a couple of pairs of dreadfully dilapidated Blucher boots). He had some pieces of armour; some China jugs and Venetian glasses; some bits of old damask rags to drape his doors and windows: and a rickety lay figure, in a Spanish hat and cloak, over which slung a long Toledo rapier, and a guitar with a riband of dirty sky-blue.

It's a prime bit of early Thackeray: the withering contempt, together with the joyfully proliferating imagination that will not let anything as narrow as contempt prevail. Fitch's every action makes him more fatuous, and more likeable. He goes out in foul weather because he believes it romantic (' "I love the storm", said Fitch solemnly'), and he wears a locket containing ringlets which he avouches, in confidence, to be relics of a Spanish girl whom he loved to madness, but which in fact, being quite without amorous experience of any description, he has been obliged to clip from the wig of the lay figure in his studio.

Fitch's original was John Grant Brine, a Scottish artist, whom Thackeray called on in his weirdly opulent Parisian atelier in 1833, and later dismissed, in a letter to his mother, as 'a second rate man, a little better than a drawing master'. Twenty-two years after *A Shabby Genteel Story* he wrote the sequel, *Philip*, and a glance at the account of Fitch there betrays quite a new note. His 'genius', we are told, made a 'little flicker of brightness', and has now been extinguished for ever, but he had 'as loving, gentle, faithful, honourable a heart as ever beat in a little bosom'. Of course the fact that Brine really had died (of consumption) in the interim helps to explain the reverential air Thackeray now adopts. But the change from crisp and exhilarating judgement to a sort of damp-eyed, whisky-and-water reminiscence is entirely typical of his deterioration as a writer.

Something comparably debilitating happened to Major Pendennis – or rather to what might be called the Major Pendennis portfolio, for Thackeray, even before he wrote *Pendennis*, had created a confrérie of old military men who are recognizably previous incarnations of the Major, without actually bearing his name. The 'model' for them was Lt. Col. Merrick Shawe, his wife's uncle, an ex-Regency buck and devoted clubman who, after a distinguished military career in India, had served on the Duke of York's staff at the Horse Guards. Captain Popjoy in *Catherine* is the first of the species, identifiable by his rich blue-black hair-dye and his curiously unpleasant eyes with 'a little pair of red watery eyeballs' afloat in them and 'sickly green pupils'. Popjoy's accomplishments are chiefly in the consumer line. 'Some six thousand bottles of wine', Thackeray estimates, have passed through him during his life, and he has played 'say, fifteen thousand games at billiards'. 'His animal functions are still tolerably well preserved, his spiritual have evaporated long since.' Here we have the rudiments of Major Pendennis, but the portrait undergoes successive elaborations. *Bob Robinson's First Love* has Gen. Sir Hugh Rolfe K.C.B. – goggle-eyed, corseted, with a yellow post-chaise and volleys of oaths 'like Vauxhall crackers', who bustles in to stop his nephew from marrying beneath him (a preliminary run-through for the opening scenes of *Pendennis* which, incidentally, antedates by three years the anecdote told to Thackeray by Miss Eliza Smith which is generally supposed to have given him the idea for the start of that novel). And in *The Book of Snobs* the dyed whiskers and tight waistband and eyes 'the colour of peeled plover's eggs' become the property of a character called Jack Spiggot, another selfish, loveless old gourmet.

The reader who had followed Thackeray to this point would feel on familiar ground when he started *Pendennis*. Like these figures the Major is an incarnation of worldliness, snobbery and self-indulgence. His eyes, like Jack Spiggot's, resemble 'plovers' eggs'. His chest, 'manfully wadded with cotton by Mr. Stultz', his factitious rich-brown hair, and his teeth, which travel with him in a small morocco box, help to make him 'juvenile and hilarious in the company of the young lords'. He would fit into *Vanity Fair* (which is a great deal more than can be said for any other character in *Pendennis*).

But as the novel proceeds Major Pendennis ceases to be a savagely ironic creation, and dwindles into an amiable old buffer, quite admirable really, with a sensible, realistic attitude to social rank. When, in the end, he triumphantly confronts his rebellious manservant, Morgan, pistol at the ready, he plainly stands for gallantry and good breeding, pitted against the impudent aspirations of the lower class ('I'm an Englishman, I am, and as good as you', the wretched Morgan whines). It is no surprise, after this, to find the Major being allocated a touching death scene in *The Newcomes*, and vowing Laura Pendennis an 'angel' as he expires. What had happened, as we have seen, was that Thackeray had taken to sucking up to lords in Major Pendennis's fashion, and found it agreed with him very well. As usual, he had his eyes open. The desire 'to go through life as a gentleman – as a Major Pendennis' is acknowledged without reserve in the correspondence, as his own particular vanity, and he can be found wryly signing himself 'Major Pendennis' in the letters of 1849. He turned himself into Major Pendennis, indeed, with considerable success, the only drawback being that Major Pendennis could never, by any stretch of the imagination, write a novel.

In the following chapters a lot of my illustrations, naturally, will be drawn from the early (and neglected) work. I shall try to show how

Thackeray put together his imaginative world, and how he filled it with light and depth, and with that strangely individual blend of enchantment and disenchantment, in the years before he stifled his talents.

2

Light and Colour

Thackeray was a born sketcher. He sketched everything and every-where – on envelopes, in the margins of letters, on his own fingernails. He retailed gleefully the rumour, circulated about him when he was in the States, that perpetual applications of phosphoretic ink had entirely worn away the nails of both his hands. At school he had always been in demand, sketching scenes from *The Mysteries of Udolpho* or *Don Quixote* for his fellow pupils. The derisive sketch was his particular forte. He would use it to subvert the most solemn scenes in his own fiction: witness the drawing of 'Capting Hosbin ded, a bullick through his Art', sent to Horace Smith's daughter, which shows George lying face-down on the field of Waterloo, with his coat-tails fixed in rigor mortis like a pair of posterior horns.

The immediacy of the sketch, its certainty and speed of line, and its seeming carelessness, as well as its power of ridicule, appealed to Thackeray's deepest preconceptions about art. He used to say in his art-critic days that a man's pictures and his sketches should never be hung together, because the sketches would inevitably be more vigorous and masterly, and would kill the pictures. He had a brilliant gift for the impromptu in words as well as in drawing. Plenty of his thrown-off things survive, mostly bawdy – like his reaction to an unusually well-developed specimen of female portraiture, ' 'Tis true 'tis titty, titty 'tis, 'tis true', or the verses he scribbled on a note from Fitz-gerald to Spedding:

> To court the fair Emily came,
> All blazing in pearls and in rubies,
> Her stomacher all in a flame,
> From her shoulder-strap down to her pubis.

And so on. Though his novels got dull, his letters and sketches never did.

Besides being impromptu, a sketch, by necessity, throws most of its subject away. What catches the artist's eye is cut out in rapid strokes, and the whole mass of circumambient fact is allowed to vanish into white paper. This aspect, too, suited Thackeray's cast of mind, which was highly impressionistic. 'Everything but impressions', he lamented,

'I mean facts, dates, and so forth, slip out of my head, in which there's some great faculty lacking, depend upon it.' Maybe there was, and critics who search the novels for errors in chronology, nomenclature, and suchlike, evidently think the lack important. Viewed from another angle, though, it was a prerequisite of his fluent, darting genius, just as extreme selectivity was the basis of his, as of any, ironic style. He was particularly scornful of the sort of fashionable portrait in which everything got painted as if it were of equal importance – boots, clocks, bell pulls, Turkey carpets, all sedulously executed, so that 'the puzzled eye scarce knows where to settle'.

The quick, unfinished feel of a sketch retains, as something worked over and framed cannot, a sense of life's haphazardness and sparkle – its 'frisky' quality, as Thackeray would have said. He liked the word 'frisky', and kept trying it out in new situations: Hodson's Pale Ale in 'neat little frisky bottles'; frisky stars in *The Bedford-Row Conspiracy*; frisky champagne at Pen and Fanny's supper after Vauxhall. And by catching its subject in momentary, chance postures, a sketch can give the impression that that particular subject has never been set eyes on before. That, too, made it absorbing for Thackeray. The strange, poetic vividness of places and people seen for the first time always intrigued him, and he tried to capture it in his style. He used to say that if you wanted to understand France you should take a boat to Calais, go ashore for two hours, and never afterwards return. (It gives us a line on what he meant by 'understand'.) For two hours, he said, everything would be wonderful and unforgettable, from the red calico bed canopies to the little French soldiers in white cockades and shakos. He felt the same when he went to the East. Landing at Smyrna, he found that he had stepped into the *Arabian Nights*. The women with their 'black nosebags' and shuffling yellow slippers, the sun through the bazaar awnings, the camels 'gingerly treading' with huge splay feet, the red mullets, grapes, melons, pomegranates, and the white worms crawling out of the figs, all thrust themselves on the senses with a suddenness and intensity beyond life.

In art and writing he admired the dash and verve that could transmit something of this experience. He found these qualities in Carlyle's prose style, which he defended excitedly in an early *Times* review, and in Daumier's caricatures for the *Charivari* – 'very carelessly drawn', Thackeray judged, but 'perfectly conceived'. Most of all he found them in Rubens, a 'magnificent master and poet', with brilliant colours and 'dashing worldly notions', who had shown how paintings could be done in a day, replacing labour and painstaking effort. He admitted that Rubens's religious paintings were not in the least piously affecting – his 'livid thief' writhing on a cross, his 'blowsy penitent' in yellow satin and glittering hair, carrying a stream of light across the picture –

but the sensuous splendour, the cold lights and warm shadows, the tints left lying 'raw' by the side of one another – 'the artist not having taken the trouble to blend them', and the speed, 'the astonishing rapidity with which he travels over canvas', filled him with exhilaration and despair. He spent hours in Antwerp before the 'Communion of St. Francis', examining the blue lips and the 'eyes rolling bloodshot with dabs of vermilion', and wondering how such reckless methods could achieve so consummate a result. It was 'scarcely more than an immense magnificent sketch', 'painted in an incredibly short space of time', yet it was patently a masterpiece.

Turner's genius, Thackeray appreciated less quickly (and not until Ruskin's *Modern Painters* had started to educate the public), but when he did it was with the same enthusiasm for what he saw as unerring rashness and haste. Reviewing the 1839 Academy exhibition, he made patriotic capital out of 'The Fighting Téméraire', but found the rest of Turner 'mad and incomprehensible'. The following year he was in two minds about 'The Slave Ship', discoursing half-facetiously about the squirted bladders of vermilion, the white lead laid on with a trowel, and wondering whether it was sublime or ridiculous. He felt it might be an idea to hang Turner's paintings upside-down, and see if that would improve them. But 'Rain, Steam, and Speed' in the 1844 exhibition entirely converted him. From dabs of 'dirty putty' slapped on the canvas, and 'smeary lumps of chrome', something new and marvellous had come into being. 'The world has never seen anything like this picture.'

Contrariwise he got annoyed about painters who cultivated exquisite finish. He strongly disapproved of Rembrandt's pupil Gerard Dou, who was reputed to have spent five days in painting a hand, and who, in the interests of exactness, used to view his subjects through a frame crossed with silk threads. Such courses, Thackeray believed, led to triviality and stiffness. In his own century the 'daguerreotype minuteness' and 'finikin air' of Richard Redgrave likewise upset him, and he suggested that Redgrave should be put on a diet of port wine and devilled kidneys to make his painting less feeble. He came to think, as his snobbishness increased, that there was something positively ungentlemanlike in laborious devotion to art, though he was forced to concede that it sometimes produced its own kind of success. The fictional outlet for this set of prejudices was the unlikely John James Ridley (generally known as J.J.) who makes his first appearance in *The Newcomes*. J.J., we are told, is a genius – and Thackeray contrives some exalted verbiage to corroborate the fact: 'O enchanting boon of Nature' etc. But he is also sickly, humble, timid and not a gentleman, being, indeed, the son of Lord Todmorden's butler. His wit is a bit slow, and he has no passion. However he is careful to draw every leaf on each tree and every hair on each animal he depicts, and by this promising expedient he eventually wins universal renown as an artist and becomes a Royal Academician. Not that his achievements bring him much pleasure, for he would much rather, Thackeray assures us, be a gentleman, and likes nothing more than to be among dashing, well-bred youths like Clive or (in the later novel) Philip, whom he admires in his spineless way (and who are both, of course, glamorous versions of the young Thackeray).

Still, this dismal creature and the social attitudes that spawned him were far in the future at the time when Thackeray was falling for Rubens and Turner and being thrilled by Carlyle's prose. His yen for writing in odd, offhand places seems to have been an effort, whether conscious or not, to get the unsettled, flashing quality that these masters could command into his own art. The notion of sitting down, day by day, in the same oppressively known work-space repelled him like something gone stagnant. Pubs and cafés suited him best, because of their bustle and racket. 'There is an excitement in public places which sets my brain working', he explained. The routine chores of plotting and planning stories suffered rather, of course. His method of composition (as J. A. Sutherland's study of the manuscripts shows) was essentially opportunistic, relying on ideas coming as he wrote, and quick reflexes that could adapt the narrative to them. Half the time he could not remember what he had written even a day or two before. We find him making a memo to read through all his Titmarsh work again in case he'd been repeating himself (he had, a great deal), and writing to his publisher to get back the start of a story he had sent in, because it had gone clean out of his head and he didn't know how to carry the thing on. The same letter contained a request to have the start of *Vanity Fair* back too, and this sort of incident has caused tremors in critical minds about whether Thackeray cared enough for his craft.

He cared, but his care was directed to different ends: not making up plots and complications, which he always found a bit footling, but trying to snatch the quick, bright things from life as the great painters had. The fear that it might not be possible in words kept nagging him. Galleries made him especially defeatist. In the Louvre he would glower dejectedly at a Carel Dujardin, noting how 'a few bladders of paint and pots of varnish' had created morning dew twinkling in the grass, and silvery vapours rising from the blue lowlands. 'You can tell the hour of the morning and the time of the year: you can do any-thing but describe it in words.' On his Irish trip, too, he felt words inadequate, as *The Sketch-Book* endlessly records. Everything was different from England – the shape of the clouds, the lights and shadows, the huge red moon over 'white purple flats', the woods 'flinging round eddies of mustard coloured leaves'. It needed Dujardin or Berghem or

Claude. Printer's ink could make no headway in picturing it. In the novels with painters in them, Thackeray gets across the sense that words are no good by making his artists think how they could do the novel better on canvas. Even the preposterous Clive Newcome has serious moments of this kind. He explains about Ethel's hair, for instance (which the novel has to settle for calling 'jet black'): 'If I painted it, I think I should paint it almost blue, and then glaze it over with lake.' Of course, once you have written that, you have in a sense achieved the thing in words, which was one way round the problem for Thackeray. Alluding to some bit of painterly technique, or some actual painting, that will help out the prose effect, is a favourite device of his. It wasn't affectation. He did it quite naturally in letters and chat. 'The very picture of Rubens's second wife in face and figyour', he wrote home jubilantly, for instance, about a pretty girl he had met in the States.

Understandably, in these circumstances, he was always getting urges to abandon writing and go back to the easel. 'Dreadfully bitten by my old painting mania', he reported himself in 1841; and later, rhapsodizing about the pictures at Vienna: 'Whenever I see them I want to shut myself up for two years and turn painter.' He wasn't good enough, as he well knew. Besides, he had doubts about painting, as about words. It was, after all, dead and still in the end. It only pretended to capture life's fleetingness in its gummy tinctures. 'That brickdust which we agree to receive as representing a blush, look at it', he insists in *The Newcomes*, 'can you say it is in the least like the blush which flickers and varies as it sweeps over the down of the cheek?' Words at least had some mobility and give in them and, being arranged in sequence, used time in their effects, whereas paintings just stood stationary. Thackeray realized he was being hard to please, and mused on the strange way in which the arts seemed to supplement and countermand one another in his experience, so that he could never quite answer for it that it was a picture, not a melody, or a sonnet, not a landscape, that he was being exposed to. He found he always wanted to criticize one art in terms of another. His ideal, insofar as he managed to settle on one, wasn't painting or writing but ballet. When he tried to find an equivalent to the brilliant architecture of the mosques in Cairo it was 'a pirouette by Taglioni' that he selected. Ballet – lit, quick, never precisely repeatable, hugely skilled but apparently spontaneous, and using real live materials for its designs – answered most of his requirements for art.

However, being fifteen stone and short of wind, he was not well fitted for a career in ballet (though he did have dancing lessons in Paris from the famous Coulon). Words were his job, and he strove to give them the immediacy of life. A start towards this was inventing new, onomatopoeic ones for noises which the old noise-words failed to distinguish between. 'Cloop', for the special noise of a wine-cork being drawn, proved handy, in view of Thackeray's subject matter. He made it up in *Men's Wives*, and returned to it frequently. Most of his other coinages are for impacts: special missiles hitting special surfaces. Tom Dale's square-toed shoes pass 'papping' down the street in *The Ravenswing*, and the women at Smyrna, more slovenly, go 'plapping' about in 'odious yellow papooshes'. 'Plapping' does for bears and water, too. The zoo's white bears in the *Roundabout Papers* 'winked their pink eyes as they plapped up and down by their pool', and Barnes Newcome's eloquence goes 'plapping on like water from a cistern'. There are also unpronounceable joke-noises, like 'grwlwlwlw' – which represents the worshipful company at a city dinner sucking down turtle soup; further special footwear noises – like the 'dismal clinting' of horses' hoofs in *The Irish Sketch-Book*; and noise-words which, though appropriated rather than coined, are rare enough to have the custom-built look of a coinage – 'flump', for instance. Things that 'flump' in Thackeray include mailbags on a ship's deck, chairs on the carpeted floor in *The Paris Sketch-Book*, and a Skye-terrier on Philip in *Philip*.

Missiles and impacts, even without special words for them, are used to force vividness into Thackeray's writing. No one forgets Becky flinging Johnson's Dictionary into Miss Pinkerton's front garden at the start of *Vanity Fair*, or Rawdon tossing his son up in his arms and bumping his head against the ceiling, and frantically begging him not to cry lest he should wake Mama. Likewise when Rawdon junior is allowed as a treat to go down among the hounds at the Queen's Crawley meet, we learn that he is excited but alarmed 'by the caresses which they bestow upon him' and 'the thumps he receives from their waving tails'. The weight and vigour and agitation of the animals, and the child's littleness, spring out at us from the thumps with the sharpness of life.

But Thackeray's normal subject matter did not allow books or children to be thrown about much. What he developed was a style that, even in unviolent moments, works in flashes or spurts that relay a lot of information and suggestion very fast, so that the reader, as in life, sees more rapidly than he understands. It was what he admired in other stylists. From George Sand's *Spiridion* he picked for praise a sentence which he translates: 'I looked into the garden; it was deserted, and the midday wind was roaming among the flowers.' Ordinary enough, you'd think. What attracts Thackeray is the terseness, and the way space is implied through movement – the wind 'roaming'. How skilfully the strokes are 'dashed in', he remarked; and a sentence in *The Irish Sketch-Book* seems to be trying to imitate the Sand effect: 'You are on a wide green plain, diversified by occasional cabbage-plots, by drying grounds with white chemises, in the midst of which the chartered wind is revelling.' Less terse: but the same attempt to create space and loneliness through air-movement; and the 'revelling' of the wind naturally transfers to the chemises, so that the idea of white clothes dancing about is conveyed without being stated.

This deft suggestiveness happens all over Thackeray. Selecting examples is like picking grains from a beach. The contexts, of course, do not need to be quick or bright themselves. At sea off Algiers he notes 'gloomy purple lines of African shore, with fires smoking in the mountains'. There it is the sense of brooding, unknown watchers that the glimpse of smoke supplies. But the thing is observed almost cursorily, while Thackeray's attention is sweeping on to the next bit of landscape, just as in a sketch it might be caught in a couple of pencillings. His metaphors and similes are put in with the same masterful carelessness – brief, unelaborate – like someone switching a light on and off to glance round an empty room. In *The Kickleburys on the Rhine*, for instance, the eye travels over the riverside scenery – towers, cliffs, and 'the green vineyards combed along the hills'. The figurative word immediately lights up the odd, foreign neatness of the hillsides, the vine-rows look quite sharp and solid. But it doesn't have the air of a word that Thackeray has much bothered over: just a monosyllable slipped in. The easy-goingness and the brilliant effect were what intrigued him in Rubens: now he can do it himself, in prose.

In the comic work the simile or metaphor has to illuminate and demolish the target at one go, while still remaining perfectly succinct and natural. Thus in *A Shabby Genteel Story* the curls of the Misses Gann are, we are informed, arranged on their shining foreheads 'damp and black as leeches'. The extreme, if oily, care the girls have taken over their coiffure, and their profound unwholesomeness, drop on the reader in one short, fat word. And as in all the examples in the last two paragraphs, the colour-words, are bare, bold and businesslike: white, green, purple, black – very Thackerayan, the way they are slapped in 'raw' (as he said of Rubens); and very important for giving the feel of swift certitude to the writing.

When Thackeray is being ironic (and he is among the greatest of English ironists), the casual air becomes vital. The tone has to be refrigerated, the detonating words craftily muted, so that the reader is almost out on the other side of them before their ridicule bursts around him. As usual, examples clamour for inclusion. There is a pleasing one in the Pumpernickel episode in *Vanity Fair*, where Thackeray is being unusually genial. On *fête* days, we learn, 'the delighted people are permitted to march through room after room of the Grand Ducal palace, and admire the slippery floor, the rich hangings, and the spittoons at the doors of all the innumerable chambers'. By the time he reaches the spittoons, of course, any reader will have realized the palace is being undermined. But 'slippery' sidles itself more innocently into the word-flow, particularly as large, well-polished floors are, in common experience, a source of awe to those on guided tours. Thackeray, as in a comic sketch, snatches the one aspect of the subject that makes it new and ludicrous.

To maintain the negligence and bravura Thackeray had to get his effects with the simplest words. They had to look easy and spontaneous. The sort of simpering learnedness that Charlotte Brontë, say, goes in for – as when she calls a sneeze in *Villette* an 'unlucky sternutation' – would have ruined things at once. But though the words had to be just common bits of currency, they had to be capable of linking into subtle compositions. Compare, as an illustration, the way Thackeray uses an ordinary word like 'hard' in describing two different facial expressions. First, the Earl of Crabs. In *Yellowplush* we see him looking 'hard and kind' at nurserymaids in the park. Here the two words tend to contradict each other. 'Hard' conveys the lustful glare; 'kind', the smiles with which the old lecher tries to mask it. The combination is quick and masterly – and looks easy because the words are so mundane. Watching lustful old men look at girls was, of course, a speciality of Thackeray's: we recall General Tufto leering under bonnets in *Vanity Fair*. The second 'hard' is used to depict little Rawdon's look in the head-bumping episode. He looked, we're told, 'in a very hard and piteous way at his father', and strove to obey his terrified injunction not to cry lest he wake Mama. Here 'hard' operates quite differently. It registers the boy's clenched effort to keep back his tears. It also suggests his startled realization that his father is afraid. He has good reason to look hard: he has just learnt something new about his parents' relationship. This power to make ordinary words do subtle things very quickly is a hallmark of Thackeray's style, and it reminds us of how he used to pore for hours over those 'dabs of vermilion' in Rubens's painting, wondering how such cheap, easy components could be combined to create a masterpiece.

Evocativeness is another gain of the speed-writing method. The brevity stimulates imagination. Crowds of people, all busily pursuing their avocations, seem to jump into being from a few snippets of language. It happens constantly in Thackeray's letters:

And now writing has made me hungry and if you please I will go and breakfast – at a Café with lots of newspapers and garçons bawling out Volla Msieur how pleasant to think of.

No customers: a café full of newspapers and waiters. But of course we fill in clientèle, chairs, trays, glasses, and all the rest of the café scene around the couple of details Thackeray notes. Eliot's 'And sawdust restaurants with oyster-shells' functions in a comparable way. Indeed, Eliot often comes to mind as a writer working similarly in evocative fragments that sometimes combine into bigger wholes, sometimes not. Brief poems like *Gerontion* or *The Waste Land* appear massively inclusive partly because of their lack of unity. Odds and ends of lives, historically and geographically remote, are intercepted like conversations overheard on an international exchange:

> And when we were children, staying at the arch-duke's,
> My cousin's, he took me out on a sled . . .

The provocative impression, too quick to quite catch and hold, of troikas and winter palaces and samovars (vaguer and better if one doesn't know that Eliot happened to be quoting Countess Marie Larisch at this juncture), is an instance of what creates the poem's suggestive aura. A corresponding technique in Thackeray accounts for the sense readers get of life being multitudinously present, when in fact his subject matter is highly selective. Barry Lyndon's memories, for example, frequently take the form of scraps and hints deployed, like Countess Marie's, to create vistas of rich but elusive living (quite possibly spurious in Lyndon's case, since he is such a liar), as when he recalls how he first met the Valdez 'with her eight mules and her retinue of gentlemen, by the side of the yellow Mançanares', or dreams of 'another drive with Hegenheim, in the gilded sledge, over the Saxon snow'.

Eliot's fascination with light-effects ('violet light', 'white light folded', 'filled with water out of sunlight', etc.) makes another link with Thackeray, who loved light, and was endlessly intrigued by its vagaries and coruscations. In the Mediterranean he kept trying to find words for the effects of 'astonishing brightness' – the palm trees in Rhodes 'with a sort of halo of light round about them'; Lisbon 'hot and shaky', as if there were an earthquake in the air. He liked to compare the sparkling atmosphere of Paris, where even the gutters made 'long, glistening lines' ('invaluable', he said, to a painter), with the smoky 'India-ink' look of London. London light was most tolerable in the early morning – 'rosy'. In *Mrs. Perkins's Ball* he admires the 'rosy' morning air while drinking coffee at a stall in Regent Circus before the rest of the world has got up; at the start of *The Virginians* the marble fauns and dryads at Castlewood 'cool themselves' in the 'rosy' sunlight, while dew twinkles on the parterres. How people or objects restricted or reflected light was the first, and often the only characteristic he noticed about them – the hulking London footman making a darkness in the cabin as he stoops through it in *The Kickleburys on the Rhine*; or the silver stubble on Major Pendennis's chin 'like an elderly morning dew'; or the little gallery of dancing girls and opera nymphs in Foker's room, lit with 'flickering illuminations' – as if they were alive – by 'dusky' streams of sunlight; or Altamont's chains, jewellery and white wristbands, 'which the illumination from the house lighted up to great advantage' during his altercation with the policeman outside the Clavering mansion; or the shining milk pots ('delightful to the eyes of a painter') which, apart from the works of art, were the one thing that took Thackeray's fancy about Antwerp. Similar pots glitter cheerily in *Vanity Fair* at moments when the main actors are occupied with loss or grief. On the day of Sir Pitt's funeral the pots of the undertaker's men flash in the sunlight from the pub doorways, and porter pots are sunning themselves on the railings when old Sedley and his wife make their bankrupt retreat to the Fulham Road. The power to bring even unpromising parts of his novels to life through light was something Thackeray never quite lost. In *The Newcomes*, for instance, Lady Clara's guilty love for Jack Belsize – not a subject that could be safely detailed – acquires some vividness simply through Jack's light-reflecting qualities. The glimpse we get into Clara's mind shows her remembering how beautiful he looked on his charger in the Royal Birthday parade, 'all in a blaze of scarlet, and bullion, and steel'. Belsize blazing sounds transfigured, like a lifeguardsman by Turner, and we get some inkling of his hold on the girl's imagination.

Thackeray's favourite literary quotations were, predictably, about light-effects. In *Pendennis* Mr. Campion's carriage entering Shepherd's Inn, with the horse flinging froth from its nostrils and the shiny bit and the groom's breeches glittering white, 'makes a sunshine in that shady place'. A pair of white kid gloves seen in the Temple, or the shirts and brooches of Negroes in the States, bring the same bit of verse (remembered from the *Faerie Queene* I iii 4) to Thackeray's mind. And 'chequered shadow' (from *Titus Andronicus*) occurs repeatedly in the art criticism as well as in *The Fitzboodle Papers* (where vine-leaves cast 'a pretty chequered shadow' over Minna's face), in the last chapter of *Philip*, and so on. Collisions of light and shade are used to print scenes on the mind. In *Henry Esmond*, when Mohun leaves Castlewood, the courtyard is split up into brightness and shadow, with a black greyhound and white spaniel to intensify the contrast, and a *memento mori* sundial as fateful commentary. Esmond remarks how this chequered eyeful has 'remained fixed' in his memory, lest we should miss the photographic effect.

Watching light meant documenting things which might not, to the unpainterly, seem very gripping – like the Paris gutters, which Thackeray apologized for dwelling on, but found irresistible. Buttons come into this category. It can safely be said that Thackeray is the leading describer of buttons among English novelists. They are frequently a great deal more important to him than either the clothes they fasten or their wearers. *A Shabby Genteel Story* has Swigby's glistering brass buttons, and a footboy 'glistering all over with sugar-loaf buttons' who brings a ray of light to out-of-season Margate. Nathan Houndsditch's lady in *The Book of Snobs* wears 'parti-coloured glass buttons, expanding from the size of a fourpenny-piece to a crown', which 'glitter and twiddle' all down her front. Jeames in *Yellowplush*, having attained wealth through railway speculation, invests in a jacket of McWhirter tartan with large mother-of-pearl buttons engraved with coaches and horses and sporting subjects. 'When I danced with Coralie de Langeac at the fêtes on the birth of the first dauphin at Versailles', boasts Barry Lyndon, 'the buttons of my amaranth velvet coat alone cost eighty thousand livres'; and Max, in *Catherine*, shows off a diamond-studded snuff box with a button wrenched from the Duke of Bavaria's coat set in it. Jos Sedley sports an apple-green coat in *Vanity Fair* with 'steel buttons almost as large as crown pieces', and when his father is ruined and falling into decay it affects his buttons, which begin to show copper through their plating, while his coat goes white at the seams. (Thackeray had written about the same coat earlier, in *Yellowplush*, only there it belonged to the fallen Deuceace – 'a shabby blue coat with white seams and copper buttons'.) Colonel Newcome's 'flashing buttons' cause 'all eyes to turn to him', we are told. But the outright winner in the button class is Foker. When Pendennis first encounters him he has basket buttons on his green cut-away coat, and a white upper coat, 'ornamented with cheese-plate buttons, on each of which was engraved some stirring incident of the road or the chase'. He later graduates to waistcoat buttons representing monkeys' heads with ruby eyes. These earn Blanche's especial admiration, and another female button-fancier is Ethel in *The Newcomes*, whose reaction to meeting Clive is 'What very pretty buttons!'

Thackeray's attachment to buttons was perfectly conscious. He enjoyed discussing changes in button-fashion, remarking in *Mr. Brown's Letters to his Nephew* that in the Prince Regent's time waist buttons were worn between the shoulder-blades, whereas by the mid century they were rapidly descending towards the heels. The course of history could be observed through button-movements. As a matter of fact Thackeray's life coincided with a revolution in button-manufacture. During the eighteenth-century the Birmingham button industry had turned out hand-made gilt or steel buttons with facets which sold for large sums. But mechanical processes gradually supervened, and in 1807 a Dane called Sanders invented the composite fabric-covered metal button which was intended to merge into the cloth on which it was sewn. In 1825 his son invented a flexible canvas shaft for this button, so that it could be more cheaply fitted.

So (except for soldiers and servants, who wear out-of-date clothes as a professional duty) bright-button-wearers belonged to Thackeray's youth. That was another reason why he enjoyed writing about them. But brightness was the main one, and if we think how buttons were later to enliven the composition of, say, Manet's 'The Fifer', we shall find it less odd that Thackeray picked on them so eagerly. He was a keen critic of buttons in the painters of his own day, remarking, for instance, in his 1840 Academy piece for *Fraser's* on the 'hideous dress with upper-Benjamin buttons' in a portrait by Stone. His eye for buttons in real life showed itself when he met Henry James. The great novelist was nine at the time, and sheathed in a tight jacket with brass buttons all down the front. Thackeray, who was on a visit to Henry James senior's house, cowed the child by telling him that in England he would be addressed simply as 'Buttons'.

Thackeray seems to have felt at times that he ought to justify his enthusiasm for buttons by making them do something in the action of his novels. When Rawdon Crawley challenges Lord Steyne, he makes preparation for impending disaster by entrusting his gold sleeve-buttons, all he has left, to Macmurdo for transmission to little Rawdon as a memento of his father. Both men weep over the pathetic trinkets, so that buttons achieve a certain tragic dignity. The elder Pendennis evidently had the same idea, for when Pen, debt-struck, is selling off his assets at university, he spares two old gold sleeve-buttons which, we learn, had belonged to his father. In *Philip* the button becomes violent. Ringwood Twysden barges into Philip at the Embassy Ball, causing one of the gold buttons on his old-fashioned coat to fly off with a dramatic 'crack!', and this occasions physical combat between the two men. Later, in a finely-lit scene, Philip strides home along the Champs Elysées at midnight, 'under the gusty trees, amidst which the lamps of the *réverbères* are tossing', and gazes fondly at one of his surviving buttons upon which Charlotte's cheek had rested. A button has erotic significance in *Henry Esmond* also. Rachel demonstrates her love for the hero by thieving one of his buttons: it is given pride of place at the novel's close: 'the only jewel by which my wife sets any store, and from which she has never parted, is that gold button she took from my arm on the day when she visited me in prison, and which she wore ever after, as she told me, on the tenderest heart in the world.'

On the lookout for highlights, Thackeray's eye also relished objects that had just come out of someone's mouth – pipes, cigars, bits of barley-sugar – which, being still covered with saliva, shone. One of his early pieces, *A St. Philip's Day at Paris* (1841), describes the Champs Elysées bedecked for Louis Philippe's birthday, with drums, squibs, lamps and a fat man in the sunshine sucking barley-sugar in 'a beautiful conical way', the 'amber apex' glistening between the eye and the sun. He never forgot the scene, and rewrote it shortly before his death in *Philip*, where Mrs. Baynes takes her little boys to the Champs Elysées, for a treat, lets them climb trees and watch Guignol, buys them 'pink sticks of barley-sugar', and observes them as, 'withdrawing the glistening sweetmeats from their lips', they point out to her the delights of the place. The peculiar intimacy of something just taken out of the mouth gave it an erotic as well as a luminous potential for Thackeray. The bewitching Minna Löwe in *The Fitzboodle Papers* lights Fitzboodle's pipe for him, sucking the amber mouthpiece seductively, and tossing her head back to blow the smoke out, until Fitzboodle grows faint with desire, and hurries home to mumble the amber mouthpiece between his lips 'like a bit of barley-sugar'. Becky, it will be recalled, later tries the same tactics with Rawdon, taking his cigar and puffing at it 'with a little scream'. When he gets it back he remarks on its improved flavour.

This association of glistening amber-colour with sex ties in, of course, with Thackeray's fixation about girls with blonde or auburn or red hair. He found them both disturbing – even repellent – and irresistible, and often tries in the early works to resolve the quandary with jocular references to 'carrotty' locks, and so forth. His wife was a red-head: it was one of the things about her he couldn't get out of his mind. 'Your little red-polled ghost pursues me everywhere', he wrote before their marriage. Becky is 'sandy-haired' and Beatrix Esmond 'auburn'. In the later writing, where the women are elevated and purified, the barley-sugar-coloured hair is sometimes transferred, for safety, to the men; but it has unfortunate results. The repeated rhapsodies on Philip's flaming whiskers make him even more ridiculous than he would otherwise be, and the sight of Colonel Newcome stroking Clive's 'yellow mustachio' with 'a look of beautiful inexpressible affection' is also hard to take as seriously as Thackeray would wish. On women the amber hair has an insidious, slightly coarse suggestiveness which keeps it interesting, and it loses this when it is stuck onto decent young gents like Philip or Clive.

Arms, though, not hair, were the part of the female anatomy that aroused Thackeray most. Their paleness and mobility satisfied his craving for reflected light, and their bareness seemed provocative, as it did to Eliot:

> Arms that are braceleted and white and bare
> (But in the lamplight, downed with light brown hair).

Bare white arms attract Fitzboodle successively to Dorethea Speck and to Minna, and Barry Lyndon first feels desire for Nora when he bandages up her arm, 'mighty round and white', after she has scratched it. Harry, in *The Virginians*, falls for Maria's round white arms which

46

she cleverly shows to advantage by playing billiards, and he dreams (with a sexual explicitness that Thackeray certainly did not intend) of 'his Maria and his horse', and 'how sweet it would be to have one pillioned on the other' and ride 'with such a pair of white arms round his waist'. Becky's 'dazzling white arms' are among her prime assets. Jos sits enraptured, gazing at them, and when she is out to inveigle Lord Steyne she arranges a barrage of candles 'in all sorts of quaint sconces, of gilt and bronze and porcelain', and sits before them with her arms floodlit, 'half-covered with a thin hazy scarf through which they sparkled'. Even when she declines into squalor and seedy hotels, her arms retain their almost phosphorescent quality. Jos finds them up several flights of stairs, shining out 'very white and fair' from the pink domino, faded and soiled with pomatum, that Becky is reduced to receiving visitors in. Rachel and Beatrix Esmond possess arms of national standing, according to Henry, who talks about them as if they enjoyed a degree of independence, like items in an inventory – 'two pairs of the finest and roundest arms to be seen in England'. Rachel's are the finer – 'my Lady Castlewood was remarkable for this beauty of her person' – and this helps to explain why Henry chooses to marry her, not Beatrix. In the scene where he passes these judgements both women have their arms daubed with white to enhance the glare – 'covered with flour up above the elbows', since they are making pastry.

These gleaming, shoulder-mounted antennae which Thackeray's women are fitted out with are not sexually attractive in any simple sense. They carry a feeling of threat and hardness – arms for arming – which complicates their allure. Thackeray had bad luck with women, as we have seen. His mother deserted him when a child; his wife went mad; his mother-in-law was a monster; Jane Brookfield thwarted him; and some other woman seems to have given him V.D. The feats of hypocrisy and meanness of which women are uniquely capable often occupy his pen. The shining arms they carry in his stories are not just light-effects, but express a particular view of the world (as, indeed, all light-effects must: Thackeray's buttons, for instance, draw attention to the cultural gulfs that lurk within minutiae – like eating peas with a knife). The separateness of women, and their need to fight or exploit men in order to survive, much impressed him. Becky and Amelia, in their different ways, both illustrate this – as do all his worthwhile females.

Lower class women were more separate and had to fight harder than others. Their sturdy arms and their greater freedom in showing them were a source of especial excitement to Thackeray, as his poem 'Peg of Limavaddy' in *The Irish Sketch-Book* shows. Peg was a maid at an inn, whose beauty put Thackeray into such a dither that he spilt ale down his trousers. The poem which celebrates this event is an odd little exercise in humiliation and regression, and records how he sat there with the liquid trickling down inside his trousers, and enjoyed hearing the big woman laugh at him, and watching her scour a kettle with her strong, bare arms. In *The Ravenswing* Morgiana's arm – also lower class – has a similar robust thrillingness as she heaves up her tankard with it – 'one of the finest round arms' covered with 'the biggest bracelets ever seen'. But the most powerful of these proletarian arms belong to Miss Fotheringay the actress, Pendennis's first love:

It was her hand and arm that this magnificent creature most excelled in, and somehow you could never see her but through them. They surrounded her. When she folded them over her bosom in resignation; when she dropped them in mute agony, or raised them in superb command . . . it was with these arms and hands that she beckoned, repelled, entreated, embraced her admirers.

Miss Fotheringay's gesticulating arms form a glistening display-cabinet (you see her 'through' them), which she carries around with her. But inside is a stupid, mercenary girl. Arms give flash and sparkle to the females Thackeray creates, and they also suggest why he thinks them rather a let-down.

Another type of display-cabinet, incidentally, that occurs so frequently in Thackeray's work that it gets to seem like a nervous tic is the bow-window of a London club with a row of faces behind it. The details vary: in *The Irish Sketch-Book* the image appears simply as 'stout men in the bow-windows of clubs'; in *Mr. Brown's Letters to his Nephew* it becomes Lord Hugo simpering out of the window of White's; in *Pendennis* 'the heads of respectable red-faced newspaper-reading gentlemen' are seen crowding the bow-windows of clubs during the London season; in *The Newcomes* old men in the window of Bay's yawn 'as widely as that window itself' – and so on. To collect all the minor variations would take hours. But basically the thing remains the same, and has the starkness of an emblem: a bulge of glass, with faces peering through it at the world beyond clubland. In its repetitiveness it provides an instance of the way in which Thackeray's art simplifies and schematizes life – as any art must – while appearing to represent its complexity. And it again shows that Thackeray's light-effects entail an interpretation of the world. The gleaming pane of glass represents his acknowledgement of a social barrier, and the faces beyond, comfortable, yet faintly comic, reflect his inclination to be ironic about social barriers and uphold them at the same time. Like bare arms, club windows are an expression of his divided feelings.

Bare shoulders which with their bony points of shoulder-blade and collar-bone make more efficient light-reflectors than bare arms, usually indicate moral unsoundness in Thackeray's women. (Blanche and Beatrix both have 'pearly' shoulders, and Blanche's – 'never easy in her frock for a single instant' – betray her fidgeting self-regard.) They are consequently less common than arms, but Thackeray uses them brilliantly as a focus in *Going to See a Man Hanged* – an eye-witness account of the execution of the murderer François Benjamin Courvoisier, which was published in *Fraser's* in August 1840.

A masterpiece of impressionistic reporting, this work draws together a mesh of light-effects (growing more garish as the sun rises), and of intensely relished physical images, so that the vividness of life stands out clamorously against the darkness into which Courvoisier is to be plunged. That he is to be, as it were, blacked-out – hooded and dropped into a dark hole from which the executioner's hands reach up to pull his legs and strangle him – is the aspect of his fate that seems most horrific to Thackeray. At the start of his account he reconstructs Courvoisier's last night from the published reports: how he ground his teeth in his sleep, was woken by the jailer at four, wrote to his mother, refused breakfast. Keenly contrasted with this is the elegant *petit déjeuner* Thackeray and his friends enjoy – coffee, fowl, sherry and soda – and the lovely scraps of the morning scene which their eyes take in as they drive to the scaffold: the drab-silk coach linings, the cigar smoke, white and pure in the clear air, the dew on the grass in Gray's Inn and the windows in a flame, and the crowd hurrying along the broad, bright street, with blue shadows marching after them. Mixing with the crowd round the gallows, Thackeray records types and faces in a seemingly disconnected way, so that the sense of waiting around for something to happen is preserved. But actually his observations distinguish rigorously (and understandably) between the spectators on the ground, like himself, and those who occupy the better vantage points who are more glaringly exposed to the early sunlight. With the groundlings he feels democratic sympathy that extends to the condemned man. The others disgust him. The group which most excites his contempt comprises several tipsy, dissolute-looking young people, with one man 'lolling over the sunshiny tiles, with a fierce sodden face', while the women of the party:

were giggling, drinking and romping, as is the wont of these delicate creatures; sprawling here and there, and falling upon the knees of one or other of the males. Their scarves were off their shoulders, and you saw the sun shining down upon the bare white flesh, and the shoulder-points glittering like burning glasses.

Thackeray's objection is not precisely moral. A young thief's mistress in the crowd, who swaps ribaldry with the standers-by, behaves quite as disreputably as the roof-top group, yet he feels attracted to her and her 'devil-may-care candour'. The harshly-lit women perched on the roof repel him because they create a cruel, raucous light-effect with their bare shoulders, besides being immodest. His sensitivity to light and his morals are intertwined.

When Courvoisier appears on the scaffold it is Thackeray's genius for rapidly-caught facial expressions that makes the scene unforgettable:

His arms were tied in front of him. He opened his hands in a helpless kind of way, and clasped them once or twice together. He turned his head here and there, and looked about him for an instant with a wild imploring look. His mouth was contracted into a sort of pitiful smile. He went and placed himself at once under the beam.

The smile is the astonishing thing. It suggests a sort of half-embarrassed resignation, like that of a child agreeing to take part in a game it has really grown too old for. Courvoisier smiles almost apologetically, it seems, at the self-destructive role he has to play, as he goes to stand under the beam.

Thackeray's response to light was too various for it to have any regular association with moral repulsion, as in this glimpse of glittering Jezebels above the gallows. But when the lights start to dazzle and cluster around women in his writing it often spells danger, as if the gleam of their jewels or flesh, or simply of pieces of metal they are holding, were an unwholesome energy darting out of them. At the catastrophe in *Vanity Fair*, when Rawdon surprises Becky with Lord Steyne, she is arrayed 'in a brilliant full toilette, her arms and all her fingers sparkling with bracelets and rings', and Steyne's diamonds flashing on her breast; and at the end of *Pendennis* Blanche has just received a serpentine bracelet, blazing with rubies, from Foker, when Pen bursts in on the couple. Likewise when Henry Esmond puts an end to Beatrix's proud hopes, by bringing her news of Hamilton's death, he finds her brilliantly lit in a room full of 'flambeaux', holding a great charger of chased gold in her 'fair arms', her eyes shining out 'like beacons of alarm'. Esmond senses the ruthlessness in the light-effect, and shouts 'Herodias!' – an allusion to the beheading of John the Baptist which Clive Newcome, who feels the same way about Ethel, repeats. He plans to paint her 'as Herodias's daughter sweeping down a stair – in a great dress of cloth of gold like Paul Veronese – holding a charger before her with white arms . . . a savage smile on her face and a ghastly solemn gory head on the dish'. There isn't, as it happens, a Veronese of Salome; but the way Clive imagines it, with a staircase and a gold robe, is very much in Veronese's style.

This example helps to show how, in the later Thackeray, the light-effects deteriorate. They tend to become stagey. Gems and various kinds of lighting-equipment are accumulated in a mechanical way when a big scene has got to be written, and anyone used to reading Thackeray will be able to tell beforehand that significant action is afoot, simply by the amount of candle-power about. In *Philip*, for instance, the brightly-lit fountain at the Embassy Ball, with oil-lamps placed around it to set off its splendour, is plainly there for Philip to kick Ringwood Twysden into, which he obligingly does. And Thackeray is by this time so sick of the whole business that he sarcastically advises his readers to arrange the flowers round the fountain 'according to their own exquisite tastes', since he can't be bothered to imagine them himself.

Young Thackeray, on the other hand, found himself swept into fantasy by light. In *The Curate's Walk*, noticing a goldbeater's sign over a door sets him wondering about goldbeaters and their work: 'Do they get impregnated with the metal? And are their great arms under their clean shirts on Sunday all gilt and shining?' It's impossible to conceive of the post-*Vanity Fair* Thackeray caring about what colour a labourer's skin was. Light takes the commonness out of common objects in the early writing – a barley-sugar stick, a woman's shoulders 'like burning glasses', or the Bluecoat boy he notices in *Beulah Spa* – 'His yellow stockings glittered like buttercups on the sunshiny grass', or a child having its hair cut off in *A Legend of the Rhine*, 'until he looked as if he was sitting in a bath of sunbeams', or a girl in Beirut whose eyes 'gleamed out like penny tapers' from the shadows she was hiding in. In these examples the light is chance and quick, and caught by Thackeray in quick, seemingly spontaneous images. The light-sources are vulgar, not gems or Embassy Balls, and they are important in themselves, poetically, not as flares for some dramatic event which the narrative is about to unroll.

The last time Thackeray was able to combine a really exciting response to light with a plot-climax he wanted to illuminate was in the scene where Pendennis takes Fanny Bolton to see the fireworks at Vauxhall. (It must have been a poignant scene to write, for, a few months before she became insane, he had taken his wife to see the fireworks – one of the rare treats he gave her – 'Isabella had her heart fixed on it', he had written to his mother, 'and she doesn't put me to much expense in way of amusements'):

How she wondered! how happy she was! how she cried Oh, oh, oh, as the rockets soared into the air, and showered down in azure, and emerald, and vermilion. As these wonders blazed and disappeared before her, the little girl thrilled and trembled with delight at Arthur's side – her hand was under his arm still, he felt it pressing him as she looked up delighted.

The fireworks express something going on inside the human actors just as surely as the bazaar fireworks in *Ulysses*, which Bloom and

Gerty MacDowell see from Sandymount beach, as she exposes her nainsook knickers to his fascinated gaze and provokes him to self-abuse:

And then a rocket sprang and bang shot blind and O! then the Roman candle burst and it was like a sigh of O! and everyone cried O! O! in raptures and it gushed out of it a stream of rain gold hair threads and they shed and ah! they were all greeny dewy stars falling with golden, O so lively! O so soft, sweet, soft!

Arthur Pendennis, of course, does not go as far as Bloom. On the brink of becoming an interesting character, he draws back and informs Fanny that they 'live in very different stations'.

The colours Thackeray ascribes to the fireworks – 'azure, and emerald, and vermilion' – are unusually ornate for him (in deference, perhaps, to the exquisiteness of Fanny's thrill). Generally, as we have noted, he keeps colour-words bare and minimal. When he combines colours in a scene, he does what he admired Rubens for doing – leaves them lying 'raw' by the side of one another to create an impression of swift mastery – 'the artist not having taken the trouble to blend them'. The lollipop-girl Fitzboodle remembers falling in love with at school, who sat with 'red cheeks' before a 'white cloth' mending 'blue worsted stockings', is typical. So is the sentence which describes Lady Clavering taking her ease: 'In a white bonnet with a yellow feather she ate a large pink ice in the sunshine before Hunter's door'. The colours in these compositions seem to acquire a clear, untouched intensity – as if exposed to full sunlight – from the stark, single words they are registered in. The crude contrasts, the refusal to mix any colour or let it blend with the next, mean that the scenes come across in vivid blocks, and more glaringly – an effect Thackeray comments on in one of his *Roundabout Papers*, where he notes how the 'blazing heaps' of oranges on street-stalls get more brilliance from the proximity of their blue-paper wrappings. It would be naive, of course, to imagine that this pigmentation, seemingly dashed-in and casual, is really the product of carelessness. Elaborate and copious colour-words are much more likely to be the sign of carelessness, as of youth, in a writer. What Thackeray's streamlined palette evinces is rigorous control.

The colours he usually limited himself to, in order to get the most resplendent effect most succinctly, were red and white. Red intrigued him. In *The Newcomes* he makes Mr. Smee give a discourse on the dangers and delights of red, and the difficulty even Rubens found in managing it, while planning to include a bit of red ribbon in his portrait of the Colonel, 'just to warm up' the design. In *Philip* J.J. notices 'how well that old woman's red cloak comes in', when staking out paintable scenes in the countryside. Red's capacity to startle is exploited by Thackeray in, for instance, *The Paris Sketch-Book*, where he recounts how he unfortunately turned up too late for the guillotining of Lacenaire, and found, when he got to the place, only some ragamuffins dancing on a puddle of red ice. Less gruesomely, the winter sun, 'hung like a red-hot warming-pan' in the 'lilac haze' over Dulwich ponds (from the *Roundabout Papers*), shows redness lighting up Thackeray's style even late in life. That Thackeray's use of red was influenced by his study of Rubens seems highly probable. In his early Antwerp period Rubens commonly employed glaring patches of red to pull together and enhance the tints of his work. The robe of the Virgin in 'St. Francis Receiving the Infant Christ', at Lille, is an instance. And in 'Christ on the Cross with Mary, John and St. Magdalene', now in the Louvre, the robe of St. John is, as Edward Dillon has put it, 'an unmitigated mass of brightest vermilion'. There is an absence of positive hues in the rest of the picture, which limits itself to greyish violets and dull greens, but because of the proximity of red the general effect is one of brilliant colouring.

The way red objects stick out from the countryside, noted by J.J., is what Thackeray exploits in *Vanity Fair* to give a panoramic sense of Belgium on the eve of Waterloo:

This flat, flourishing country never could have looked more rich and prosperous than in that opening summer of 1815, when its green fields and quiet cities were enlivened by multiplied red coats: when its wide *chaussées* swarmed with brilliant English equipages: when its great canal-boats, gliding by rich pastures and pleasant quaint old villages, by old chateaux lying amongst old trees, were all crowded with well-to-do English travellers.

The phrase 'multiplied red coats' makes focus-points break out on the broad generalized green countryside, so that the eye is made to feel it could take in the whole landscape synoptically, as in a canvas. To handle his European subject, Thackeray had to manage these rapid vistas, and his concentrated colour-sense – especially his red – stops them getting vague. *Vanity Fair*'s description of Gaunt House is another instance of big sweeps of time and space being pinned down with red spots:

Peering over the railings and through the black trees into the garden of the Square, you see a few miserable governesses with wan-faced pupils wandering round and round it, and round the dreary grass-plot in the centre of which rises the statue of Lord Gaunt, who fought at Minden, in a three-tailed wig, and otherwise habited like a Roman Emperor. Gaunt House occupies nearly a side of the Square. The remaining three sides are composed of mansions that have passed away into dowagerism – tall, dark houses, with window-frames of stone, or picked out of a lighter red. Little light seems to be behind those lean, comfortless casements now: and hospitality to have passed away from those doors as much as the laced lacqueys and link-boys of old times, who used to put out their torches in the blank iron extinguishers that still flank the lamps over the steps. Brass plates have penetrated into the Square – Doctors, the Diddlesex Bank Western Branch – The English and European Reunion, etc. – it has a dreary look – nor is my Lord Steyne's palace less dreary. All I have ever seen of it is the vast wall in front, with the rustic columns at the great gate, through which an old porter peers sometimes with a fat and gloomy red face – and over the wall the garret and bedroom windows, and the chimneys, out of which there seldom comes any smoke now. For the present Lord Steyne lives at Naples, preferring the view of the Bay and Capri and Vesuvius, to the dreary aspect of the wall in Gaunt Square.

Here time and space slip and slide with a litheness entirely Thackerayan. From Gaunt Square in the Regency period, one avenue strikes back past lacqueys and link-boys and three-tailed wigs to the Roman Empire, and another shoots forward to the time of writing and current commercial usurpers of the Square like the Diddlesex Bank. And from the spatial oppressiveness of the Square, with the governesses and their pupils wandering dementedly 'round and round', a line springs out to the Bay of Naples and Vesuvius. The red window frames and the porter's red face are the only dabs of colour, breaking the gloom and fixing the Square for the eye as times and places dissolve around it.

As against red's warmth, white, used alone, was sinister for Thackeray. In the béguinage at Ghent, for instance, he saw 'a couple of old ladies in white hoods tugging and swaying about at two bell ropes', while five hundred others, in white veils, sat mutely contemplating, and it struck him as frightful – 'white, and ghastly. Like an army of tombstones by moonlight'. Nuns, or any species approaching them, always upset him – enforcing that apprehension of woman's separateness and armedness that glinting white arms and shoulders also aroused. In Ireland, not far from Carlow, he met 'a couple of cars drawn by white horses, and holding white Quakers and Quakeresses, in white hats, clothes, shoes, with wild, maniacal-looking faces, bumping along the road'. Their religious extremism (which he always hated) and their 'hideous white raiment' coalesce in his mind. In *Denis Duval* the perilous scene in which the crazed Madame de Saverne gets out onto the beach with her baby, and almost drowns it, shimmers with whiteness – the moon over the sea, the 'tide of silver' pouring up the sand, the white slipper on the path which showed where the mad woman had gone, and her form 'glimmering out of the dark' in its white wrapper. The episode had a special horror for Thackeray, being

based on his wife's attempt to push their daughter Anny into the sea
when they were staying at Margate in the early stages of her insanity.

But red and white flagrantly juxtaposed constitute the standard
Thackerayan colour-combination, as much a mark of his style as club-
windows or buttons, and there with the same eye-rinsing intent. As
you follow the reds and whites through his career, you notice, as with
other light-effects, a tendency towards the mechanical. Where before
there had been an eager response to garishness and odd angles and
low life, you find yourself landed with a sort of candy-striped routine.
Typical of the early colouring is the comic climax of *The Fatal Boots*
where Stubbs, in the butcher's moonlit back-yard, is confronted by
two 'white, ghastly-looking' sheep's carcasses and a 'great gutter' of
blood. Thackeray drew special attention to the effect of moonlight on
the dead sheep when writing to Cruikshank about the illustrations.
Not a subject much in the later Thackeray's line. Nor is the superb
Lady Gorgon from *The Bedford-Row Conspiracy*, who resembles a
'healthy, broad-flanked, Roman-nosed white dray-horse' clad in
'flame-coloured satin', and whose feelings cause seismic tremors in
her person: 'An immense heave of her ladyship's ample chest was
perceptible. Yards of blond lace, which might be compared to a foam
of the sea, were agitated at the same moment, and by the same mighty
emotion. The river of diamonds which flowed round her ladyship's
neck seemed to swell and to shine.' Also contributing to the red-and-
white violence of *The Bedford-Row Conspiracy* are the ears and collar
of William Scully, M.P. – 'his ears looming over his stiff white shirt-
collar as red as fire'. Such ears intrigued Thackeray, and he returned
to them. He gave them to Joseph Swigby in *A Shabby Genteel Story*,
for example, who arrives for tea with 'his great ears shining over his
great shirt-collar delightfully bright and red'. And touring the Low
Countries in 1843 Thackeray noted down another sighting of 'fat men
with large white shirt collars sawing under great raw ears'. Ears –
now looming, now shining, now being sawn – show Thackeray reacting
to the observed world with originality and unstuffiness. Things a dull
eye would regard as trivial become central. Images are found that
make them radiant and weird – the chef's hat in *A Little Dinner at
Timmins's*, for instance, contrasting with his crimson velvet waistcoat,
and so white that it 'looks as if it had been just skinned', or the cab-
boy's 'long dusky white hat – that looked damp and deep like a well'
in *Cox's Diary*.

In *Vanity Fair* and *Pendennis*, red and white are still used with
power, and still at times with a feel for the surprises that come jumping
out of the commonplace. Becky's life explodes with a flash of red and
white when Rawdon, bursting in on her, flings the diamonds at Steyne
and leaves a 'burning red mark' on his 'white, bald, shining forehead'

which he bears to his dying day. In the bustle of departure on the morning of Waterloo Amelia, white-faced and in a 'white morning dress' follows George about, helplessly trying to be useful. She:

had taken up a sash of George's from the drawers whereon it lay, and followed him to and fro with the sash in her hand, looking on mutely as his packing proceeded. She came out and stood, leaning at the wall, holding his sash against her bosom, from which the heavy net of crimson dropped like a large stain of blood.

The big operatic pose, full of portent and psychological depth, springs directly from Thackeray's alertness to queer yet mundane red-and-white conjunctions. So does the moment in *Pendennis* when Fanny Bolton, cast off by Pen and affianced to the malodorous Huxter, is greeted by Pen when they meet at the Derby, and notices, among his other refinements, 'the circle on his white forehead that his hat left when he lifted it'. Tenderness and desire blend in the noticing. Pen's delicate skin, lovingly spied, sets Fanny thinking unthinkable thoughts. And the red-and-white glimpse has the oddness that, elsewhere, would turn comic, like red ears over a white collar.

By comparison the later red-and-whites are hackneyed. Thackeray pounds away at the known expedient in hopes that it will animate his writing. Lady Castlewood in *Henry Esmond* is a red and white composition, from her face – 'daubed with white and red up to the eyes, to which the paint gave an unearthly glare' – down to her 'white pantofles with red heels'. But it looks like what it is – historical-novelish high-colouring: it is quite unrelated to anything freshly or genuinely seen. Beatrix, who is supposed to be beautiful, is given a similarly grotesque complexion, as if Thackeray were describing a clown: 'her complexion was as dazzling white as snow in sunshine; except her cheeks, which were a bright red, and her lips, which were of a still deeper crimson.' Worse still, in *The Newcomes*, with its elevated claptrap about Ethel's 'glorious colour of rich carnation and dazzling white', we drop into stuff that has never passed through the imagination at all. It is partly having his perceptions represented by such bursts of cliché, with the pretence that they signify 'the ardour of a painter', that makes Clive Newcome so fatuous a figure.

Thackeray's manipulation of light and colour falls off, then. Slovenly formulas replace the quick, bright perceptions. It affects the very bones of his writing. For it would, as I have suggested, be over-simple to regard light and colour as optional extras, unconnected with meaning. To a large extent they determine what meanings can be purveyed. The importance, for Thackeray, of the arresting light-effects that people make with their clothes and bodies, for instance, relates both to a watchfulness and to a detachment from them, as people, that permit irony to operate. Similarly, the definiteness of his colouring, with its hard contrasts and unqualified tones, is of a piece with the peremptoriness and certitude that irony roots in. More tolerant, concessive or involved meanings could not co-exist with light and colour as Thackeray apprehends them.

Fixing on light-effects that would strike others as incidental (and, contrariwise, missing what ordinary people regard as essentials) were, it should be added, not mannerisms that Thackeray cultivated for his fiction, but long-established traits. No doubt his short-sightedness was a factor in developing this light-attracted vision. His one clear memory of his childhood home in India was of a portrait of his grandfather that hung there, in which he recalled not the sitter but 'above all how the stick was painted, which was made to look as if it was polished and shone'. And when he bought his wife's engagement ring he noticed the brightness of the stone, not the black setting, and did not realize, until it was pointed out to him, that what he had bought was a mourning ring.

3

Commodities

When, in *Yellowplush*, the Hon. Algernon Percy Deuceace is confined in the Fleet Prison, Jeames, his manservant, promptly deserts him, in response to a bribe from the Earl of Crabs. Thackeray intended this as a more realistic account of menial loyalty than Dickens had provided in Sam Weller, and he alludes to the Fleet episode in *Pickwick* lest we should miss the comparison. The moment of taking the bribe, a £50 banknote, is a moving one for Jeames: 'My fingers trembled a little as I took the pretty fluttering bit of paper', he recalls. Of course, the note is extremely important to him as cash – five times larger than any sum he has previously possessed – and its moral significance is not wholly lost on him either. But it is a highly Thackerayan touch that he should see it, at this crisis, as simply a bit of paper. The thingness of things, their intractable otherness, intrigued Thackeray, as did the decisive role they play in all human activities. Animating things, pretending they had some sort of latent life in them, struck him as a cheat – a whimsical concession to human weakness that blunted the tragic absurdity of life. This was one of the factors he resented in Dickens and his imitators. 'Every object in the world is brought to life and invested with a vulgar knowingness and outrageous jocularity', he complained. The very trees 'squint, shiver, leer, grin and smoke pipes'.

In his own writing things regain their status as things. He likes to expose the ways in which people meddle with them and twist them into extensions of their personalities. Letters, especially, provoke him to this. The physique of letters – their weight, colour, smell; the look of their wax and script – occupy him as much as the personal meanings their senders have tried to graft onto them: sometimes more. We know that Blanche's letters to Pendennis arrive in 'pretty little satin envelopes', written 'in a delicate hand' on 'pink scented paper', but their contents are rarely divulged. Nor do they need to be, for the stationery alone reveals Blanche as a scheming minx. It is practically impossible, in Thackeray, to write a decent letter on pink paper. Miss Griffin's ill-judged love-letters in *Yellowplush* are rose-coloured, and smell like a barber's shop. Howard Walker in *The Ravenswing* inscribes his invitation to the Crump family on pink notepaper, and as a further indication of his hideous tastelessness, places it in a filigree envelope sealed with yellow wax. When Rawdon writes to his wife from prison requesting her help, Becky returns 'a beautiful letter, highly scented, on a pink paper with a light green seal' – to match her eyes – composed entirely of falsehood, much of it in French. Note-paper's tendency to betray those who foist their human interests upon it is illustrated, too, by Pen, who spends hours kissing the 'musky satin paper' of Miss Fotheringay's letters, though unbeknown to him they were written by her friend Miss Rouncy, Miss Fotheringay being more or less illiterate.

An appreciation of the texture of his mail is part of Major Pen-dennis's elegantly organized life. We first find him at breakfast in his club, savouring through a gold eye-glass, the collection of 'large solemn dinner cards', 'neat little confidential notes', and communi-cations on 'thick official paper', that has recently arrived through the post. Mrs. Pendennis's letter, with its country postmark, and Arthur's, written 'in a great floundering boy's hand', with 'supplementary wax sputtered all round the seal', are placed on one side by the Major, as unfit to mix with the fasionable London stationery.

The personal look which letters acquire is most poignantly dis-credited by Thackeray when he describes the last one George Osborne wrote to his father – delivered at the Russell Square house weeks after George's death:

The great red seal was emblazoned with the sham coat of arms which Osborne had assumed from the Peerage, with 'Pax in bello' for a motto; that of the ducal house with which the vain old man tried to fancy himself connected. The hand that signed it would never hold pen or sword more. The very seal that sealed it had been robbed from George's dead body as it lay on the field of battle.

The object which George regarded as his individual insignia is being put to other uses by people to whom he is not so much as a name, and its emblem and ludicrously inept motto were never his anyway. It is cruelly appropriate that the monument which old Osborne places on the church wall to commemorate George should likewise lack any real connection with his dead boy. The mourning marble figure and Latin quotation are standard items from what was, in wartime, a rather busy production line:

The sculptors of those days had stocks of such funeral emblems in hand; as you may see still on the walls of St. Paul's, which are covered with hundreds of these braggart heathen allegories. There was a constant demand for them during the first fifteen years of the present century.

In this way objects in *Vanity Fair* repeatedly withdraw into a stark, commercial dimension from the clutches of people who want to cherish or humanize them. Similar withdrawals, though less frequent, occur in the later novels. Thus the silver coconut-tree table-ornament in *The Newcomes* ('whereof the leaves were dexterously arranged for holding candles and pickles') retains its protrusive and ridiculous existence among the members of the Newcome household, quite refusing to merge, though their attachment to it is so eager that Mrs. Mackenzie tries to carry it off in her trunk when the Newcome fortunes tumble.

Being unable either to appropriate objects or to carry on without them, humans are placed in an ironic position, which Thackeray liked to prod at and juggle with. Naturally the objects he concentrated on were those people rub up against most, like commodities and clothes. Trees, mountains, and suchlike stirred him very little, unless someone started commandeering them for a human use. The only tree that gets more than passing attention in his novels is the hollow one in *Pendennis* which Blanche and Pen use as a letter-box; and typically we are not told what sort of a tree it is. Flowers did not strike him as significant until they were made up into bouquets and buttonholes. To profess an enthusiasm for nature's remoter aspects appeared to him a mere affectation. Of a nautical number among Procter's *English Songs* he observed: 'How absurd it is to write about the Ocean in Upper Harley Street, and say you would "ever be" there. Nobody really likes it.' It was a reasonable complaint, for Procter had, as a matter of fact, never set eyes on the sea at the time when he wrote the offending verses. Becky pretends an interest in the stars, in order to captivate the bewildered Rawdon:

'O those stars, those stars!' Miss Rebecca would say, turning her twinkling green eyes up towards them. 'I feel myself almost a spirit when I gaze upon them'.

'Oh – ah – Gad – yes, so do I exactly, Miss Sharp', the other enthusiast replied.

One enthusiast is a liar, the other a fool, and admirers of the stars were likely, in Thackeray's view, to fall into these two categories.

An exception to his general negligence of the natural world is the gooseberry bush. The arbitrariness is perfectly in character. Critics who call him 'realistic', though right to a degree, leave out of account not only the narrow limits he sets to his world, but also the way in which certain objects within it acquire a mesmeric prominence, which a realist would find puzzling. Gooseberries and gooseberry bushes recur in his writing with a frequency that seems out of all proportion, given the absence of other specified greenery. Like pink writing paper, they have a fixed moral standing, being habitually associated with innocence and childhood. Young Barry Lyndon first tentatively kisses his cousin Nora among the gooseberry bushes, and Eliza's pink frock among the gooseberry bushes captures her admirer's heart in *Bob Robinson's First Love*. Miss Tickletoby's little pupils are fed on gooseberry pudding, and in *Meditations on Solitude* Thackeray muses upon youth's strong appetite for gooseberry fool. His own childhood memories probably came in here. One of his earliest letters, written at the age of six to his mother back in India, reports 'I can eat Granmamas Goosberry pyes famously'.

No record survives of his grandmother drying washing on her gooseberry bushes, but that is a common role for the innocent shrub in his works. The Shum house in *Yellowplush* is a scene of easy-going domesticity, full of dishclouts and girls in torn pinafores eating bread and treacle, and it has four gooseberry bushes in front of it covered in washed linen. A neat little Swiss cottage with a garden where children hang pinafores on the gooseberry bushes figures in *Rebecca and Rowena*. The tranquillity, simplicity, and general saintliness of the life that Mrs. Pendennis and Laura lead at Fairoaks is likewise guaranteed by their gooseberry bushes having clothes drying on them – a feature which the odious Mr. Wagg derides when he comes on a visit from London. More clothes on bushes soften the blow in *Vanity Fair* when the old Sedleys, after the collapse of their fortune, creep off to bury their heads in Mr. Clapp's little cottage near the Fulham Road. It turns out to be one of those deliciously seedy bits of London that Thackeray and Dickens both have a way of stumbling on, with doll's-house-sized houses, and the sounds of jingling spinets drifting out of the open windows on summer evenings. And, to complete the idyll, 'the shrubs in the little gardens in front bloom with a perennial display of little children's pinafores'.

By becoming clothes-horses, gooseberry bushes qualify as commodities, which is why they fit into Thackeray's vision when the rest of the natural world won't. Commodities were an unfailing stimulant to him, though not everything about them stimulated him equally. He was not concerned with their manufacture, for instance. Tracing the resplendent window-display of Victorian wealth to its sources in mills and factories and mean streets of disease-stricken dwellings was not an enterprise that impressed him as at all enticing. His imagination kept returning, rather, to the relations, or failed relations, between commodities and consumers.

To stress the promiscuity of commodities – their disinclination to become personal items, however much their owners might want them to – he alludes incessantly to the stores from which they come and the brand names under which they are marketed. To annotate his stories you need a commercial directory of early Victorian London. Howell and James's (of Regent Street) and Gunter's were his favourite emporia, but scores of smaller vendors are cited, or invented, along with their addresses, specialities and usual advertisements. The carriages and flunkeys outside Howell and James's, like the women dripping with baubles inside, are a perpetual feature of his metropolitan scene. Mrs. Bumpsher in *Our Street*, for instance, whose husband is in wholesale stationery, parades rubies, ribbons, cameos and Valencienne lace 'as if she were an immense sample out of Howell and James's shop'. Becky, too, glitters with spoil from Howell and James's, including so many watches that 'her apartments were alive with their clicking' (a dead kind of aliveness, Thackeray implies). Among these 'a little bijou marked Leroy, with a chain and cover charmingly set with turquoises, and another signed Breguet, which was covered with pearls, and yet scarcely bigger than half-a-crown', were donated by General Tufto and George Osborne respectively. 'If Messrs. Howell and James were to publish a list of the purchasers of all the trinkets which they sell', comments Thackeray, 'how surprised would some families be.' What Becky's admirers regard as their intimate advances are seen as commercial operations, following lines as well trodden as a department store. Personal expression through gifts is impossible in a world of commodities, for the goods bear the public stamp of manufactured articles. Becky, when we are introduced to her watches, is totting up their value as realizable assets on the eve of the battle.

The sameness of the dinners people give is another side to the impersonality of the commodity world that Thackeray enjoys noting. In his stories about middle-class upstarts everything, from footmen to salt-spoons, gets hired at the same catering establishments, so that at every social gathering 'the same cutlets, fish and cucumbers, the same lumps of Wenham Lake ice', are carried round by the same greengrocers got up as butlers for the occasion and working at an hourly rate. It's typical of his early work that these hired menials arouse his curiosity more than the guests, who, like the fare, are standardized. In *Mrs. Perkins's Ball*, for instance, he finds himself considering how the pastrycook's men must despise the dowagers 'chumping away at plates of raised pie', since they see them at it night after night.

Higher up the prefabricated-food ladder one reaches Gunter's of Berkeley Square. Charles Honeyman in *Pendennis* tries to make an individual impression on Rosey and her mother by giving them lunch from Gunter's, complete with bouquets and a large pineapple, while Pen offers inferior ices and dessert from Partington's in the Strand. Gunter's supply wedding cakes for Thackeray's wealthier marriages. Jeames, in *Yellowplush*, orders his there when he comes into money, and the wedding of Clara and Barnes in *The Newcomes* is also dignified by 'a cake decorated by Messrs. Gunter with the most delicious taste and the sweetest hymeneal allusions'. Their union is, needless to say, quite loveless. Gunter's icing-sugar plaudits have an impersonal currency, like Becky's watches. Arranged marriages were anathema to Thackeray, of course, who sympathized with his mother over the way her family had tricked her into marrying his father. In his novels they are presented as elevated trade-conventions, with crowds flocking to see the Gunter's cake, the service of plate at Handyman's, and the diamonds being set for the bride, and with a bishop superintending 'the sale of the girl's person' at St. George's, Hanover Square.

But there is a danger in all this of making Thackeray sound dourly prejudiced against commodities. In fact, as the detailing of Becky's watches suggests, he loved them, even while he saw through them and their prizers. His rapturous accounts of shop windows bring to mind Mann's Felix Krull learning, through plate glass, to know the appurtenances of a high and discriminating way of life:

the bottles, the hair-brushes, the dressing-cases, the boxes with plates and cutlery and collapsible spirit stoves of the finest nickel; fancy waistcoats, magnificent ties, sybaritic underclothes, morocco slippers, silk-lined hats, deerskin gloves, and socks of gauzy silk strewn in seductive display.

The shops in the Palais Royal in Paris were Thackeray's Mecca – the glowing centre of commerce's rainbow world: 'those shops where the beautiful dressing-gowns used to hang out, more splendid and gorgeous than any tulips', 'that wonderful bonnet shop at the corner of the Gallerie Vitrée', resplendent with 'ravishing plumes of marabouts, ostriches and birds of paradise'. The thing that upset him most, going back to Paris after the 1848 Revolution, was to find these shops deserted and shut up, and squads of soldiers in the square showing 'dingy undervestments'. It is this side of Thackeray that Barbara Hardy strangely ignores when she claims (in *The Exposure of Luxury*) that he viewed commodities 'as sententiously and didactically as the Book of Daniel'.

It was a delight to him to imagine the riches of commerce being heaped on a beautiful woman. He instinctively connected love with buying things. 'For a kiss from such a dear creature as Amelia', he proclaims in *Vanity Fair*, 'I would purchase all Mr. Lee's conservatories out of hand.' The orgy of purchasing with which Rawdon celebrates his acceptance by Becky, though it has its comic side, is presented as a likeable and wholly human outburst:

He ordered in a piano, and half a nurseryhouse full of flowers: and a heap of good things. As for shawls, kid gloves, silk stockings, gold French watches, bracelets and perfumery, he sent them in with the profusion of blind love and unbounded credit. And having relieved his mind by this outpouring of generosity, he went and dined nervously at the club.

Thackeray wanted his women to revel in commodities. It was part of their lovable frivolity. Amelia's spending spree at the milliners and linen-drapers shows that she is not above the pleasure of buying pretty things, and, Thackeray adds, 'Would any man, the most philosophic, give twopence for a woman who was?' Squandering money expressed, for him, exuberance and vitality. Towards the end of his life, at the time of the massive success of his magazine, the *Cornhill*, a friend found him in Paris, beside himself with joy, and had to restrain him from buying 'a pocketful of diamonds' in the Palais Royal. In his journalism he often conveys the excitement of seasons of the year and suchlike natural happenings by transmuting them into events in the world of commerce. Spring is the time when 'Gunter and Grange come forward with iced creams and champagne', ducks and green peas burst out, and Dyer's embroidered pocket handkerchief advertisement appears. Country air (at Major Ponto's place, in *Snobs*) smells like *millefleurs* in Mr. Atkinson's shop.

His attitude to possessions was far from moralistic. He saw how the universal lust to own things led people into self-deceiving situations where his irony could play upon them, but he didn't think the desire wrong. Over this, he firmly contradicted the Christian view. Despite 'Vanity Fair', he was decidedly not a Bunyan. 'You have chapter and verse telling you to give up *all* to the poor', he wrote to his mother, who was extremely devout, 'and you don't – and you would be wrong if you did – Common sense being stronger in this case than chapter and verse.' Renunciation of worldly goods would, he believed, bring everyone to the condition of 'lousy Capuchins' clattering begging-boxes: 'what a world it would be!' He was both too attached to commodities to consider them wicked, and too self-aware not to realize the vanity of this attachment.

Sherrick, the most intriguing minor character in *The Newcomes* (where, admittedly, the competition is not strong), owes his being to Thackeray's imaginative urge to create a religion that depended wholly on commodities. Sherrick (alias Shadrach) owns the wine-vaults under Lady Whittlesea's Chapel and also, as it emerges, the mortgage of the chapel itself. He has showy horses, a box at the opera, and a mysterious past. According to rumour he was once an orange boy, and afterwards a chorus singer in the theatres, and Mrs. Sherrick, who also sings, is said to have had brilliant triumphs at La Scala and the San Carlo. Together they transform Lady Whittlesea's with a view to improving the clientèle. Flowers are imported from Covent Garden and a painted Flemish window from Wardour Street. Labels of faint green and gold, with long Gothic lettering, are introduced to give the place a medieval look, and Mrs. Sherrick sings Handel 'in a sort of nun-like costume'. Honeyman, the incumbent, is instructed to cough, on the grounds that women like a consumptive parson. These measures are perfectly successful. The chapel is soon filled 'with bonnets of the newest Parisian fashion', and Sherrick's pockets rattle with coin. Far from being condemned, he is presented as a resourceful and fair-minded figure.

A congregation of bonnets is quite in Thackeray's style. Of the commodities people annex to create their personalities, the most obvious are clothes, and clothes for Thackeray meant essentially hats, boots and gloves. Those, anyway, are the items he selects with obsessive regularity to display the finances and morals of his characters. He believed hats, boots and gloves the best barometers of social change. Poverty, he argued, always attacks the extremities to begin with: 'the coverings of head, feet and hands are its first prey'. Thus boots were not a joke to him, as they were to Dickens. A man's relations with his boots – the design he chooses, and what he cleans them with – are crucial to his destiny in a Thackeray novel. In the early work the morally reprehensible figures can be readily identified by their varnished boots. Deuceace, in *Yellowplush*, keeps a 'beautiful museum' of them, and the disgustingly familiar Mr. Slang in *The Ravenswing* sprawls with them on the furniture. They are popular, Thackeray points out in *Men's Wives*, with Frenchmen, who habitually clink along boulevards in them as they 'grin and chatter' about chaste English ladies. Wagstaff in *The Partie Fine* notices that the shady swell Fitzsimons sports high-heeled varnished boots ('I hate those varnished boots', Wagstaff muses). To compound the offence, Fitzsimons's moustache is lacquered with what Wagstaff suspects is the same varnish. 'Little lacquer-tipped jean boots' distinguish the Marquis of Carabas's son in *Snobs*, as does a shirt 'embroidered with pink boa-constrictors'; and though Jos in *Vanity Fair* cannot wear varnished boots since, as Thackeray explains, they have not yet been invented in 1815, his polished Hessians shine with great brilliance, and are likened to the boots in Warren's Blacking advertisement (by Cruikshank), which had a man shaving himself in them.

The perky, amiable clerks and commercial travellers in the early stories, on the other hand, are never seen in varnished boots – or, indeed, in real boots at all. 'We chaps in the City on £80 a year contented ourselves with Bluchers', Sam Titmarsh recalls in *The Great Hoggarty Diamond*, and what with a cheroot and one of Dando's glossy silk hats 'really looked quite the genteel thing'. Bluchers were half-boots, called after the Prussian field-marshal at Waterloo, and despised by toffs. Thackeray in his cockney art-critic days allied himself with the Blucher-wearers, referring to 'us poor fellows with Bluchers and gingham umbrellas'. However, in the social up-grading to which he subjected his novels after *Vanity Fair*, the Blucher and the varnished boot changed sides. Pendennis's varnished boots appear to advantage in the Derby Day scene beside the Bluchers of his coarse-grained rival Huxter, and Major Pendennis glories in a boot varnish 'incomparably better' than any competitors, the secret recipe for which is known only to his manservant Morgan. In *The Newcomes* the more normal moral qualities of shoe-leather start to reassert themselves. Clive's friends favour varnished boots, but so does the treacherous little absinthe-drinking dandy Barnes Newcome, whose footwear the hero appropriately punishes. 'I brought my heel down on his confounded little varnished toe', boasts Clive, 'and gave it a scrunch which made Mr. Barnes shriek out one of his loudest oaths.' By the time of *Philip* boots have come full circle. Philip's 'vulgar' Bluchers are contemned by the snobbish Mrs. Baynes, and approved of by Thackeray.

Thackeray keeps on about varnished boots partly because they are light-sources, of course, like buttons. Varnished boots on horseback especially caught his eye, being higher up in better light and moving quicker. Again and again he describes, or recollects, scenes in which they glitter – sometimes redoing the same scene twice as if to get the light more accurately (as in *The Newcomes* Chapter 43, for instance, and *Philip* Part II Chapter 7). Typical are Clive's friends of the Life Guards Green, exercising their 'magnificent thoroughbred horses' in Rotten Row, 'scarcely touching their stirrups with the tips of their varnished boots', and kissing 'the most beautiful primrose-coloured gloves' to the ladies they pass. The tips 'scarcely touching' have the speed and mastery that always captivated Thackeray, whether in a stripe of light across a Rubens or a pirouette by Taglioni.

Gloves – primrose coloured like the Life Guards', lemon-coloured, lavender-coloured, white – sprout all over Thackeray, with (for him) unusually flowery tints, and makers' names and prices attached. *An Interesting Event*, for instance, turns on the fate of a pair of 'beautiful white French kid, No. 8½', purchased at Houbigant's for three and sixpence; and Master Clavering's miniature yellow kid in *Pendennis* are the creation of Privat in the Rue Neuve St. Augustin (where Thackeray and his wife lived when first married). Gloves, like boots, may seem niggling items to heed, but ignoring them means missing Thackeray's visual and moral build-up. When you go through his works from start to finish, you find that gloves undergo precisely the same social revolution as boots. In the jaunty milieu of the early tales and sketches Berlin gloves (inferior articles, made of dyed wool), or at best kid gloves kept clean with india-rubber, are the favoured wear. Thackeray in *Men and Coats* jokes about his own old 'sausage-fingered' Berlins, bulging out at the ends and 'concaved like spoons'. To sneer at Berlin gloves is the mark of the undergraduate snob, in *Snobs*. But by the time he wrote *Pendennis* Thackeray could hardly bring himself to mention Berlin gloves without giggling circumlocution. Bungay's footmen wear gloves 'of the famous Berlin web', and the hands of the policeman who accosts Altamont are 'enclosed in gauntlets of the Berlin woof'. It shows Pen's high, generous nature that he should not only wear kid gloves of the most exquisite kind (lavender-coloured ones, stitched with black), but should also 'scorn' base economies like cleaning them for reuse; while in *The Newcomes* Mrs. Mackenzie proves her mean-mindedness by cleaning hers. In *Philip* gloves, like boots, revert to their old virtuous shabbiness. The hero is a mass of disintegrating haberdashery, with hands 'as red as raw beefsteaks' bursting through the seams of his 29-sou gloves in a way that is meant to put his honest manliness beyond doubt, and to distinguish him from his mincing little rival, who is swankily *'bien ganté'*.

With hats – the third tell-tale covering nominated by Thackeray – we come to a more restricted area. Women's hats, particularly garish turbans and bonnets with bird-of-paradise feathers, interest him far more than men's. In his writing, women who are past their prime, or in reduced circumstances, advertise, while seeking to conceal, their condition by topping themselves with monstrous decomposing creations. Thus Jemima, in *Yellowplush*, appears beneath 'a faded yellow velvet hat, with a wreath of hartifishl flowers run to seed, and a bird of Parrowdice perched on top of it, melumcolly and moulting, with only a couple of feathers left in his unfortunate tail'; and at the other end of Thackeray's career Mrs. Baynes, in *Philip*, preserves 'a dreadfully old performance, with moulting feathers, rumpled ribbons, tarnished flowers, and lace bought in St. Martin's Alley'. The care women take in safeguarding these fearful parodies of their own decline adds pathos to the satire. In *Vanity Fair* Mrs. Major O'Dowd leaves for Belgium with her 'famous yellow turban' locked in her husband's tin cocked-hat case, and the bird of paradise wrapped in brown paper.

But women's hats did not need to be old in order to dismay Thackeray. New hats could be just as bad, because of the vulgar attempt to appropriate the beauty of objects that they represented. This is demonstrated by Mrs. Cox in *Cox's Diary*, who flaunts 'a large fantail gauze with ostrich feathers, birds of paradise, artificial flowers, and tags of muslin or satin scattered all over it'. We have seen how enthralled Thackeray was by the 'wonderful bonnet shop at the corner of the Gallerie Vitrée', with its 'ravishing plumes of marabouts, ostriches and birds of paradise'. As objects, masterpieces of the milliner's art, he found the things entrancing. But when women stuck them on their heads, the result was frequently preposterous. Thackeray's varnished boots and exquisitely-tinted gloves are often let down by their wearers, too, as we have seen. Once people use commodities they lose their pristine perfection and become implements in the human system of self-aggrandizement. Besides, few people were beautiful enough, he found, to use the really high-class commodities at all. The hat which General Baynes buys for Emily MacWhirter in *Philip* drives this point home. Emily is a good woman, and there is nothing intrinsically wrong with the hat:

the sweetest thing you ever saw! green piqué velvet, with a *ruche* full of rosebuds, and a bird of paradise perched on the top, pecking at a bunch of the most magnificent grapes, poppies, ears of corn, barley &c., all indicative of the bounteous autumn season.

Thackeray phrases it so that there is no mistaking the disastrous effect of the hat on Emily. Its only appropriateness lies in its autumnal emphasis. Yet we are expressly informed that Baynes bought it in the Palais Royal 'at the corner shop under the glass gallery' – the very shop where Thackeray used to admire those ravishing bonnets, before they were impaired by contact with unworthy female heads.

One bit of woman's headgear became so spoiled for him by personal association that he could never think of it as a separate and harmless commodity at all, but always depicts it on malign misses or matrons. This was the *ferronnière* – a chain worn round the head, suspending a jewel in the middle of the forehead, and called after Leonardo's *La Belle Ferronnière*. Up with the fashion, as usual, Thackeray is cited in the Oxford Dictionary as the first user of the term (in a *Fraser's* article of 1840). In fact he had described a fellow-lodger in his Parisian hotel, back in 1834, as 'a long Miss Brooke with grey hair and a *ferronnière*, who looks as if she had committed murder'. The withered and predatory Miss Gam in *Dennis Haggarty's Wife* is addicted to cheap ornaments, 'brooches, *ferronnières*, smelling bottles', which would have been enough to warn poor Haggarty off, had he been a reader of Thackeray, even without her 'excessively bare shoulders'; and in *A Shabby Genteel Story* Mrs. Gann's 'large red turban' and smelling bottle 'attached by a ring to a very damp, fat hand', combine with a *ferronnière* in sullying her. One of Thackeray's surviving sketches of his mother-in-law shows her with a *ferronnière* (as well as a turban and massive nose), which accounts for the taint this trinket suffers in his work.

The *ferronnière* is not unique in being an authentic article from Thackeray's past. So is almost the entire wardrobe he depicts in his fiction, which is persistently nostalgic in drift. When he was young, as he loves to recall, there were still dandies about and dazzling brocade waistcoats and tall stocks with cataracts of satin and blue-and-gold handkerchiefs. The varnished boots and many-hued gloves, like the bonnets in the Gallerie Vitrée, belong to this world. While he had youth and money it had been at his feet. He did not begin writing till his mid-twenties, by which time he had squandered his way through more luxury than most people manage to lay hold of in their entire lifetime. The sudden loss of his fortune brought a sense both of the deceitfulness of commodities and of their painful desirability. Hence the vacillation we keep feeling in his work between their beauty as objects and their vanity as possessions. Hence, too, the repetitiveness and particularity of the luxury articles he harks back to as he writes. They have the unaccountableness, as well as the distinctness, of personal memories.

The silver dressing-case, which pops up in story after story, bears this out. As a youth Thackeray bought 'a grand silver dressing-case, so as to be ready for the beard which was not yet born', and the youths in his fiction whose precocious elegance he wants to bring out (Barry Lyndon, Bob Robinson, Adolphus Simcoe, Foker, Clive Newcome, Harry Warrington, etc.) are all accordingly equipped with silver dressing-cases. As a possession it is redolent of vanity. But it is also a shiny luxury article of fascinating intricacy (one of those noted by Felix Krull in shop windows, we recall), with its multiple dishes, boxes and bottles, all silver-topped (except Adolphus Simcoe's, who has had to pawn his tops, and is left with the cut-glass parts). Being needlessly elaborate, it has the self-justifying quality of pure expense, which is another reason why Thackeray likes it. Also its intimate relations with its user make it (like George Osborne's seal) the kind of possession which people mix up with its possessor. Thus Dr. Firmin gives Philip a dressing-case, advising him that 'it looks well on a man's dressing-table at a country-house . . . I have known women come in and peep at it'. For the women, the man's sexual appeal spills over into his commodities, and can be surreptitiously tasted when he is away. Really, of course, dressing-cases are as feebly attached to owners as any other objects, and Rawdon, estimating what he can leave Becky if he falls in battle, instructs her to pawn his, which he has never paid for anyway.

The most expensive commodity conveniently taken around and shown off, though, isn't a dressing-case but a vehicle, and vehicles are voluminously present in Thackeray, bearing much of the weight of characterization and social drama. Typically, almost at the climax of *Vanity Fair*, when Dobbin and Amelia have had their row, and Dobbin is leaving, we are reminded that Dobbin's carriage, which is being wheeled into the courtyard, cost only six pounds. It is a reaffirmation of his unshowy worth. Vehicles provide the poor with all they generally see of the rich, and the rich with all they generally see of the poor. Gorgeous equipages penetrating into dingy neighbourhoods, and being gawped at by the loiterers, are a recurrent subject, and the gawping is often two-way. When Miss Crawley, for instance, visits Amelia in Bloomsbury, the flunkeys hanging onto her carriage wonder at the locality in which they find themselves, and take the Sedleys' black footman to be 'one of the queer natives of the place'. Not that Bloomsbury would have seemed a poor neighbourhood to most people, but the incident helps Thackeray to map the social distance between Sedleys and Crawleys. The Bareacres' chariot and fourgon, lashed to the deck of the ship going to Germany, emblazoned with coronets and heaped with shining imperials, represent conspicuous expenditure of the most irresponsible kind, as Thackeray remarks, but they also belong to a class of objects that he found irresistible. Brightness, colour, grace and speed combine to captivate him, together with exquisite manufacture. Witness the description of a cab in *The Irish Sketch-Book*:

The cab was of lovely olive-green, picked out with white, on high springs and enormous wheels, which, big as they were, scarcely seemed to touch the earth. The little tiger swung gracefully up and down, holding on by the hood, which was of the material of which the most precious and polished boots are made. As for the *lining* – but here we come too near the sanctity of private life.

The sprightly detailing (with the suggestion of almost feminine delicacy about the cab's inside) typifies the heightened response to objects in the early work: his later books are much more vapid about their vehicles. And the scarcely-touching wheels, like scarcely-touching boots and stirrups, radiate the quickness and lightness Thackeray coveted. Not surprisingly, he likened his own style to 'a jaunty yellow park-phaeton'.

Horse-transport appealed, too, because steam-transport had, in his lifetime, begun to replace it. He loves remembering the stage-coaches of his boyhood – the roadside inns, tenantless now, and the cold veal pies at Bagshot, and the waiters in black tights. Changes of fashion in carriages were measures of time for him – in *Snobs*, for example, he shows young Ponto and Gules in the stables mocking Ponto's four-wheeled cruelty chaise and 1824 chariot. Up-to-dateness like this conveys the writer's expertise, his grasp of the commodity market. So does the rampant profusion of vehicle-types he specifies: Captain Rook's neat britzka, Mrs. Berry's smart calash, General Sir Hugh Rolfe's yellow postchaise, Rawdon's stanhope, Foker's black tandem with red wheels, cruelty vans driven by stout females in bustles, hired flies full of Jewish families in flaming polkas and flounces, Lord Mohun's chaise in *Esmond* – 'swift as a Laplander's sledge', the diligence of Laffitte, Caillard & Co., that took you from Boulogne to Paris in twenty-five hours, the old *coucous* that plied between Paris and

Versailles before trains came. The list is endless, and from the distinctive names we get a sense of an author urbanely cognisant of coach-building and horseflesh, and of the social nuances that gather round them. Actually, insofar as horses were concerned, the impression was quite illusory. Thackeray admitted in one of his letters that he didn't know a horse from a cow. But he sounds as if he knows, which is what counts in the writing, because he is able to use the right names for things.

The names imply control, as names always do, and characters unable to use the names are shown floundering – as when Amelia is puzzled by Jos's Anglo-Indian 'buggy', and still more puzzled when her father jocularly explains that it is 'a one horse palanquin'. Commodity name-dropping in Thackeray extends, of course, beyond vehicles, and is vital to his tone. It makes an exception to his normal, chatty diction, but serves the same end, since it suggests easy mastery, So the reader keeps finding himself up against odd words for kinds of tobacco ('latakia', 'canaster'), or for fabrics and laces and bits of costume ('tabinet', 'guipure', 'philibeg'), and having to recognize that 'rappee' is a kind of snuff, and a 'doodheen' a pipe, and that 'a great *bouffé* of Varinas' means cigars – all of which occur in just a few pages of the *Fitzboodle Papers*. True, Fitzboodle is exceptionally urbane, even for Thackeray, being the third best whist-player in Europe, and able to order a dinner in every Western language. But the exotic names, keys to the commodity-realm, are pervasive in the early writing, and their dwindling is symptomatic of the slackness that overtakes the later.

Brand-names are a similarly sophisticated device that Thackeray is versatile at using. They can give the writing a circumstantial, authentic air – as when Rawdon, noting down his effects, puts not 'gun' or 'saddle' but 'my double-barril by Manton', 'my Laurie'; or as when, in *Lovel the Widower*, it is not mere jam that Mrs. Prior the landlady filches but Morel's Raspberry. Or they can imply connoisseurship – as when, in *The Fat Contributor Papers*, it is a new 'Lincoln and Bennett' that blows off, rather than a hat. They can give a ludicrous cast to high deeds – as when in *The Tremendous Adventures of Major Gahagan* the Major disguises himself as a native and infiltrates the enemy camp covered in Warren's Blacking and Burgess's Walnut Ketchup. Or they can bring fantasy engagingly to earth – as when in Thackeray's fireside pantomime, *The Rose and the Ring*, the shoe which helps, Cinderella-fashion, to identify Rosalba has 'Hopkins, Maker to the Royal Family' stamped inside it. There are, too, trade-names that carry with them a permanent cloud of affectation – Delcroix's, for instance, whose macassar oils and essences provide Rook in *Captain Rook and Mr. Pigeon* and Major Pendennis and Charles Honeyman with their spurious fragrance. (Honeyman, anointed with perfumes

71

'into which a thousand flowers have expressed their sweetest breath', seems almost murderously gross as a result of his careful toilet.)

Trade-names have, too, a self-congratulatory air that attracts Thackeray's satire. Rowland's Kalydor, made by Rowland's of Hatton Garden, specialists in skin ointments, dentifrices and depilatories, struck him as an especially pompous product. He painstakingly alludes to pustules, whenever they occur, as 'those marks which Rowland's Kalydor is said to efface'; and the dashing George Delamere in *Rolandseck* is revealed, at the end of the story, as a traveller for Rowland's. Rowland's advertised in the monthly numbers of *Vanity Fair*, and with his zeal for commodities it's not surprising that Thackeray should have hit on the idea of writing a novel in which advertisements were incorporated into the text. His *Plan for a Prize Novel* in *Punch* is made up entirely of sentences like 'Lady Emily was reclining on one of Down and Eider's voluptuous ottomans'; and in the middle of *Mr. Brown's Letters to his Nephew* he drags in an advertisement for his own dentist, Mr. Gilbert of Suffolk Street, whom he had found commendably painless.

Prices, like names, suggest an informed, pertinent stance, and stop incidents shading into fantasy. Thackeray's anecdotes of his youth are inextricably wound around with memories of how much things cost. *Picture Gossip*, for instance, resavours the bundles of Torlonia's 4-baiocchi cigars he used to smoke with his painter friends in Rome as they drank Orvieto by the Pantheon Portico, and the scene comes up again in *The Newcomes*, by which time the cigars are half a baioccho more expensive. His Paris recollections wistfully return to the 15-sou coffee and breakfast at the Hotel Poussin, the bedroom at 30 francs a month, and so on. An eating guide to Paris in the 1830s could be quickly got together from his writings – the 2-franc house in the Rue Haute Vivienne, the 30-sou menu in the Passage Choiseul – and dinners, especially in his early stories, are scrupulously itemized and priced, like the one Wagstaff in *The Partie Fine* is obliged to pay £4 18s. 6d. for at Durognon's in the Haymarket. Expenditure and debt play a crucial role in all his longer and most of his shorter fictions. But by the time we come to *The Newcomes* the circumstances are sloppily adumbrated, if at all. Colonel Newcome's financial crash is one of those vague economic données that we come to expect in a Dickens novel, as remote from human control or understanding as meteorological phenomena. With the younger Thackeray, though, an accurately-kept account book is close behind the writing, and pokes into it firmly from time to time. Typically in *The Book of Snobs* old Ponto's talk of impending bankruptcy is backed up by the production of his son Lieutenant Wellesley Ponto's regimental tailor's bill, which lists twenty-two items, including a gold-laced dress jacket at £35, a pelisse trimmed with sable at £60, a regulation saddle at £7 17s. 6d., the whole coming to £347 9s. 0d. (expensive but, as it is explained, the 120th Hussars in which Wellesley has his commission is a champagne-and-claret regiment, not a port-and-sherry light-infantry outfit).

By surrounding his people with commodities – priced, catalogued, bearing trade-names and maker's labels – Thackeray strands them in a richly equipped but impersonal universe, and it is one of his purposes to show how they strive to satisfy their human needs – for love, for personal definition, for survival – by shifting commodities around and giving them to one another. The patent-medicine addicts, invariably women, are among his most abject fools, disintegrating into lists of repellently named quack nostrums which Thackeray makes up with increasing wildness and unlikelihood. Lady Blanche, in *Snobs*, swallows quantities of Gambouge's Universal Medicine, boxes of Parr's Life Pills, and inhales Squinstone's Eye-Snuff for headaches. Lady Southdown in *Vanity Fair* recommends Podgers' Pills, Rodgers' Pills and Pokey's Elixir. It wasn't just funny. Early nineteenth-century medicine was, by our standards, horribly rudimentary. The simplest scientific aids were either unknown or neglected. The stethoscope, for instance, was not even introduced into England before the third decade of the century, and it was not until the mid century that the clinical thermometer became established as a precise and regular means of observation. The medical profession was chaotic and inefficient. The establishment of the Register of qualified practitioners and of the General Medical Council took place only in 1858, and it was 1875 before an Act was passed setting up medical officers of health and responsible sanitary authorities. During the latter half of the century the death-rate of many towns was reduced by something like 50 per cent. Thackeray's women, desperately cramming themselves and their loved ones with useless medicaments to stave off pain, were a tragic spectacle as well as a ludicrous one. He recognized this, of course. The two elements come together in the great row between Amelia and her mother over Daffy's Elixir. They blend, too, in Thackeray's account of a visit to old Mrs. Buller at Richmond:

Her false teeth looked ghastly in her mouth and her chestnut wig over her wrinkled old forehead. Dear old haggard eyes how beautiful they were, even in my time – and how kind and affectionate she has always been to me. O Thackeray she said what a hardship it is to live to be old – and then she added with a sigh I have one hope left and that is – *blue pill and cod-liver oil*. It was tremendous the satire.

Thackeray wasn't much of a Christian, as we've seen. But Mrs. Buller, clinging to her commodities as the grave gaped, staggered even him.

What he usually notices, at death, is the heartless way commodities survive. As objects, they last longer than human love or pain. Their durability intrigued him. Death, for him, means loss of control over one's commodities, as life means manipulation of them. The smallest gestures of the bereaved bring this home. When Major Pendennis comes to Fairoaks at his brother's death, for instance, he is shown into the darkened drawing-room, and drinks a glass of wine from a bottle which, only four days before, had been opened for his brother. In *Vanity Fair* Jos, dining with old Osborne, embarrassingly asks where his host got his excellent madeira, whereupon the Osborne butler reminds his master, in a whisper, that it used to belong to Jos's father, whose funeral we have just been witnessing. What the survivors cannot eat, drink or reuse, they push out of sight. When Sir Pitt dies, his invalid chair is 'wheeled away into a tool-house in the garden', and the members of the Crawley family treat his body as another unserviceable commodity, 'packing it up in gilt nails and velvet', before putting it into the ground.

Old Sedley's death is marked by the survival of another material object besides madeira, and Thackeray gives the point general application:

As you ascend the staircase of your house from the drawing towards the bedroom floors, you may have remarked a little arch in the wall right before you, which at once gives light to the stair, which leads from the second storey to the third (where the nursery and servants' chambers commonly are) and serves for another purpose of utility, of which the undertaker's men can give you a notion. They rest their coffins upon that arch, or pass them through it so as not to disturb in any unseemly manner the cold tenant slumbering within.

The plunge from straggling chat about house-layout to a dead body contrives to reproduce the sense of alienation that comes upon us when friendly, familiar objects are suddenly seen to be quite detached from their moribund handlers, ourselves. Betjeman, the modern poet most realistic about death, notices it too. In his poem 'Devonshire Street W.1', a patient who has just learnt that he is fatally ill leaves the specialist's consulting room, with the terror of his predicament dawning upon him, and is struck by the unseemly composure of the material world – 'The opposite brick-built house looks lofty and calm' – and by its enviable nullness:

the iron nob of this palisade
So cold to the touch, is luckier now than he.

The new light which, as Thackeray proceeds, breaks around his innocent little staircase arch, issues from the same chilling consciousness.

Auction sales are the places at which commodities that have survived their owners congregate most plentifully, and there is a high frequency of them in Thackeray. Besides watches, Becky receives from General Tufto 'many very handsome presents, in the shape of cashmere shawls bought at the auction of a French general's lady'. The impression one gets is not so much of women sloughing off clothes, as of clothes sloughing off women. Thackeray liked going to sales: 'such sights suit the gloomy temper of my soul and besides are good for my purposes as a tradesman and satirist', he explained to Lady Blessington. Not long afterwards Lady Blessington's own furniture at Gore House came under the hammer, and Thackeray, who joined the crowd at the public view, was seen to be weeping, though he wrote half-facetiously to Jane Brookfield afterwards about the 'picture of Wanaty Fair' it presented. Sales made him tearful and cynical by turns, and what repeatedly strikes him at them is the way objects revert to their commodity-staus, shrugging off their private affiliations. 'How changed the house is', he writes of the Sedley sale in *Vanity Fair*. 'The front is patched over with bills, setting forth the particulars of the furniture in staring capitals. They have hung a shred of carpet out of an upstairs window.' The 'staring' capitals have the blatant, shameless look that turns a possession back into a commodity; and the 'shred' of carpet suggests a dinginess, which a possessor would hide, being unfeelingly publicized.

Describing sales, Thackeray regularly falls into characterless auctioneer-language, so as to show the familiar objects shrinking into commodities again: 'the rich, chaste and appropriate planned furniture, by Dowbiggin', for example, or 'the rich and splendid electrotype ware'. This is one element in the haunting passage that describes the closure of the Russell Square mansion after old Osborne's death:

The house was dismantled; the rich furniture and effects, the awful chandeliers and dreary black mirrors packed away and hidden, the rich rosewood drawing-room suite was muffled in straw, the carpets were rolled up and corded, the small select library of well-bound books was stowed in two wine-chests, and the whole paraphernalia rolled away in several enormous vans to the Pantechnicon.

The words show Thackeray's imagination lured on by the deserted furniture: the 'black' mirrors 'hidden', as if their failure to reflect the old faces were shameful or frightening; the drawing-room suite 'muffled', as if echoes or footfalls from the old life might otherwise still be heard; the books stowed in wine-chests, as bulk goods now, not for reading. Indeed, the ease with which old Osborne's effects slip back to being catalogue-ware suggests that they were never really owned. He had not enough personal warmth to permeate his possessions. They were simply objects, bought to enhance his prestige.

The treatment portraits get at sales epitomizes the callousness of the commodity world. Jos Sedley's, and later, in *Philip*, Dr. Firmin's, are both knocked down, amid laughter, for a few shillings. (In *The Newcomes*, typically, the auction sale is washed out by sentiment: Pen, narrating the affair, and coyly attributing his generous actions to 'a friend of the family', purchases the Colonel's swords, 'for which no single dealer present had the heart to bid'; and J.J. secures the Colonel's portrait for Clive – no one laughs.) When Dobbin at the Sedley sale buys Amelia's piano for her (just as Woolsey at the Walker sale had bought Morgiana's piano for her in *The Ravenswing*), it shows the untrustworthiness of commodities as love-tokens, for Amelia believes that it was George's gift, and when she discovers the truth it instantly loses all value in her eyes.

Whereas auction sales display the accumulation of commodities that a departing owner leaves in his wake, it is not unknown for Thackeray's characters to anticipate the sale, and regard their fellow men as a kind of mobile boutique. Isadore, Jos Sedley's valet, confident of a French victory at Waterloo and the consequent slaughter of the English in Brussels, occupies his thoughts, as he helps Jos through his complicated daily toilet, in reallocating the articles with which Jos is hung about. The silver essence bottles and toilet nicknacks are destined for Isadore's young lady; while the frilled shirts, gold-laced cap, frogged coat, gold-headed cane, sleeve-buttons and boots with brass spurs will decorate his own person, as will Jos's ruby ring, after it has been converted into ear-rings (*'Corbleu!'* Isadore muses, 'what an effect they will make in the Allée Verte!'). With robust cynicism Thackeray goes on to suggest that Isadore's viewpoint is common not only among servants but among intimates and 'dear relations' as well, though their victims naturally remain unaware, 'as you see one of Mr. Paynter's assistants in Leadenhall Street ornament an unconscious turtle with a placard on which is written "Soup tomorrow" '.

Nor is it just a matter of rapaciousness. Harmless and innocent characters think of other people as commodities because, having always lived among commodities, they have had their ideas of the desirable and of the elegant moulded by them. Their innermost feelings are enmeshed in commodity-standards. Even Dobbin's love for Amelia, which is as near as anything in *Vanity Fair* comes to being a respectable emotion, demonstrates this:

Very likely Amelia was not like the portrait the Major had formed of her: there was a figure in a book of fashions which his sisters had in England, and with which William had made away privately, pasting it into the lid of his desk, and fancying he saw some resemblance to Mrs. Osborne in the print, whereas I have seen it, and can vouch that it is but the picture of a high-waisted gown with the impossible doll's face simpering over it – and, perhaps, Mr. Dobbin's sentimental Amelia was no more like the real one than this absurd little print which he cherished. But what man in love, of us, is better informed? or is he much happier when he sees and owns his delusion?

The last question gives a new turn to the subject. For whereas to regard a person as a bundle of commodities might seem, to a champion of human dignity, an impoverishing delusion, Thackeray is prepared to entertain the possibility of its being an enriching one. If commodities cannot return love, they cannot disappoint it. Loving a high-waisted gown and a doll's face will hurt Dobbin less, in the long run, than loving a woman as selfish and unworthy of him as Amelia.

Besides, Thackeray's eager response to the beauty of commodities helped him to see that they might, in some circumstances, both attract and deserve more love than human beings. Little Rawdon Crawley's feelings for his mother provide an illustration of this. To him she is:

like a vivified figure out of the *Magasin des Modes* – blandly smiling in the most beautiful new clothes and little gloves and boots. Wonderful scarfs, laces, and jewels glittered about her. She had always a new bonnet on: and flowers bloomed perpetually in it: or else magnificent curling ostrich feathers, soft and snowy as camellias. . . . Sometimes when she was away, and Dolly his maid was making his bed, he came into his mother's room. It was as the abode of a fairy to him – a mystic chamber of splendours and delights. There in the wardrobe hung those wonderful robes – pink and blue, and many-tinted. There was the jewel-case, silver-clasped: and the wondrous bronze hand on the dressing table, glistening all over with a hundred rings. There was the cheval glass, that miracle of art, in which he could just see his own wondering head, and the reflection of Dolly (queerly distorted, and as if up in the ceiling), plumping and patting the pillows of the bed.

Rawdon, like Dobbin, substitutes a fashion model for a real person. He loves not his mother but her clothes and jewels. However, this is the wiser course, for Becky can neither merit nor return his affection, and if Rawdon knew what she was really like he would be overwhelmed with anguish. The metal hand on which she keeps her rings is, and is plainly meant to be, an apt representative of her motherly tenderness. Rawdon's mistaken viewpoint is a happy one, and his sensitivity to the loveliness of his mother's things is not presented as either despicable or valueless. Like his childish wonder at the mirror's distortions, it shows a fresh and vivid consciousness, ripe for life. And it is plainly shared by Thackeray, who gloats upon Becky's clothes as ecstatically as her son – those bonnets, reminding us again of the bonnets in the shop at the corner of the Gallerie Vitrée, with feathers, petals and snow downily interfusing, and blanching and softening one another, – 'feathers, soft and snowy as camellias' – as he compacts the words around them. Moreover, Becky does not look a fright in her bonnets, as Emily MacWhirter did in hers. If no more than a fashion model, she is a superb fashion model, and fulfils one of woman's timeless roles as a displayer of commodities.

True, Thackeray adds to the passage quoted a brief coda about Mother and God and the hearts of little children, which portrays Rawdon as a poor, lonely mite, 'worshipping a stone'. But this, by comparison, is merely a moist concession to the Victorian reader's pieties – and inaccurate, besides, for Rawdon was not worshipping a stone but a hat.

Thackeray is, then, the novelist of commodities, and of people apprehended through them. In Thackeray 'You belong to your belongings' (as old Lady Kew remarks in *The Newcomes*). Boots and dressing-cases, gloves and hats, vehicles and stationery, are not incidentals but pivots in his writing. He shows their involvement in the great human transactions like love and death, and in the formation of human values. It is through their names and prices that he impresses reality upon us. Their relations with people were, to him, infinitely suggestive of irony, pathos and absurdity; for like other nineteenth- (and twentieth-) century men he was caught between the Preacher and the Machine – between deeply-ingrained religious and philo-sophical attitudes that contemned material possessions, and a civiliz-ation devoted to the manufacturing of them; between the vanity of beauty, and the beauty of vanities. It is typical of Thackeray that the largest accumulation of commodities he witnessed in his lifetime – the International Exhibition of 1851, housed in Paxton's Crystal Palace, and covering 20 acres of Hyde Park – should have impelled him to write two opposed poems. The one is a grandiose celebration of the trophies of industry and the 'blazing arch of lucid glass' beneath which they are displayed. The other, in comic Irish, sees it all as meaningless heaps of teapots, canons, coffins, dental instruments and suits of clothes, in a palace made of windows.

4

Food and Drink

Nothing meant more to Thackeray than food, except perhaps drink. If there were a blue riband for the most committed consumer among major English authors, he would win it comfortably. 'Guttling and gorging' were, he claimed, vital for his work. He wrote from 10 o'clock to 6, and then needed 'the quantum of wine' and rich comestibles, in order to keep up his enthusiasm for life. He invented new recipes himself, among them a highly praised one for boiled pheasant with *soubise* sauce, and he cultivated gourmet friends like Abraham Hayward, author of the *Art of Dining*, and Richard Monckton Milnes, who allegedly observed, when near to death, 'My exit is the result of too many entrées'. The house he finally built for himself at Palace Green, Kensington, had a cellar stocked with fine vintages – including, as he boasted to an acquaintance, 300 bottles of '41 and '48 claret – and he planned elaborate dinners there on Sunday evenings. Menus for these survive in his diary, a representative one featuring turtle, pickled salmon and turbot, cold sirloin and hot venison, suckling pigs and peas, savoury jelly and sweet, dry champagne and 'first chop claret'. He was, as his enemies remarked, a 'big blubber man', his weight varying between 15 and 18 stone.

Over the years he acquired an intimate knowledge of cuisines in Paris and other European cities, and the cosmopolitan air of his writing benefits from this. The Trois Frères Provençaux in the Palais Royal and the Rocher de Cancale in the Rue Montorgueil were the brightest stars in his culinary firmament, but lesser lights like the Bedford at Boulogne, the Dessein at Calais, and the Hôtel de Suède in Brussels, get due recognition, as does the Grand Laboureur in the Place de Meir at Antwerp, where they made a peculiar kind of jam tart, called Nun's Tarts, to which Thackeray was devoted. A rare moment of deep feeling intervenes in *The Newcomes* when he reports that the Grand Laboureur has been pulled down. He manifested his discrimination and his resolute pursuit of pleasure in ferreting out specialities: the pale old East India madeira at the Rocher, the pineapple rum and other West Indian produce at the Hôtel des Américains in the Rue St. Honoré, the 'capital eels' and fried gudgeon fresh from the Seine at the Marronniers at Bercy. On his Mediterranean trip he discovered, and recorded for his readers' benefit, superior kebabs at Mechmet Effendi's near the Rope Bazaar in Constantinople, and good raisin wine on sale at the Armenian shops for two piastres a bottle. Similar gastronomic hints make his fictions seem more solid and more fully experienced. Writing home to Pen, Clive Newcome recommends the *huîtres de Marenne* at the Café de Paris, while in Rome he singles out the mezzo-caldo at the Café Greco for praise, and gives the ingredients – rum, sliced lemon, pounded sugar and boiling water. Though he was convivial by nature, Thackeray's epicureanism could take furtive forms. On one occasion he came across the remainder of a 'wonderful bin of port' in the cellar of the Gray's Inn Coffee-House, and by negotiation with the landlord managed to consume every drop himself, slipping off to his treasure, 'with all possible secrecy short of disguise', whenever he thought a bottle would do him good.

Contemporary improvements in nutritional science attracted his notice. He reviewed cookery books, and publicized the French dietician Alexis Soyer, who appears under various names in his stories. Soyer was chef at the Reform Club, went to the Crimea to advise on cookery for the army, and later replanned the catering in British military hospitals. However, food for Thackeray was not merely something to eat but an incentive to elegance. His friend Allingham recalls dining with him at the Palais Royal, and the enjoyment he registered at every little incident, beginning with the waiter's flourish on setting down their dishes of Ostend oysters. *The Book of Snobs* is severe about Scottish holiday-makers who shut themselves away in dismal huts provisioned with canisters of portable soup and hermetically sealed *fricandeaux*. Such behaviour abrogated the ceremoniousness of feeding, in Thackeray's eyes.

Food and drink intermingled in the formation of his most delicate human relationships. 'I am in the middle of a great bowl of raspberries and cream', he wrote to his wife just before they were married, 'and wishing for my little gourmande to share it with me.' Looking back on their happy days together in 1849, after she had become insane, he composed what many consider his best poem, 'The Ballad of Bouillabaisse', recounting a visit to Terré's Tavern in the Rue Neuve des Petits Champs where they used to dine. The red-cheeked *écaillère* is still, he finds, opening oysters at the door; the Chambertin with yellow seal is still recommended; and they still serve the medley of:

> Green herbs, red peppers, mussels, saffron,
> Soles, onions, garlic, roach and dace,

with which his memories of his lost wife are fused. In rather the same way, his love for Jane Brookfield was mixed up with jam tarts. They first met when Brookfield took him home to dinner unexpectedly, and

Jane sent out to a confectioner's for some tartlets, which Thackeray joked about, and continued to joke about for several years, referring to 'the dear old twopenny tart dinner' as a sort of toothsome bond between them.

To the modern reader it occurs to ask whether Thackeray, when indulging himself, ever remembered his starving fellow-creatures. The honest answer seems to be that he did, but tried to forget them again as soon as possible, as most of us do. In *The Irish Sketch-Book* the contrast between the hunger of others and his own ingestion is at its most alarming. He describes women pulling weeds and nettles from the hedges for food – 'on which dismal sustenance the poor creatures live, having no bread, no potatoes, no work' – and yet, in a couple of pages, he is complaining about the 'plentiful and nasty' dinner served to him at Waterford – 'raw ducks, raw pease, on a crumpled tablecloth' – without, seemingly, any twinge of guilt. Generally it is the spectacle of others' gluttony, rather than his own, that awakes his social conscience. In a paper for the *New Monthly* of July 1844, he recalls the only city dinner he ever attended – the universal gurgle as the worshipful company sucked in their turtle soup, and the gruesome sight of old, waddling citizens stretching out their plates for second helpings of the venison and the 200 quarts of early peas, at 25s. a quart, which they were consuming. 'There were thousands in London that day without bread', Thackeray interjects. But, typically, he grows suspicious when he hears himself moralizing, recoils ('This is growing serious'), and changes the subject. He wrote the thing up again for *Punch*, though, three years later, in one of his most brilliant and scathing virtuoso pieces, *A Dinner in the City*. Here the bloodshot citizens with their decaying tusks, and their winking, twitching decrepitude galvanized by greed, and the 'dizzy mist of gluttony' that surrounds them, fuse into a macabre spectacle; and the sight of the tearoom afterwards, with the guests wolfing buttered muffins 'until the grease trickled down their faces', is recognized as a final outrage to human decency: 'who is it that *can* want muffins after such a banquet? Are there no poor?'

It was writing for *Punch* that encouraged such reflections. In his determination to 'go in a higher class' after *Vanity Fair*, Thackeray suppressed them. Of course, to speak of himself 'guttling and gorging', as he often did, itself implied a kind of shamefaced shamelessness on the subject of food and drink. Apart from any concern for the poor, he had his own health to worry about. He keeps complaining in his letters of his awful digestive disturbances, and Chester Jones, a Clinical Professor at Harvard, who has investigated Thackeray's medical history, finds that the recurrent illnesses of the last third of his life were greatly aggravated by his 'extreme dietary indiscretions'. Thackeray himself knew this perfectly well. 'Can't I, for Heaven's

81

sake, be moderate?', he lamented. He couldn't, it seems. He ate his last dinner on 23 December 1863, came home after midnight, and was struck down by one of his violent retching attacks, which resulted in the rupture of a cerebral blood vessel. So his gormandizing was the death of him.

But if his eagerness about food and drink did him no good morally or medically, its effect on his writing was wholly beneficial. It was an unfailing source of vitality and precision. His gastronomic experience was immensely varied, and his response to the taste, texture and fragrance of foodstuffs abnormally sensitive. Consequently his appetites provided him with a rich shadow-world of flavours and distinctions into which he could dip for images to fix people and events. His scenes spring to life around their eatable and drinkable bits – as at the start of *The Paris Sketch-Book*, where the vigour and activity aboard the cross-channel steamer are concentrated in the 'red raw Cheshire cheese', boiled beef and pickles, and 'little dumpy bottles of stout' which 'fizz and bang about with a spirit one would never have looked for in individuals of their size and stature'. Memory, too, crystallized around comestibles. The parts of his boyhood that had faded least were the lollipops, the hardbake, the brandyballs and alicompaine of forty years ago, and the mixture of liquorice, brown sugar and water shaken up to a froth, which he used to carry around in a bottle in his pocket. His normally rapid style expands into Proustian lingerings as he strives to convey the exact taste of, for instance, the coffee and toast he bought on his way home for the school holidays in the summer of 1823: 'a peculiar, muddy, not-sweet-enough, most fragrant coffee – a rich, rancid, yet not-buttered-enough delicious toast.' About food he is at his most unexpected and evocative. The feel of incidents and people regularly comes across through his allusions to edibles, as when he lets slip the remark, in *Men's Wives*, that he once saw a friend in Germany eat five larks for his breakfast before fighting a duel, or complains that Courvoisier's hanging 'weighs upon the mind like cold plum pudding upon the stomach', or describes Aunt Lambert in *The Virginians* as 'one great syllabub of human kindness'. In *Strictures on Pictures* he makes play with the parable of the Prodigal Son and the killing of the fatted calf, speculating on the difficulty of constructing a menu entirely of calf, and eventually producing an elaborate one, with dishes ranging from stewed veal, brown sauce and force-meat balls to calves' foot jelly. This treatment of biblical material would certainly have struck some of his readers as blasphemous, but then his exaltation of food and drink, and of allied pleasures like cigar-smoking, represented a challenge to religious prejudices against carnal indulgence, as well as to Victorian reservations about the propriety of bodily functions.

Snappy similies drawn from food recur, especially in his art-criticism and early stories, as a way of establishing the irreverent Titmarsh persona. He scoffs at Turner's 'pea-green skies' and Hill's stags on their 'spinach pastures', and the dog in a Stone painting with 'no more bones than an apple dumpling'. Rhubarb is a prominent simile-material. Jowler's half-caste wife in *Gahagan* and Eglantine's coat in *The Ravenswing* and Mrs. Houndsditch's gloves in *Snobs* and Dr. Firmin's flock wallpaper are all rhubarb-coloured. Pitt Crawley has 'gooseberry-coloured' eyes, and Mrs. Baynes's garnets in *Philip* resemble 'gooseberries set in gold'. An old gentleman with a 'salmon-coloured' face also features in *Snobs*, and Mrs. Cox goes 'red as a glass of negus' in *Cox's Diary*. Fright turns the clerks in *The Great Hoggarty Diamond*, and old Abednego in *Little Spitz*, as yellow as parsnips, and on various occasions in *The Newcomes* it makes Barnes as pale as a turnip and as yellow as cream cheese.

In these food images the crudity and cockney-flavour is part of the point. Root vegetables and laxatives set the tone. But when Thackeray applies himself more seriously to food, it becomes spiritual. Elusive fragrances waft the reader into realms scarcely foodlike at all, as at the whitebait dinner in *Philip*, with 'the smell of *friture* of flowers and flounders exquisitely commingled', or in his earlier rhapsody on the 'almost angelic delicacy of flavour' to be found in flounder-souchy, 'as fresh as the recollections of childhood'. The innocence of eating – pure, sensuous, unalloyed by the intellect – intrigues because it involves, too, innocent victims, in the shape of the food. An ogreish mock-sympathy with what he is eating often augments the pleasure in Thackeray's culinary passages. He gloats over the sacrifice. The trout he remembers eating, fresh from Derryclear Lake, on his Irish trip – 'rich, flaky, creamy' – are commemorated like human infants. 'The world had not time to spoil these innocent things before they were gobbled up with pepper and salt, and missed, no doubt, by their friends.' There is facetiousness here, of course, but in Thackeray, as in other writers, facetiousness is a pointer to unspoken complications in his thought.

Whereas elegant eating transmutes into an innocent encounter with innocence, practically disembodied in its refinement, like religion, Thackeray's descriptions of bad food or drink depend for their disgustingness on organic associations. Brandon, in *A Shabby Genteel Story*, refuses to stomach 'bleeding beefsteak or filthy reeking *gigot à l'eau* with a turnip poultice', and the Twysdens' 'clammy' port is deplored in *Philip*. Among the more repellent eatables offered to Thackeray in Ireland were 'one very lean mutton chop and one very small damp kidney, brought in by an old tottering waiter' at Ballinasloe. Real bodies, with glands, wounds and secretions, are what these

examples urge upon the reader's notice, the waiter's 'tottering' state
even bringing forward for a moment the suspicion that the small damp
kidney was recently his. The impulse towards uplift, aroma and spiritu-
ality is, by contrast, manifest in Thackeray's account (from *Memorials
of Gormandizing*) of the *perdreau aux truffes* at the Café Foy – one of
his finest bits of food-writing:

Presently we were aware of an odour gradually coming towards us,
something musky, fiery, savoury, mysterious – a hot, drowsy smell,
that lulls the senses, and yet inflames them, – the truffles were coming!
Yonder they lie, caverned under the full bosom of the red-legged bird.
My hand trembled as, after a little pause, I cut the animal in two . . .
The poor little partridge was soon a heap of bones – a very little heap.
A trufflesque odour was left in the room, but only an odour. Presently
the cheese was brought: the amber sauterne flask had turned of a
sickly green hue; nothing, save half a glass of sediment at the bottom,
remained to tell of the light and social spirit that had but one half-hour
before inhabited the flask. Darkness fell upon our little chamber: the
men in the street began crying *'Messager! Journal du Soir!'* The
bright moon rose glittering over the tiles of the Rue Louis le Grand, opposite, illuminating two glasses of punch that two gentlemen in a
small room of the Café Foy did ever and anon raise to their lips.

The management of space is delicately suggestive here. As appetites
are stilled, and the faculties relax, the viewpoint shifts from cramped
concentration on 'caverned' truffles, floats through the window, and
above the rooftops, whence, soulfully moonlit, we look back at the
darkened room with its sediment and heap of bones. The spiritual
ascent of Thackeray's partridge and truffles contrasts significantly
with a famous dish from modern fiction, Virginia Woolf's *Bœuf en
Daube* in *To the Lighthouse*:

an exquisite scent of olives and oil and juice rose from the great brown
dish as Marthe, with a little flourish, took the cover off. The cook had
spent three days over that dish. And she must take great care, Mrs.
Ramsey thought, diving into the soft mass, to choose a specially tender
piece for William Bankes. And she peered into the dish, with its shiny
walls and its confusion of savoury brown and yellow meats, and its bay
leaves and its wine, and thought, This will celebrate the occasion.

Virginia Woolf, diving into her soft mass, works in a direction quite
contrary to Thackeray's. The spiritual quest, for her generation, is
downwards, plumbing the psyche, groping among the tender nerves
and filaments. For Thackeray's it is still a matter of heavenward
aspiration, which is what his partridge achieves.

Another difference is that Virginia Woolf's beef is dead and sexless.
Thackeray's 'inflamed' senses, and his trembling hand approaching the
'full bosom' of the 'poor little partridge' imply, though, a desecration
that is, if covertly, erotic, so that it is no surprise when he goes on,

immediately after the quoted passage, to discuss the relative merits of eating and women as pleasures, coming down on the side of eating. A wise choice, since few women would allow him the sensuous liberties he takes with his truffled partridge. The degree of sexual enjoyment included in his eating is at times quite blatant. 'How plump and tender the rogue's thigh is', he remarks of a chicken at the Trois Frères, 'Half a dozen cuts with the knife, and yonder lies the bone – white, large, stark naked, without a morsel of flesh upon it, solitary in the midst of a pool of melted butter.' That his attachment to food was in part a compensation for his loss of poor Isabella, whose place the plump chicken is here supplying, we have already conjectured. But, more importantly, his writing taps, through food, a reservoir of sensuousness which would have been unthinkable, in the Victorian period, had he dealt directly with sexual experience. At the same time, the sensuousness became transfigured and subtilized by his epicurean imaginings.

He conveys the enticing delicacy of women through the food they eat. Ethel Newcome's birthday party, with its 'gentle refection of sponge-cakes, jellies, tea, and the like', implies an infantile reluctance to digest anything beyond soft foods and liquids, though Ethel is approaching marriageable age. Young unmarried ladies should not, Thackeray asserts in one of his cookery-book reviews, be allowed down to dinner at all, but should receive their nourishment in the nursery. Rich meats and strong flavours have a virile potency, which it would be immodest to let young women near. To render them exquisite enough for the feminine palate, they must have their grosser associations bleached out of them, or so Mirobolant (alias Alexis Soyer) believes in *Pendennis*. He decides that only white dishes, 'spotless as the snow', are appropriate to Blanche's name and nature. For her dinner he serves up *potage à la Reine Blanche*, 'as white as her own tint – and confectioned with the most fragrant cream and almonds', white fish, sweetbread and chicken, 'opal coloured plover's eggs', and a heart-shaped ice with cut-paper bridal veil and wreath of orange flowers. Women who are hearty eaters, especially if they venture upon meat, occasion comic embarrassment. Fitzboodle, in *The Fitzboodle Papers*, is greatly upset by Ottilia's keen appetite, and watches her with horror consuming German sausages and Westphalia ham. The more she eats, the redder her nose grows. An odour of 'oniony sandwiches' hovers around her, together with 'reeking reminiscences of roast'. Eventually Fitzboodle works out that she eats meat twenty-one times a week, and concludes that to marry her would be marrying 'a sarcophagus'.

Cakes, jellies, and other childish fare, provide a more spiritualizing female diet, especially if they can be imbibed through some means less coarse than mastication. Fitzroy Timmins, in *A Little Dinner at Timmins's*, gazes through the plate glass of Fubsby's the caterers at the girls who work within, and fancies that they have grown so beautiful simply from living in the same atmosphere as the pineapples, blancmanges, creams, preserved fruits and golden ginger. For sustenance they might occasionally nibble off the side of a strawberry, Fitzroy feels, and if very hungry a rout cake or macaroon. In the end, he imagines, they get to such a pitch of loveliness that they become 'complete angels', with deliciously-scented wings, and fly away over the trees of the square as the policeman touches his hat.

Fitzroy's fantasies are quizzically viewed by Thackeray, of course. The airy ascent, like that of his truffled partridge, intrigues him. But he knows that women and food inter-relate more solidly. Fitzroy enters Fubsby's one day to find the girls at tea over stale bread and butter, and his passion vanishes. Mirobolant is deluded, too, in thinking Blanche delicate enough for his delicacies. Becky Sharp is the girl most taken up with food in Thackeray, and at the big moments in her career is regularly to be found putting things into her own and other people's mouths. She manipulates her victuals with brio and cunning, and they, more than any other single factor, conspire to envelop the reader in her provocative and adept personality. Apart from a gruff aside or two about her 'famous frontal development' Thackeray can't, without sending contemporary readers into convulsions of outraged modesty, say much about the sensuous joys Becky's body offers, so it has to be done through the eatables and drinkables. Becky gets a grip on Sir Pitt with a White Hermitage and a superlative salmi of pheasant which, being a brilliant cook, she has prepared herself; and when Miss Crawley has gorged herself sick on hot lobster it is Becky who is called in to manage the gastronomic emergency. She superintends Miss Crawley's invalid diet, and at the same time sweeps poor, twittery Miss Briggs into her net, almost entirely through her masterful way with foodstuffs:

Briggs was so much choked with emotion that she could hardly take a morsel of meat. The young person carved a fowl with the utmost delicacy, and asked so distinctly for egg-sauce, that poor Briggs, before whom that delicious condiment was placed, started, made a great clattering with the ladle, and once more fell back in the most gushing hysterical state.

'Had you not better give Miss Briggs a glass of wine?' said the person to Mr. Bowls, the large confidential man. He did so. Briggs seized it mechanically, gasped it down convulsively, moaned a little, and began to play with the chicken on her plate.

'I think we shall be able to help each other,' said the person with great suavity.

On the surface Becky only means help each other to food. She's about to send the servant away, so as to get Briggs to herself. But of course she means Briggs's 'help' to extend considerably further than that. The scene is a food-forte, with Becky displaying her fine control of fowls and of big men and of Briggs's feeble capacity for alcohol.

When Becky is setting up as a hostess, Lord Steyne and his male friends come to her house 'to finish the night', where she keeps, Thackeray notes, ices and coffee for them – 'the best in London'. Her elegant tickling of bodily desire is implied through her provisions, rather as the wicked high jinks which we are supposed to conclude Lord Steyne gets up to in his *petits appartements* off New Gaunt Street are conveyed through the fact that in the little private kitchen 'every saucepan was silver and all the spits were gold'. Without restricting his novel to the pornography-market, Thackeray could not go into the implements with which an elderly nobleman's *cabinet de plaisir* might in reality be equipped, so he has to get across his air of devilish abandon through the cooking pots.

Even when Becky is outwitted over food, she is marvellously adept at turning the situation to her own advantage. In order to attract Jos Sedley she pretends an interest in everything Indian, and is persuaded by Sedley *père*, who likes practical jokes, to try some curry:

'Do you find it as good as everything else from India?' said Mr. Sedley.
'Oh, excellent!' said Rebecca, who was suffering tortures with the cayenne pepper.
'Try a chili with it, Miss Sharp,' said Joseph, really interested.
'A chili,' said Rebecca, gasping. 'O yes!' she thought a chili was something cool, as its name imported, and was served with some. 'How fresh and green they look!' she said, and put one in her mouth. It was hotter than the curry; flesh and blood could bear it no longer. She laid down her fork. 'Water, for Heaven's sake, water!' she cried.

Old Sedley roars with laughter, but Becky gathers her wits and her culinary memories and stages a comeback:

She would have liked to choke old Sedley, but she swallowed her mortification as well as she had the abominable curry before it, and as soon as she could speak, said, with a comical, good-humoured air –
'I ought to have remembered the pepper which the Princess of Persia puts in the cream-tarts in the *Arabian Nights*. Do you put cayenne into your cream-tarts in India, sir?'
Old Sedley began to laugh, and thought Rebecca was a good-humoured girl.

So that wins *him* over, and Becky proceeds to use the chilis to initiate some sexual stirrings in Jos's somnolent frame, by bringing the conversation poutingly round, a few days later, to her burnt mouth and Jos's cruelty to her:

'I shall take care how I let *you* choose for me another time,' said Rebecca, as they went down again to dinner. 'I didn't think men were fond of putting poor harmless girls to pain.'

'By Gad, Miss Rebecca, I wouldn't hurt you for the world.'

'No,' said she, 'I *know* you wouldn't,' and then she gave him ever so gentle a pressure with her little hand, and drew it back quite frightened.

With his physique and intellect, errors in the choice of food are almost the only peril Jos could defend a girl against, so Becky makes him feel masterful by keeping the talk in this area, and her seductive hint about putting girls to pain is a bait for his masculine sadism, should he happen to have any. It is not her fault that she doesn't enmesh Jos. What ruins her plans is the bowl of rack punch he gets tipsy on at Vauxhall. 'That bowl of rack punch was the cause of all this history', Thackeray comments, lest the alimentary basis of his novel should be missed, and he proceeds to explain how Jos's rack punch influenced the fates of all the principal characters.

Of course, Becky gets Jos in the end, and, we are given to understand, poisons him – a final proof of her cunning with foodstuffs. Throughout the book they are her arsenal for worming her way into people's confidence, from the time when she allays Mrs. Blenkinsop's suspicions by evincing 'the deepest sympathy in the raspberry jam preserving', to the time when she obediently swallows Lady Southdown's 'black dose', to get herself accepted in that quarter. But foodstuffs impress her energy and vivaciousness on the reader as well. Becky at Brighton, munching prawns while she dictates Rawdon's letter to Miss Crawley; Becky with her breakfast chocolate, which Rawdon is trained to take up to her, jubilantly waving the black-edged missive that announces Sir Pitt's death; Becky in the German hotel among students and bagmen and Bohemians, with a bottle of brandy and a plate of cold sausage clinking under the coverlet of her bed, where she has hastily shoved them on the arrival of Jos – these scenes charge her part of the book with richness and savour. They glaringly distinguish her from the pale Amelia, whose purity is preserved by eating hardly anything at all. So little does she care about food, indeed, that at the opulent wedding feast that George lays on, she has no inkling what to do with the tureen of turtle, and has to be checked from serving Jos 'without bestowing upon him either calipash or calipee' (i.e. the turtle's edible bits).

A less appealing aspect of Becky's gourmandize is that she eats people. This is part of a recurrent Thackeray nightmare. From early in the 1840s, if not earlier, sirens, with sinisterly white arms and shoulders, and surrounded by blanched human bones, haunt his imagination. Unlike the Homeric sirens, Thackeray's have fish's tails, and instead of just drowning their victims, they devour them. These ghoulish beauties appear first in *The Artists* (from *Heads of the People*, 1840–1), where they masquerade as models and eat young painters. They are glimpsed, too, in *The Newcomes*, in connection with la Duchesse d'Ivry – 'I fancy a fish's tail is flapping under her fine flounces, and a forked fin at the end of it'. The obsession comes up again in *The Virginians* with Maria (one of Thackeray's most elaborate sirens, with 'fishpool' eyes, to mesmerize victims, and a tail that 'trails' horribly, and new dentures to crunch bones with), and in the essay on ogres in *The Roundabout Papers*, and in *Lovel the Widower*, where there are mother-in-law sirens, too, hiding behind the rocks and egging their daughters on. What prompted this slimy fancy in Thackeray, one can only guess. If the mother-in-law sirens are a clue, maybe we should look for the explanation in his own marriage. The sight of Isabella, demented and flapping around in the sea, after she had jumped from the steamer on her way to her mother at Cork, may have been shock enough to fuse marine life and awful, unsatisfactory women in his mind. Certainly he came to think of marriage to Isabella as a trap, which he had ruinously fallen into. Anyway, the idea that women had a fishy horror concealed beneath their skirts, and might swallow you, was persistent with him. He took an interest, naturally, in real-life mermaids, and collected stories about them in Ireland, where, he found, they were frequently sighted, had fair hair (like Becky) and screamed offensively when shot. A woman attracted to water inevitably arouses suspicions in his stories. Blanche, in *Pendennis*, passes herself off as a water-nymph called Undine, which should warn one that she's a bad lot, though poor Harry Foker, her victim, is fatally unable to hit on the right word for her. 'She sings', he tells his friends, 'like a – whatdyecallum – you know what I mean – like a mermaid, you know, but that's not their name.' Becky sings charmingly, too, and is an excellent swimmer – even planning, while at Brighton, to swim under water and surprise Briggs in her bathing-machine. Her expertise is understandable, for she has a fish's tail, though it can't be seen normally:

Those who like may peep down under waves that are pretty transparent, and see it writhing and twirling, diabolically hideous and slimy, flapping amongst bones, or curling round corpses. . . . When, however, the siren disappears and dives below, down among the dead men, the water of course grows turbid over her. . . . We had best not examine the fiendish marine cannibals, revelling and feasting on their wretched pickled victims.

It doesn't really work as part of the novel, whatever its qualities as a plunge into loathsomeness. Thackeray can't glue a fish's tail onto Becky, or make us believe that her lively delight in food has anything to do with pickled corpses. His reading public will not permit him to explain what Becky really does to men, and so (as with Lord Steyne's saucepans) he has to make do by pretending that it is something nasty in the kitchen.

Miss Fotheringay in *Pendennis* is more successfully damaged in the reader's eyes through her low feeding habits, though Thackeray also makes her encounters with food radiate her sturdy sense. She eats mutton hash, drinks brown stout, cleans her shoes with breadcrumbs and calls pie 'Poy'. 'Them filberts is beautiful', she advises Mr. Bows – and calling food beautiful (she calls beefsteak and punch 'beautiful' as well) is one of the things that make it and her unbeautiful, just like Lil's friend in *The Waste Land*, who tells how she was asked home to gammon dinner 'to get the beauty of it hot'. She packs Pen's love-letters up at the end of the affair like 'a parcel of sugar' – nourishingly unsentimental.

Meanness over food is a disastrous handicap to a Thackeray character – witness the sordid fuss Mrs. Mackenzie makes at the end of *The Newcomes* over the servant's alleged pickings from the beef and pudding. Thackeray never wrote anything more acute: the ghastly domestic row pitched so shamingly, and so believably, on the wretched eatables that the reader finds himself tugged into the embarrassment of it. Contrariwise, generosity with food bespeaks deeply lovable qualities, so that Thackeray is able to negotiate the potentially awkward business of Dobbin becoming young George's stepfather by means of the engaging scene at Pumpernickel, where George consumes 'schinken, and braten, and kartoffeln, and cranberry jam, and salad, and pudding, and roast fowls, and sweet-meats', and Dobbin 'joked the boy, with a great deal of grave fun pointing out dishes which he *hadn't* tried, and entreating him not to baulk his appetite'. Dobbin's warmth and maturity are vouched for by his not taking a moralistic attitude towards George's gluttony. Thackeray himself loved treating children to food, and he shows how sane and natural it is to express one's joy in them by stuffing them with delights. With a child, gorging carries no moral opprobrium, and Thackeray can make even adult gluttons appealing by regaling them with childish foodstuffs. Thus Jos Sedley, downing 'a couple of plates full of strawberries and cream, and twenty-four little rout cakes, that were lying neglected in a plate near him', is indulgently viewed by the reader, because he seems not quite grown-up. General Tiptoff, dying 'full of honours, and of an aspic of plover's eggs', appears a good deal less endearing, since the contents of his stomach are not such as would normally appeal to children.

Jam tarts, particularly raspberry tarts, are the food which children in Thackeray relish most. It is virtually impossible for him to imagine childhood without them. Tarts were prominent in his own schooldays, as he recalls in *Cruikshank's Gallery*, and the scene in a school play-ground where an adult visitor, probably military, hands out a sovereign tip which is converted into jam tarts, recurs frequently in his writing. Tarts meant, for him, innocence and vulnerability. Thus Fanny Bolton, out for a treat at Vauxhall with her adored Pen, owns to 'a partiality for raspberry tart', which Pen quickly gratifies, and Dobbin longs for Amelia 'as the poor boy at school who has no money may sigh after the contents of the tart-woman's tray'. 'Tart', incidentally, was a low word for 'woman' as early as the mid-eighteenth century (see Charles Brietzcke's Diary for 1765, *Notes and Queries* ccix 66) and this may confer a defiant purity on the boyhood tarts in Thackeray. He was the first, according to the Oxford Dictionary, to use the formation 'tart-woman', and he makes Fitzboodle, at school, fall in love with the girl who sells tarts, so some compounding of pastry and more adult pleasures was going on in his mind, as Dobbin's desire for a jam-tart bride indicates.

While childish gluttony is to be encouraged, making a mess of food can't be forgiven. When a child is staked out for condemnation in Thackeray, it tends to get its edibles over itself and others, like Master Francis Clavering, who lathers his face and hands with *meringues à crème*, besides knocking wine over Pen's waistcoat. Food and drink applied externally have a peculiar repulsion, because of the physical grossness involved – the obverse of the spiritual ascent Thackeray's fine foods achieve. Thackeray draws on this to make people ludicrous or disgusting. Gahagan, while helping a nobleman to *poulet à l'Auster-litz*, sends seven mushrooms and three greasy *croûtes* over his whiskers and shirt frill, and Giglio in *The Rose and the Ring* shoots goose-stuffing and onion sauce into his rival's eye. Barry Lyndon throwing claret into Quin's face, and Clive into Barnes Newcome's, and William dousing Sampson's wig with port in *The Virginians*, carry these *haute cuisine* custard-pie antics into the serious novels. Food also taints if you have trade-associations with it, or so Thackeray's snobs think. Rich tripe butchers and sugar-bakers abound, and Thackeray's own social shifts can be traced from his changing attitudes towards them. Foker, as a brewer's son, and Dobbin, as a grocer's, both suffer at school. Dobbin's fees, it is rumoured, are paid in kind, and the boys regard him as the representative of so many pounds of tea, sugar and plums. They call him 'Figs', so that when he vanquishes Cuff in the great school fight it is a sort of victory for dried fruit.

Without food, Thackeray's novels would fall apart, and this is true from the very beginning of his career. His first published tale, *The Professor*, concerns a man with an insatiable appetite for shellfish, and much of it happens in an oyster-shop, where the gleaming gas on ruby lobsters (Thackeray's earliest lobsters), and the waitress-heroine

Adeliza flying here and there with rolls, pats of butter, and a vinegar bottle with a perforated cork, radiate cockney spiritedness. In his best writing character and action continue to depend on food to a prodigious extent. And even in his decline the scenes clustered round food have a vividness and subtlety others lack – as in the beautifully gauged sequence from *The Newcomes*, where Lady Ann and her children turn up at Miss Honeyman's lodging-house in Brighton, and fall out over Lady Ann's imperious meal-orders, and make it up again over the chicken Miss Honeyman roasts for fractious little Alfred.

But to recognize the responsibilities that devolve on Thackeray's fictional food is to go only half way. His thinking about art and literature was also fundamentally affected by his attachment to the pleasures of the palate, and we need to see how. To begin with, he didn't want art to exist in a hallowed atmosphere, isolated in the sanctity of museums and cushioned from real experience. He wanted it to be a part of life, like eating and drinking, and to be treated with the same familiarity. The idea of the art-lover as a rarefied being struck him as ridiculous. In his picture-reviews he presents himself munching ham sandwiches and drinking gin-and-water at Lord's Coffee House, or nipping out of the National Gallery for ice and mock turtle at Farrance's, and the intent of these digressions is to show that the pleasures of art and food should not be segregated but richly intermingled. *A Pictorial Rhapsody* starts with an account of dinner at the Clarendon, during which one of the company goes to sleep with his head in a dish of raspberry ice, and it goes on to criticize the inhumanity and bloodlessness of Greek art, clearly meaning the sensuousness of the food-scene to back up this criticism. The largest dinner of Thackeray's life was (as he enjoyed recalling) eaten in Brussels after coming out of the Musée des Beaux Arts:

1, green pea-soup; 2, boiled salmon; 3, mussels; 4, crimped skate; 5, roast-meat; 6, patties; 7, melon; 8, carp, stewed with mushrooms and onions; 9, roast-turkey; 10, cauliflower and butter; 11, fillets of venison *piqués*, with asafoetida sauce; 12, stewed calf's ear; 13, roast veal; 14, roast lamb; 15, stewed cherries; 16, rice-pudding; 17, Gruyère cheese, and about twenty-four cakes of different kinds. Except 5, 13, and 14, I give you my word I ate of all written down here, with three rolls of bread and a score of potatoes. What is the meaning of it? How is the stomach of man brought to desire and to receive all this quantity?

Thackeray leaves one in no doubt that, in his opinion, producing food that can be bolted in such bulk is as much a province of the fine arts as painting the pictures which gave him an appetite for eating it.

To say that his favourite novels are as good as raspberry tarts (as he does in the *Roundabout Papers*) is, for Thackeray, high praise. He develops the theory that 'novels are sweets' – literary equivalents of jellies and other confections, and similarly bad for one if taken in excess. He finds it illuminating, too, to trace 'the hidden analogy between liquors and pictures', likening Claude, for instance, to a bottle of Château Margaux – 'calm, fresh, delicate' – and Poussin to a 'heavy, sluggish' Romanée Gelée. Such comparisons can easily be mistaken for vapid pretentiousness – the whimsies of the wine-snob – but in Thackeray they relate to a pugnaciously-held belief that the satisfactions of art and of appetite are truly linked, and bring the same parts of the human organism into play. The pretentiousness, he felt, lay on the side of the art worshippers, who liked to think that their gratifications took place in some higher realm than the everyday. Eating and drinking were, for him, quite as dignified as painting or music. To disparage them because they appealed to the senses was absurd, for so did all arts: 'the senses are the arts'. 'All enjoyments', he insisted, 'are sensual enjoyments' – whether they take the form of champagne and oysters, or Taglioni dancing the mazurka, or looking at pictures. Indeed, it seemed to him hypocritical to deny that, in certain circumstances, even the greatest art offers pleasures inferior to those of feeding: 'Shakespeare and Raphael never invented anything to equal Ay and oysters at 5.30 on a hot day.'

It followed that the superior claims made for artists and writers – the romantic tendency to regard them as 'priests of nature' – met with scant sympathy from Thackeray. Artists, he asserted, were tradesmen, just like grocers or sellers of figs. They had no special right to consideration, or to maintenance at the public expense should they prove unable to vend their wares. This was a theme he frequently recurred to, evidently relishing the howls of rage that it elicited from the literary and artistic fraternities. It should be noted that he did not put forward such views only after he had become a successful author, when they might appear little more than taunts, but when he was himself struggling and in want.

A further corollary of the equation of art with food was that it allowed artistic 'value judgements' to be seen as, in reality, mere matters of taste, on a level (as Thackeray remarked) with the preference of mutton to lollipops. He realized that what such judgements reflect are the prejudices that class, income-group and cultural background have infixed, and he resented attempts to impose the tastes of one element in the community upon another. 'How much income tax must a man pay, in order to have a decent love of art?' he demanded, when the *Athenaeum* alluded to the low artistic standards of the masses. He felt that the workman should be allowed to have his 'green parrot with a bobbing head', and the intelligentsia, who could not make do with less than Milton, should have Milton. This was not a condescending view for, as we shall see, he would almost certainly have preferred a green parrot to Milton himself.

True, there are some weaknesses in Thackeray's theoretical position, and in his analogy between tastes in art and food. He might, for instance, have noted that artistic value judgements lack the dependability of food preferences, since it is possible, by verbal persuasion, to get people to change their opinion about art (most literary criticism directs itself to this end), but not about mutton or lollipops. However, this does not affect his main point, which is that no verifiable (or, for that matter, momentarily plausible) basis exists for believing it meritorious to prefer art to food, or 'high' art to 'low'. In reading, his own taste was for the low. His favourite authors included Paul de Kock, whose spicy tales of Parisian life, with their *'sémillantes, frétillantes, pétillantes grisettes'* (as Wagstaff puts it in *The Partie Fine*), were, it will be remembered, also enjoyed by Molly Bloom ('Nice name he has', Molly thought). Thackeray liked de Kock's 'simple tricks for exciting laughter' and his vulgar style, and defended him against critics who thought he wasn't 'artistical' enough.

Whereas the pleasure which food and low art give is unmistakable and genuine, Thackeray felt that high art entailed a good deal of sham – sham sentiment, sham morality and sham religion. French neo-classical painting, with its emphasis upon the violent deeds of antiquity, epitomized 'the bloated, unnatural, stilted, spouting, sham sublime' that art snobs had taught people to admire. Getting models to ape the death-throes of classical persons such as Eudamidas or Hecuba, and painting them, was, he argued, a fatuous affectation, for plainly the artists could not care about Eudamidas or Hecuba, at this distance in time, and besides they were, for the most part, quite ignorant both of ancient civilization and of Greek and Latin literature:

How were they to be inspired by such subjects? From having seen Talma and Mademoiselle Georges flaunting in sham Greek costumes, and having read up the articles Eudamidas, Hecuba, in the *Mythological Dictionary*. What a classicism, inspired by rouge, gas-lamps, and a few lines in Lemprière, and copied, half from ancient statues, and half from a naked guardsman at one shilling and sixpence the hour!

Similarly, the religious art of the Nazarene School, headed by the German expatriates Overbeck and Cornelius, which the French were zealously imitating, and which was later to contribute to the formation of the Pre-Raphaelite Brotherhood, roused Thackeray to an exposure of its 'absurd humbug'. As he saw it, it had nothing to do with religion, or even with a decent historical feeling for the biblical personages and their era, but depended on a few fads and dodges, handed on from one painter to the next, and easily reduced to a formula:

First, take your colours, and rub them down clean, – bright carmine, bright yellow, bright sienna, bright ultramarine, bright green. Make the costumes of your figures as much as possible like the costumes of the early part of the fifteenth century. Paint them in with the above colours; and if on a gold ground, the more 'Catholic' your art is. Dress your apostles like priests before the altar; and remember to have a good commodity of crosiers, censers, and other such gimcracks, as you may see in the Catholic chapels, in Sutton Street and elsewhere. Deal in Virgins, and dress them like a burgomaster's wife by Cranach or Van Eyck. Give them all long twisted tails to their gowns, and proper angular draperies. Place all the heads on one side, with the eyes shut, and the proper solemn simper. At the back of the head, draw, and gild with gold leaf, a halo, or glory, of the exact shape of a cart-wheel: and you have the thing done.

Thackeray's objection to both these varieties of art was basically the same: they hoodwinked people. The art-experience made them feel they were being devout or classical, and gave them a better opinion of themselves, when they were merely conniving in a fraud. A thoroughly false view of culture and of religion ensued. The public were persuaded to forsake their own unexalted, commonsense enthusiasms, and feel ashamed of them, but they received nothing authentic in return.

Byron, whom Thackeray detested, and Goethe, about whom he had at best mixed feelings, seemed to him to be leaders in this business of making people deny their own identities. *Don Juan* is read by Sam Pogson in *A Caution to Travellers*, and indeed by all Thackeray's second-rate dandies, and they learn from it that seduction is 'a very correct, natty thing', whereas without it they might have developed some decent, sensitive notions about the opposite sex. In this, Pogson and his kind illustrate the endless gullibility of the human species:

The silly animal is never content; is ever trying to fit itself into another shape; wants to deny its own identity, and has not the courage to utter its own thoughts. Because Lord Byron was wicked, and quarrelled with the world; and found himself growing fat, and quarrelled with his victuals, and thus naturally grew ill-humoured, did not half Europe grow ill-humoured too? Did not every poet feel his young affections withered, and despair and darkness cast upon his soul?

As Thackeray saw it, each writer trails in his wake a horde of impressionable Pogsons, busily twisting themselves to fit the moods and manias of the master. It is a view of human behaviour that observation amply bears out, though, of course, other romantics have taken Byron's place since Thackeray's day, from Marx to Marcuse. Thackeray's scepticism about the fake emotions romanticism induces links him with Flaubert. Emma Bovary, half swooning with passion at *Lucia de Lammermoor*, is a female Pogson: 'The heroine's voice seemed simply the echo of her own consciousness, and all this fascinating make-believe a part of her own life.' Because romantic ideologies are seldom practicable in daily life, grotesque disparities open up between the devotee's creed and conduct, and Thackeray touched on this point in his portrait of the public executioner from *The Paris Sketch-Book*, who spends his leisure time blubbering over *The Sorrows of Werther*.

The most prolific breeding-ground for such sham sentiment was, he believed, the social-conscience novel, as developed by Dickens. For one thing, he despised the bogus philanthropy that induced comfortably-off readers, who had every intention of remaining comfortably-off, to grow lachrymose over fictional accounts of workers' woes. For another, he felt that you could not have a political question fairly debated in a novel, since the author was at liberty to invent characters and motives, in order to revile or revere them. The whole structure was rigged. Moreover, none of the sentimental novelists, it seemed to him, had devised any feasible scheme for bettering the poor, or shown the political and economic acumen that might lead one to expect such a scheme was forthcoming. The happy endings, tacked onto their stories of suffering, were enough to expose the shallowness of their social concerns:

At the conclusion of these tales, when the hero or heroine has been bullied enough – when poor Jack has been put off the murder he was meditating, or poor Polly has been rescued from the town on which she was about to go – there somehow arrives a misty reconciliation between the poor and the rich; a prophecy is uttered of better times for the one, and better manners in the other; presages are made of happy life, happy marriage and children, happy beef and pudding for all time to come; and the characters make their bow, grinning, in a group, as they do at the end of a drama when the curtain falls, and the blue fire blazes behind the scenes.

This was not the way, Thackeray protested, in which men who were seriously engaged in the question of the conflict between capital and labour met and grappled with it. His scepticism in this area seems healthy, and still relevant. For, even today, readers of conscience-stirring novels feel, when they find themselves siding with the oppressed, that they are taking up a righteous stand on a social issue, and experience the self-applause that such a consciousness brings, when they are merely engaged in idle amusement.

The most poisonous brand of sham politics, to Thackeray's way of thinking, came from writers who set themselves up as statesmen, and fostered nationalistic aspirations in their countrymen. In the early 1840s seeds of the conflict between France and Prussia that, thirty years later, was to leave 156,000 Frenchmen and 28,000 Germans dead on the battlefield, were already being sown by the literary men of both nations. Thackeray, writing in the *Foreign Quarterly Review*, picked on Victor Hugo's *Le Rhin* (1842) as typifying this mode of irresponsibility. The book describes Hugo's holidays in the Rhineland, and incorporates a study of the balance of power in Europe, full of grandiose fancies, which Thackeray cuts to shreds. Hugo concludes that the Rhinelanders are pining to become Frenchmen, and speculation upon how he might have descried this, without being able to read or speak German, prompts some of Thackeray's livelier sarcasms. With his account of Hugo's visit to the tomb of Hoche, the French general who defeated the Prussians in 1793, Thackeray's tone hardens:

He says that after looking a while at the stone, and peering into the vault, he heard a voice coming from it, which uttered these words 'Il faut que la France reprenne le Rhin'. . . . Let us hope, however, for the interest of humanity, and of at least five hundred thousand human creatures who must bloodily perish by gun and bayonet, in case this voice that M. Hugo heard out of the hole really *were* a celestial one – let us hope there is some mistake on the poet's part.

The reduction of Hugo's visionary *mise en scène* to 'the hole' is worthy of Swift. And if Thackeray, as things turned out, rather miscalculated the casualties, the wholesomeness of his protest can't be questioned.

Thackeray's aversion to the sham in art meant that he had serious reservations about tragedy. He disliked it because it imposed a fixed, doom-dogged view of the world, and entailed people making themselves miserable for no good reason. He did not care for Racine, though he could see that his 'sparkling undertaker's wit' had a lugubrious kind of appeal, and he, like Tolstoy, thought Shakespearean tragedy over-rated. Personally, he declared, he would be glad to see a stomach-pump brought on for Romeo in the fifth act, and would have Mrs. Macduff and her little ones come in from the slips at the end, to state that the account of their murder was 'a shameful fabrication of the newspapers'. He found *King Lear* 'a bore', especially the part where Lear curses his children, which reminded Thackeray of the 'cut-throat imprecations' in the *Book of Psalms* – another work he couldn't stand. To the criticism of Shakespeare he brought an obstinate rationality, and a desire to test the plots and motivation against what he took to be realistic standards of likelihood. Thus the play scene in *Hamlet* struck him as an unthinkably crass device for someone of Hamlet's social and intellectual standing to have resorted to:

Suppose our beloved monarch were to lose Prince Albert and marry his brother the Duke of Saxe Cobourg two months after Albert's death, suppose I say a company of actors going to Windsor and acting

a play by the desire of the Prince of Wales full of the grossest allusions
to widows marrying, to marriage with a deceased husband's brother
and so forth – what a noise there'd be! What a pretty strategem for a
clever Prince to employ.

Thackeray's insensitivity to Shakespeare may appal. It is probably
best regarded as willed. He refused to be moved, because the spectacle
of bogus suffering, put on a stage for the delectation of a crowd,
offended his reason. He reacted faithfully, if myopically, to one truth
about tragedy, which is that it takes pleasure in the horrible, and this
is what lies behind his irony in *Pendennis*, when he relates how 'the
group of slaughtered personages' at the end of *Hamlet* attracted 'immense shouting and applause' from the crowd.

For people to upset themselves over literature or drama at all is,
rationally, absurd, and the emotions they give way to are not real,
but knowingly prompted by fictions. This situation worried Thackeray.
He was suspicious of artistic attempts to agitate his feelings. With
novels, he customarily looked at the last paragraph first, so he said,
and when he found it starting with 'There is a fresh green mound in
Brentford churchyard . . .', or suchlike, would shut the book at once.
In his walks round the Louvre, when he came upon Delacroix's ghastly
masterpiece, based on an incident in *Don Juan*, which shows ship-
wrecked men drawing lots to find which should be eaten first, he made
a practice of turning round and looking at 'a fat woman with a par-
roquet', hung opposite, to cheer himself up – 'for what's the use of
being uncomfortable?'

The agonies and ecstasies of art repelled him as falsifications. They
involved people flinging themselves into exaggerated postures, and
belied life as it was lived. In painting, literature and sculpture, all
magnitude and elevation – idealized figures, exalted themes, acres of
canvas, aggregations of masonry – left him with a suspicion that real
human creatures had been lost sight of and betrayed. This accounts for
his reservations about Milton ('Great daring geniuses' like Milton
are rare, 'Heaven be thanked for it', he observed in *An Exhibition
Gossip*), and, indeed, for the worrying feeling, which sometimes overcame him, that most of what is esteemed as art by the cognoscenti is
worthless pretentiousness. 'There is very little Art that's the fact', he
wrote to Kate Perry from Naples in March 1854:

not that great blustering hulking Colosseum for instance, nor those
simpering Canovas, sickly Guidos, swaggering Caracci – only bits
here and there. I went yesterday to see the Farnese Hercules . . . O
the great coarse bumptious old braggart! Playing a smart piece on the
piano, or cutting a neat figure of eight on the Serpentine, or writing
a review, are really as good as that thumping piece of skill. There are
avenues of worthless marble and canvas here and at Rome.

As a matter of fact he reveals, at the start of this letter, what has really been on his mind – namely his daughters' illness (they were convalescing at the time from scarlet fever) and, by association, 'that day fifteen years ago when their little sister died at sunrise'. This was his second child, Jane, whom he had lost when she was eight months old in March 1839. He had never forgotten her, or the pang of that bereavement. Indeed, he could not bring himself to believe her really dead. One of his other daughters records that he 'always expected to find his little Janie somewhere', and when he was near to death himself he took comfort in the thought that he would not be 'left without a child'. For years he noted the anniversary of Jane's death in his diaries, and it was this date that prompted the thoughts about art in the Kate Perry letter. The Colosseum, and the other vaunted artefacts, were having to compete in his thoughts with something profound, ineradicable and everyday – the death of a child, and he recognized them, in that context, as windy impostures.

He sought, in art, the genius of common life – an ordinariness and a keen observation, that would not be punctured by confrontation with reality. He found this, eminently, in George Cruikshank, and his essay on Cruikshank's achievement constitutes a catalogue of the things Thackeray (or the early Thackeray) expected of art. He liked Cruikshank because he hadn't 'a morsel of mysticism', and because his world was low and lively. It was populated by run-of-the-mill people – dustmen, charity-children, policemen – and it often depended for its verve and precision on eating and drinking. Cruikshank's miller wolfing bacon-rashers 'frizzing and smoking' from the gridiron was an embodiment, for Thackeray, of Cruikshankean gusto; and the girl in 'Philoprogenitiveness', making a Yorkshire pudding for her swarming siblings with the gravy from two mutton chops hung on a string before the fire, represented Cruikshank's loving documentation of life's unremarkable processes.

The department of art furthest removed, in Thackeray's view, from Cruikshank and the decent, solid pleasures of food and drink, was that which dealt with battle. His qualms, here as elsewhere, are understandable. The process of fitting human slaughter into words and phrases at all can be seen as a betrayal of humanity, an acquiescence, carrying with it a concession that the unspeakable can be spoken. Language steals from life. The particularity of another's pain is blunted and made acceptable by translation into linguistic forms. Thackeray realized this, and consequently sham warfare was, of all literary shams, the most disgusting to him. In his *Chronicle of the Drum*, poets rhyming 'in fashion picturesque' about carnage, and historians like Sir Archibald Alison, turning it into 'classic prose', are shown to be obscenely engaged. The battles in Scott's novels, where

'everything passes off agreeably', attracted his ridicule, as did belliger-
ent rhetoric wherever he encountered it. One of his funniest reviews
is that of Georg Herwegh's poems in the *Foreign Quarterly*. Herwegh
was a German revolutionary poet, and a friend of Karl Marx, who,
when called up for military service, found the discipline irksome, was
insubordinate to an officer, and fled to Switzerland to avoid punishment.
Thackeray, in a mischievous but not wholly inaccurate account of
Herwegh's early career, attributes the poet's flight to his distaste at
having to share a bed in barracks with coarse countrymen from the
Black Forest, and other such indignities of soldiering. He proceeds to
quote from Herwegh's poems, which seethe with fiery rant, and
comments: 'It will be seen that, though Herwegh the man is disin-
clined to military service, Herwegh the poet has a great appetite for
war.' His conclusion is that the German poet's calls to arms may be
discounted as shoddy fake: 'Many a set of conspirators have sung such
a ditty on the theatrical boards, and so shouting "Death!" have
marched off with tin battle-axes to drink small beer in the slips.' As
things turned out, Thackeray was unjust to Herwegh who, five years
later, led a column of German working men in the 1848 rising,
managed to get them cut to pieces, and narrowly escaped himself to
Switzerland. However, Thackeray's contention that warlike poetry is
a boyish make-believe, which actual warfare quickly puts out of
countenance, would scarcely be challenged nowadays, though it took
Owen, Sassoon and their war to press the point home.

Painting warlike pictures likewise struck him as a juvenile business,
inspiring bogus bravado in artist and spectators alike. He admitted that he went in for it himself, in his younger days, and once
started work on a canvas of Waterloo, with lifeguardsmen locked in
combat and a cuirassier having his head cut off, until, as he joked in a
letter, he began actually to fancy himself a hero. This episode in his
career is burlesqued in *The Newcomes*, where Clive executes a massive
battle piece, depicting General Wellesley charging the Mahratta
Artillery at Assaye. The group in the foreground consists of Clive's
friend Fred Bayham bestriding the corpse of a cab-horse, which has
been dragged into Clive's studio for the purpose, and remains there
until the landlady and the rest of the lodgers complain of the stench,
whereupon the model is carted off by the knackers. The dead steed's
aroma represents unglamorous reality upsetting arty notions of death.

Thackeray's impatience with sham was bound, eventually, to alienate
him from fiction altogether – and did. His honesty drove him to despise
his art. We can see this happening already at the end of *The Newcomes*,
where he comments wryly on the unreal rewards and punishments that
novelists deal out to their characters – 'bags of sovereigns, which
won't buy anything' for the good, and 'awful blows, which do not

hurt' for the wicked. In *The Virginians* his disillusionment becomes more pronounced. Halfway through the account of Maria and Harry's love-affair, he breaks off and delivers a testy lecture on the uselessness of writing or reading such stuff: 'Whole chapters might have been written to chronicle all these circumstances, but *à quoi bon?* . . . I am surprised, gentlemen and ladies, you read novels any more. What is the good of telling the story?' The honest answer was that Thackeray was receiving £250 a month from his publishers for telling it; and he does not shirk – indeed, he seems rather to enjoy – bringing this aspect of the matter to his readers' notice. In *Philip* he interjects:

Ah! How wonderful ways and means are! When I think how this very line, this very word, which I am writing, represents money, I am lost in a respectful astonishment . . . I am paid, we will say, for the sake of illustration, at the rate of sixpence per line. With the words 'Ah! How wonderful' to the words 'per line', I can buy a loaf, a piece of butter, a jug of milk, a modicum of tea – actually enough to make breakfast for the family.

That he is providing himself with food and drink is the reality behind the fiction, and food and drink are alone real enough to make the fiction worth pressing on with. The passage has an intriguing circularity – earning money by explaining that it is earning money – and its viewpoint appealed to Thackeray because it blew fiction's gaff. Writing fiction became so far from an end in itself that he wished he could hire a 'competent, respectable and rapid clerk' to do his novels for him, under his general direction, arguing that there was 'a great deal of carpenter's and joiner's work' in novels, which any 'smart professional hand' could supply.

It seems a desperate position for a novelist to have been brought to, but Thackeray's tone remains quite resilient, indeed flippant. This characteristic tone, and his disparagement of art, have angered some critics, who consider him a traitor and a philistine. More justly, as this chapter has tried to show, he may be regarded as a sceptical and rational hedonist (sceptical enough to be sceptical of hedonism much of the time), who found humankind's endless capacity for giving itself airs – in literary and artistic, as in other matters – tiresome. His flippancy was a prophylactic against the self-prizing posture of more solemn styles. It advertised his nonchalance. He once said that he liked to see people asleep over his books: the rest would do them good. To have felt affronted would have been, in Thackeray's code, to give way to a typically self-centred human reaction. Judgements in art and literature were, after all, purely personal.

Thackeray's championship of this view constitutes a more important contribution than we might at first suspect to the debate about the function of art which occupied so many educated minds in the Victorian period. His contribution is important because it is negative, realistic and subversive, in an area where assertiveness, unreality and idealism were the general rule. Anyone, in any age, who believes that there are functions that art should fulfil is ultimately imposing upon art his own preconceptions about the desirable ordering of society. It is surprising how few art-theorists in the nineteenth century realized this. Thackeray, though, seems to have done so, and his rejection of prescriptive attitudes to art, and of the notion that judgement might be objective, is altogether singular. We may contrast him most strikingly, perhaps, with Matthew Arnold. With social ideas that incorporated sweetness and light (and flinging the ringleaders of civil disturbance from the Tarpeian rock), Arnold drew up touchstones (or pieces of poetry that he liked) by which, he asserted, the genuine article might be recognized. Having thus satisfied the rage for certainty that so deluded his age, Arnold ventured to prophesy that poetry would come to replace 'most of what now passes with us for religion and philosophy'. Few prophecies have proved so mistaken. Thackeray would never have fallen into such vagaries, because he would have realized that Arnold's touchstones were purely arbitrary, and because he knew that certainty was not to be found in life. His position, if less hopeful than Arnold's, is more adult and courageous.

5

Theatre

It seems odd that someone so wary of sham as Thackeray should have had a passion for the theatre – and odder still that ballet, opera and pantomime, the theatre's most unreal forms, should have been his favourites. Still, they were; and it's clear that their extravagant, transparent sham partly accounted for their appeal. Pleasure in them was not impaired by any obligation to take them seriously. 'How I long for a sight of a dear green curtain again', he wrote to Fitzgerald:

after going three times a week to the play for a year one misses it so. O the delight of seeing the baize slowly ascending – the spangled shoes which first appear, then as it draws up, legs stomachs heads, till finally it ends in all the glory of a party of 'musqueteers' drinking – a dance – an inn with an infinity of bells jingling or a couple of gay dogs in cocked hats with pieces of silk dangling out of their pockets for handkerchiefs. Yet another month, and all this paradise will be in my reach.

It's easy to see, from the way Thackeray talks, that without the patent falsity paradise would not be half so enjoyable, because one would not be at liberty to feel superior to it. He had no aspirations towards being an actor, as Dickens had, and Dickens's tempestuous involvement in amateur theatricals and dramatic readings – his 'triumphs before the Hoperatives at Manchester', as Thackeray put it – moved him only to disdain. He saw the stage as a lighted box, with himself on the outside. In the box, magic happened; the world was transfigured. But the watching satirist had (and wanted to have) always at hand the complicated, melancholy pleasure of knowing that the magic was just gas and greasepaint, and fairy-land a fake.

The need for resplendently unreal theatre explains Thackeray's adulation of 'the exquisite young Taglioni', as he called her, whom he first saw dance in Paris in 1829, and who always remained his idol. The young folks, he feared, as he aged, would never see 'anything so charming, anything so classic' again, and when he imagined his later heroines he found himself picturing Taglioni as she had been – so that Ethel Newcome finishes a waltz 'panting, and smiling radiant', we learn, 'as many hundred years ago I remember to have seen Taglioni, after a conquering *pas seul'*. To understand his enthusiasm, it helps to know something of Marie Taglioni's career.

She had her debut in Paris in 1827, and within five years she had revolutionized ballet. Together with Véron, the manager of the Académie Nationale de Musique, she created the romantic formula of *ballet blanc* – ethereal, airborne, gleaming vaguely through transparencies. The first glimpse of the new art came in the cloister scene of *Robert le Diable*, staged in 1831 – a spectral dance, with moonlight, provided by gas jets hooked in the flies, turning the *corps de ballet* into a floating, milky cloud. The gas was a novelty – they still had oil lamps at the Comédie Française. Even today we can get an idea of the scene's effect, because it remained unaltered for forty years, and Degas, in 1872, put it on canvas.

Marie took up the shimmering style triumphantly in 1832 when she appeared in *La Sylphide*, the ballet with which her name was ever afterwards linked. Set in the wild land of the Waverley Novels, it told of a Scottish peasant haunted by an intangible, sylph-like creature with wings attached to her shoulders, and muslin underwear puffing out her short dress of white crêpe. This dress, the *tutu*, created for Marie, became the received garb for romantic ballet, replacing the Greek tunic previously in favour; and gnomes, salamanders, undines, elves and peris immediately took over ballet (as Théophile Gautier, one of Marie's admirers, observed) from the figures of classical myth who had prevailed hitherto. At its finale, *La Sylphide* becomes a flying ballet, with hosts of winged spirits carrying their dead leader, Marie, off on the ends of wires – a dangerous business; at one performance two sylphides were left dangling above the audience, and had to be freed by a stage-hand on a rope.

Marie did not only change ballet, she changed women. With the advent of the *tutu*, as Louis Maignon records in *Le Romantisme et la Mode*, all kinds of frills were introduced into dresses and bodices to render them rustling and billowy, and to give women a seraphic, ideal appearance. Likewise, Marie's other great role as the nixie or water-elf of German folklore in *La Fille du Danube* made wave-coloured taffetas all the rage. *La Fille du Danube*, which came out in 1836, had an under-water second act, and maybe contributed to Thackeray's strange feelings about sirens and waterproof women. Spirit roles fitted Marie because she was a prodigy of lightness. All observers agree that, when dancing, she seemed to be in flight. She moved in great bounds, and alighted without the slightest noise – her father, it was said, had threatened to curse her if he ever *heard* her dance. She cultivated soul and uplift, whereas her rival, Fanny Elssler, was an exponent of the fleshly style, all hip-wiggling and provocativeness. The controversy between Taglionists and Elsslerites divided

Paris, Thackeray's position being clearly indicated in *The Paris Sketch-Book*, where he compares the excitement generated by Fanny Elssler's 'flesh-coloured stockinnet pantaloons' to the sort of thrill people get at a public execution.

Marie's success story was a romantic phenomenon in itself. She married a count; she had a manor near Lake Como and a palace in Venice; she charmed kings and emperors. Audiences went wild at her performances. In Russia, the Bolshoi Theatre had to turn thousands away; in Vienna she was recalled forty-two times on her opening night, and followed home by a crowd who fought for the flowers she tossed from her balcony. She was the first dancer for whom bouquets were thrown on the stage – a thing unheard of in the theatre before. Yet she was by no means beautiful. Sallow-faced, and almost hunch-backed, she suffered from emaciation, and had abnormally long arms. It was spitefully said that she could put on a garter without bending down, and dance a *pas de Châle* with her arms as the only property. The queerly-accentuated arms of Miss Fotheringay, and other Thackerayan women, seem to have evolved from Marie's lengthy members.

It's typical of Thackeray's restless scepticism that, when he set about depicting Marie as a dancer, it was her plainness rather than her enchantment that he stressed. In 1836 he published, under the pseudonym Théophile Wagstaffe, a set of drawings, with captions, burlesquing scenes from Didelot's ballet *Flore et Zéphyre*, in which Marie had performed with Perrot, the celebrated male dancer and pupil of Vestris. Perrot was abnormally ugly, as even admirers like Gautier admitted, so Thackeray had fertile ground to work on. His studies in *Flore et Zéphyr* (*sic*) are highly perceptive as ballet commentary. Indeed, Taglioni's biographer, André Levinson (who does not realize that Wagstaffe is Thackeray), considers that they teach more about the dancer's technique and Didelot's choreography than any of the adulatory tributes. But Thackeray's main purpose is to expose the hideous irrationality of two adults romping around with each other in short skirts, and purporting to express grief, anxiety and suchlike emotions by bounding in the air and waggling their feet. To have come to accept these conventions is, the satirical half of Thackeray wishes to impress upon us, an abandonment of intellect and innocence. Tolstoy was to make a similar point when he showed Natasha at her first opera. Fresh from the country, the girl is ashamed of what she observes on the stage – the trees made of glued canvas and painted cardboard, the fat man in tights pretending to be a lover, the bare-legged dancers leaping and kicking. She is sorry for the players, imagining the audience will feel as derisive and bewildered as herself. The rapturous applause amazes her, but eventually she gets sucked into the sham and enjoys it. Tolstoy's account, dwelling on the half-naked women in the boxes, and the scantily-clad dancers, intimates that sexual corruption is contagiously present at such performances, and that Natasha succumbs to it.

Thackeray felt the same, though he was less upset about the moral taint than about the self-delusion involved. That people should be corrupted didn't particularly surprise him. The world being what it was, he didn't hope for anything else. But he thought they should at least have the sense to see what was happening. He enjoyed ballet himself, but he did not pretend that watching young women show their legs was a high spiritual pleasure, and he was, accordingly, suspicious of Marie Taglioni's more soulful admirers. Thus one drawing in *Flore et Zéphyr* shows Taglioni executing a *développé à la grande seconde* 'to deplore Zéphyre's absence' (as the caption informs us), which entails standing on one leg, with the other stretched out at hip-level, while men in the audience leer up her skirt. This male propensity is innocently illustrated by Harry Foker in *Pendennis*, who brings the conversation round to ballet during dinner:

'Seen Taglioni in the Sylphide, Miss Amory? Bring me that souprame of Volile again, if you please (this was addressed to the attendant near him); very good: can't think where the souprames come from; what becomes of the legs of the fowls, I wonder? She's clipping in the Sylphide, ain't she?' and he began very kindly to hum the pretty air which pervades that prettiest of all ballets, now faded into the past with that most beautiful and gracious of all dancers.

Taglioni sets Harry thinking about legs, and legs good enough to eat, quite naturally. *La Sylphide* ministers to his appetites, Thackeray wishes us to see, in much the same way as *suprême de volaille*, and this, so long as it is recognized, does not at all prevent the ballet or its dancer from being beautiful, according to Thackeray's view of art. When he first saw Taglioni, it was her legs that appealed to him: 'the most superb pair of pins' he had ever seen, as, with his usual frankness, he told his mother.

He felt it should be realized, too, that girls dancing for the gratification of men expressed something about the relationship between the sexes that high-mindedness might like to gloss over. It brought out the sultan that squats in every male, and the slave that fawns and cringes in every woman. The harem was a subject which, throughout his work, Thackeray's mind kept flitting back to with a certain fondness; and one of his most savoured theatrical memories was of the ballerina Marie-Louise Duvernay in *La Bayadère*:

How well I remember the tune to which she used to appear! Kaled used to say to the Sultan, 'My lord, a troop of those dancing and singing girls called Bayadères approaches', and, to the clash of cymbals, and the thumping of my heart, in she used to dance.

The ballet gave Western man a chance of feeling like the masterful voluptuaries of the orient, with girls exhibiting themselves at his command. Further, there was a distinct appropriateness about this, Thackeray realized, for middle-class Victorian society did indeed attempt to keep its women ignorant, powerless and decorative, like dancing-girls, and Laura, in *The Newcomes*, is given a short tirade against male supremacy, in which she explicitly likens 'young women in our world' to 'Bayadères . . . whose calling is to dance, and wear jewels, and look beautiful'. Significantly, one result of Taglioni's revolution in ballet was the eclipse of male dancing. Not a single great male dancer emerged between Perrot and Nijinsky. Ballet became essentially girls parading before men.

Thackeray saw the situation with clarity. It did not in the least spoil his enjoyment of ballet, or of young women, whom he frankly regarded as 'pretty little sentimental gewgaws', boring if clever. He knew that Laura described Victorian social injustices accurately – after all, he wrote her tirade for her – but he believed those injustices answered to something deeply ingrained in the nature of the sexes. Women, he often said, enjoyed being cowed, and of course they alone had the angelic patience necessary for tending the needs of the male. Probably most men still think like Thackeray, though they would be more circumspect about admitting it, simply because honesty on the point is likely to make women less docile and manageable. At all events, Thackeray would have felt it hypocritical to pretend you did not like having lightly-clad women making submissive gestures in your direction – and hypocritical, too, to deny the element of male brutality and female degradation that such a pleasure entails. Both ingredients are present, and are fused with the garish excitement of the theatre, in the scene from *Pendennis* where we are shown Lord Steyne in his proscenium box at the Museum Theatre, with a *corps de ballet* consisting of 'a hundred and twenty lovely female savages in palm leaves and feather aprons' dancing before him, all ogling his box, and with his hirelings, Wenham and Wagg, at his side, ready to slip behind the scenes and make an assignation with any female savage who takes his fancy. The ballerinas, Thackeray recounts:

Mademoiselle Sauterelle, or Mademoiselle de Bondi (known as la petite Caout-chouc), . . . when actually up in the air quivering like so many shuttlecocks, always kept their lovely eyes winking at that box in which the great Steyne sate. Now and then you would hear a harsh voice from behind the curtain cry 'Brava, Brava!' or a pair of white gloves wave from it, and begin to applaud. Bondi, or Sauterelle, when they came down to earth, curtsied and smiled, especially to those hands, before they walked up the stage again, panting and happy.

We have seen how much Thackeray depends on gloves, but this is one of his best pairs – pallid, prehensile and sinister, like their owner, as they stretch out towards the excitedly panting girls.

Though enraptured by ballet, then, Thackeray loved to demonstrate the murky sources of its charm. Doing so helped to preserve his sense of control and superiority. The idea of life behind the scenes, the tawdry back end of theatre's magic box, constantly stirred his imagination, too. The final drawings in *Flore et Zéphyr* take us into the dancers' dressing rooms. Flore is hobnobbing with two raffish-looking male visitors, and Zéphyre shoving snuff up his nose, while a servant brushes his wig. Forays backstage had been a customary licence for Thackeray as a wealthy young wastrel, and they revealed (insofar as he has left us word of them) beauty and violence, as well as squalor. Once, behind the scenes at the opera, he recalls in the *Roundabout Papers*, he saw the famous soprano, Gertrude Sontag, 'let her hair fall down over her shoulders' – 'such hair, such eyes'; and once, after the ballet at the King's Theatre, his diary records, 'I saw the rivals Brugnoti and Heberle – plastered with rouge and looking like she devils more than graceful women'. Lurid glimpses of this sort also slip themselves into his fiction. Following the bespangled ballet-scene in *Pendennis*, for example, Wenham goes backstage on an errand for Lord Steyne, and finds the theatre manager 'cursing the ladies of the corps-de-ballet', with his fist 'clenched in the face of one of the offending coryphées'. O'Rourke, in *Philip*, lets out some gossip about a back-stage debauch, with one ballet dancer smearing the cream from a Charlotte Russe over the face of another, which sounds a lot livelier than anything that happens in the novel proper. Clive Newcome falls for a dancer at Drury Lane, only to discover that, in the light of day, she is scraggy and yellow-faced (like Taglioni), and inhabits a back-parlour smelling of onions. 'Can there be any more dreary object than those whitened and raddled old women who shudder at the slips?' Thackeray mournfully inquires, 'Over this stage of Clive Newcome's life we may surely drop the curtain.' This spinsterish recoil typifies, of course, the late Thackeray's concessions to Victorian hypocrisy, with which *The Newcomes* is plentifully stocked. In reality whitened, raddled women, or men for that matter, old or young, fascinated him, and he could hardly keep his pen away from them or the wild frolics he fancied them enjoying in the theatre's dimmer recesses. Hence the garish phantasmagoria which the backstage goings-on present to the eyes of Cox in *Cox's Diary*:

Fancy scores of Jews, with hooked noses, and black muzzles, covered with rings, chains, sham diamonds, and gold waistcoats. Fancy old men dressed in old night-gowns, with knock-knees, and dirty flesh-coloured cotton stockings, and dabs of brickdust on their wrinkled old chops, and tow-wigs (such wigs!) for the bald ones, and great tin spears in their hands mayhap or else shepherds' crooks, and fusty garlands of flowers made of red and green baize. Fancy troops of girls giggling, chattering, pushing to and fro, amidst old black canvas, Gothic halls, thrones, pasteboard Cupids, dragons, and such like. Such dirt, darkness, crowd, confusion, and gabble of all conceivable languages was never known.

No question, here, of the raddled old troupers or their entourage being 'dreary'. The scene was written before respectability inclined Thackeray to muffle his imaginative excitements. The whole theatre-sequence in *Cox's Diary* is brilliantly executed. Cox and his wife have never seen opera or ballet before, and, like Natasha, they are thunderstruck by the indecency, the sham, and the applause. Cox's matter-of-fact account of the antics on stage prefigures Tolstoy's, though it is Tolstoy translated into comic cockney. Further, the set-up in Thackeray is really the more complicated. For Tolstoy presents Natasha's innocent vision as the correct one. But Thackeray, loving opera and ballet, but also loving seeing through them, selects as his innocent spectator the coarse Cox, whose viewpoint we can neither quite endorse nor quite dismiss.

For Thackeray, then, behind-the-scenes life meant dirt and violence and beauty. It was fantastic and alluring, the meeting place of dream and of the waking world, where strangely-garbed and painted figures swarmed and revelled. It was low and mysterious, located beyond the area-railings of middle-class decency, down unwholesome mews and alleyways and up dilapidated flights of stairs. Coarseness, ignorance and duplicity pervaded it, as Pen's Miss Fotheringay amply manifests, but also resourcefulness and vigour, and a down-to-earth attitude towards the shams of art, and this Thackeray naturally found seductive. It took the lid off the magic box. Though sordid it engendered human warmth – the frowsty comfortableness of curl-papers and cribbage and punch, which Maria descends into when she marries the actor, Hagan, in *The Virginians*. And it was sexually emancipated. Its women flouted the conventions of dress and conduct which embraced their subservient sisters like a damp corset, and they were exiled from respectable society in return. They frankly showed themselves off to men for money, and they generally took care to be knocked down to the highest bidder. Hence they laid bare the connections between sex and cash which more fastidious people spent their time trying to cover up.

In this robust world, Becky Sharp was born. But before he created her, Thackeray depicted another girl with theatre in her blood,

Morgiana in *The Ravenswing*, who has some of Becky's characteristics, and for whom Thackeray's admiration is undisguised, though as usual his admiration incorporates a fair amount of levity and disparagement as well. The story is in Thackeray's breezy early manner, and teems with theatrical tittle-tattle. Just as Becky's mother was a dancer in the French opera, so Morgiana's mother Mrs. Crump, née Budge, now landlady of the Bootjack Hotel, danced on the French stage as Miss Delancy, and called her daughter after her celebrated role in the *Forty Thieves* (the once popular musical drama that Jos slips off to see in Chapter IV of *Vanity Fair*). The Bootjack bar is plastered with ballet prints, including *La Sylphide*, and Miss Budge as Morgiana 'in the act of pouring, to very slow music, a quantity of boiling oil into one of the forty jars'. Morgiana herself was often on the stage as a child, 'in Little Pickle, in Desdemona, in Rosina, and in Miss Foote's part where she used to dance'. She has beautiful eyes – the size of billiard balls, her votaries vow – and an amazing head of hair which, at the point in the story where she intends to entrap a husband, she lets down:

Removing a sham gold chain which she wore on her forehead, two brass hair combs set with glass rubies, and the comb which kept her hair together, – removing them, I say, and turning her great eyes towards the stranger, and giving her head a shake, down let tumble . . . a flood of shining, waving, heavy, glossy, jetty hair. . . . It tumbled down Miss Morgiana's back, and it tumbled over her shoulders, it tumbled over the chair on which she sat.

We recognize in the dramatic moment Thackeray's treasured behind-the-scenes glimpse of Sontag letting her hair down – 'such hair, such eyes'. Indeed Morgiana's destined husband, a swell called Captain Walker, reacts in precisely the same way – 'Such hair! – such eyebrows! – such eyes!' Morgiana, like her sham gold and glass rubies, belongs to the backstage regions of Thackeray's imagination, and even her hair, though genuine, is converted into a theatrical property: she is frequently cast in 'hair parts', where it can appear dishevelled.

Morgiana marries Captain Walker, but retains several other admirers, among them her singing master Signor Baroski, whose infatuation she is perfectly aware of, but does not discourage, thus reaping the benefit of 220 guineas-worth of unpaid-for singing lessons. In private she mimics the singing master's manner of rolling his eyes, and performs 'Baroski in love' for the amusement of her husband and mother. This mimicry also aligns her with Becky, who, to divert her father's friends, does dialogues with her doll in imitation of Miss Pinkerton which are 'the delight of Newman Street, Gerrard Street, and the artists' quarter' and who, after a visit to Chiswick, ungratefully adds Miss Pinkerton's sister, Miss Jemima, to the act:

for though that honest creature had made and given her jelly and cake enough for three children, and a seven-shilling piece at parting, the girl's sense of ridicule was far stronger than her gratitude, and she sacrificed Miss Jemmy quite as pitilessly as her sister.

As Captain Walker's wife, Morgiana, like Becky, has her carriage and her box at the opera, and entertains 'the most fashionable manhood of London'. But Walker's finances are as nebulous as Rawdon's. He is eventually arrested for debt, and Morgiana's servants react to the disaster by offensively demanding wages, and plundering her house of its table-knives, cambric handkerchiefs and similar movables. It is, in effect, an early draft of the scene where Becky's servants rebel after Rawdon's arrest, and Becky's maid Mademoiselle Fifine clears the dwelling of its trinkets and silverware.

But if Morgiana's capers and comeuppance resemble Becky's, she is in other ways very different. She becomes a celebrated singer, whereas Becky is hissed off the stage in Strasburg when she tries to earn her living that way, and she remains faithful to her husband, who lives off her earnings. Her dog-like devotion to Walker sets Thackeray wondering about the gullibility of wives – how they can wake every morning to find the same dull, ugly face snoring beside them, and believe it divine – and what this trait brings to mind is not Becky but Amelia's obstinate love for George Osborne. And indeed, Morgiana is plainly an ancestor of Amelia in some respects. She has a Dobbin, in the person of Mr. Woolsey, a tailor from Conduit Street, who lacks her husband's flash elegance, but loves her before her marriage and proves his loyalty to her after it. At the sale of Walker's effects he buys and gives back to Morgiana her cherished rosewood piano and music books, just as Dobbin does for Amelia at the Sedley sale. And Woolsey gets his Amelia in the end. *The Ravenswing* concludes with a letter written by the author from a hotel in Coblenz:

Only yesterday, as I was dining at this excellent hotel, I remarked a bald-headed gentleman in a blue coat and brass buttons, who looked like a colonel on half-pay, and by his side a lady and a little boy of twelve whom the gentleman was cramming with an amazing quantity of cherries and cakes.

Here, of course, we have the Pumpernickel scene from the end of *Vanity Fair*. The similarities extend to minute particulars. Woolsey's stepson leaves the table, after his huge feast, carrying off some macaroons with him, just as Dobbin's stepson little George Osborne does. And Morgiana's faithful tailor, looking 'like a colonel on half-pay', looks like what Dobbin is by the time he gets to Pumpernickel. Yet *The Ravenswing* was published in 1843, two years before *Vanity Fair* is usually thought to have begun to take form in Thackeray's mind. What it amounts to is that Amelia and Becky, the good and evil angels of *Vanity Fair*, were originally the same person, called Morgiana Crump. When Thackeray sliced Morgiana in half, Amelia got the wifely virtue and the second husband, while Becky got her stage-tricks and dancing mother (and also her huge eyes – 'very large, odd and attractive', Becky's are). This division of Morgiana's proceeds is intended, by the prim part of Thackeray, to taint Becky socially and morally. But the effect of her theatrical connections is quite otherwise. They vitalize her. Her mimicry, for instance, may be ungrateful, but it turns life's drearnesses into gaiety. When Becky accepts Lady Southdown's tracts and medicine, and then puts on an imitation of her benefactress in nightcap and gown for Lord Steyne and his friends, she achieves, as Thackeray admits, something that had always eluded Lady Southdown herself: 'for the first time in her life the Dowager Countess of Southdown was made amusing'. Becky's childhood among the painters and Bohemians sounds hardy and amicable compared with anything Amelia could have experienced. When Miss Pinkerton, taken in by her *ingénue* airs, presents the sixteen-year-old Becky with a doll, we're shown her and her father laughing over it 'as they trudged home together', and the stalwart verb puts them at once in a more hale relation to life than all the Miss Pinkertons in the universe.

Becky, alone in the novel, has known hunger as a child, and has shown her mettle in its presence: 'Many a dun had she talked to, and turned away from her father's door; many a tradesman had she coaxed and wheedled into good humour, and into the granting of one meal more.' The tales envious Mrs. Bute carries to Miss Crawley – that Becky used to fetch gin from the public-house to her father, and keep the studios laughing with her 'fun and mimicry', and work as a dancer at the opera and as painter's model – only make her past seem sturdier; just as when, much later, she comes across her maternal grandmother who is a box-opener at a theatre on the boulevards, it spins a thread binding her to the confrérie of artists and entertainers which stretches across Europe and plies its vagabond trade under propriety's nose. Becky proves her histrionic skills too, of course, in the lordly charades at Gaunt House, and twirling round the ballroom afterwards is applauded 'as if she had been a Taglioni'. But she gets quickly sick of high life. 'How much gayer it would be', she thinks, 'to wear spangles and trousers and dance before a booth at a fair.' She is incorrigibly a demi-mondaine, and finds the life she loves not at Gaunt House but in the Elephant Hotel among pedlars, punters, vaulters, tumblers and students. Thackeray puts into her his wildest imaginings about the half-lit Bohemian world. Was she a Russian spy at Töplitz? Was she ejected from St. Petersburg by the police? Rumours fly about her like sparks. She has too much life for the novel fully to encompass her. True, Thackeray sometimes gets nervous about the power of what he has created, and throws out sops to morality by turning Becky's theatrical expertise into a stick to beat her with. At the ballet in Brussels, for instance, we are sourly informed that 'there was no dancer that went through her grimaces or performed her comedy of action better' than Becky. But patently the words represent so meagre a morsel of what Thackeray feels about the ballet or Becky that the stick drops harmlessly from his hand, like the fish's tail which he else-where tries to pin on her. Nor is he more successful in allocating to Amelia any of the theatrical glamour that enwraps Becky, though he does attempt it. In the opening pages we are advised that Amelia can sing like 'Mrs Billington, and dance like Hillisberg or Parisot'. But the opera stage and the French dancers at the Haymarket seem such a world away from Amelia's pale charms that the effort to bring them together soon wilts.

There is never another Becky. Her type was thrown out when Thackeray cleaned himself up after *Vanity Fair* and resolved to become more refined. Miss Fotheringay, for all her burliness, is a thinner creation – chaste and filial, and fitted out with those droll lapses in grammar that Thackeray's middle-class readers liked to associate with actresses. Becky's corrosive intelligence and literary skills and gift for languages – everything that made her a danger to the class above her – have been expurgated. Fanny Bolton, the other lower-class woman in *Pendennis*, is perfectly tame. She inherits a few tinselly bits of Becky's theatrical magic, in that her mother used to dance at the Wells as one of Mrs. Serle's famous forty pupils, and Fanny, under Mr. Bows's tutelage, hopes to emulate her parent's triumphs. But Thackeray does not allow this part of Fanny to grow.

Not until the end of his career do we get a faint reflection of Becky in Elizabeth Prior, the ballet-dancer turned governess of *Lovel the Widower*. *Lovel* was a rewriting of an unsuccessful drama, *The Wolves and the Lamb*, which Thackeray had penned in 1855. It presents an amalgam of the young Thackeray's passions, sunned by the years, and mulled over in his wandering, darting late manner; and in its oblique-ness and nuances and allusions to a misty imbroglio of past loves and losses, it generates a far richer fictional density than the play which begot it. Elizabeth, the heroine, has Becky's colouring – 'a rough, tawny-haired filly of a girl, with great eyes' – and shares her stage-skills. She used to dance under the name of Bessy Bellenden in the *corps de ballet* at the Prince's Theatre, among the 'Sea-nymphs, or Bayadères, or Fairies, or Mazurka maidens (with their fluttering lances and little scarlet slyboots)'. Six years of slavery as a nursery governess have taught her cunning, and she is almost as polished a hypocrite as Becky herself. She pretends love for Batchelor, the narrator of the story, and also for Lovel's butler, though she is actually engaged in an amorous correspondence with the household's medical attendant, and eventually succeeds in marrying her employer, Lovel. Batchelor, though, comes to realize that her artifice and dissimulation are blameless, being forced on her by poverty. In this respect she represents an exculpated Becky. Likewise when Lovel's outraged relatives discover that their governess has starred in *The Bulbul and the Rose* wearing a ballet dress and spangles, and demand her instant dismissal, Lovel's defiance of them marks up a victory for the Bessy Bellendens and the Beckys against the Mrs. Butes.

However, Bessy Bellenden can be redeemed only because she was never really wicked, or not in the expensive manner that virtue finds it hardest to forgive. Becky Sharp's forays into marble halls are quite unparalleled in Elizabeth Prior's hard-working little life. The bought sex and lordly debauch which were always, for Thackeray, an enticing ingredient of theatre's backstage thrill, are hived off, in *Lovel the Widower*, onto one of Bessy's dancing colleagues, Miss Montanville. It is she who acquires the familiar perks of Thackeray's fallen women – the cottage in Regent's Park, the brougham, and the groom with the gold-lace hatband, and she comes to a bad end, falling off a rainbow during one of the theatre's spectacular montages and breaking her leg, so that she can dance no more. Becky, who herself began as a sub-division of Morgiana Crump, is thus subdivided in her turn, and the part of her which decency could not stomach is summarily maimed by the late Thackeray.

Opera and ballet provided, then, one of the great germinating-grounds for Thackeray's imagination. The two arts coalesced in his mind – understandably, because it was the practice at the time for theatres to stage an opera and a ballet as parts of the same evening's entertainment, and the ballet dancers spilt over into the opera. Panto-mime, his third love, had dancers too – indeed, Miss Montanville's abrupt exit from her profession in *Lovel* occurs during the fairy scene in the Prince's Theatre Christmas pantomime, a gorgeous affair with a dove-drawn aerial chariot and a Revolving Shrine, through the roof of which Miss Montanville drops, almost damaging Miss Bellenden who is seated within clad in spangles.

The early nineteenth-century pantomime, it should perhaps be explained, had three main parts. The opening was a dramatized fairy-tale of the Mother Goose or Jack and the Beanstalk type, in which the actors wore huge masks. These they threw off during the second part, the transformation scene, when the Fairy Queen appeared and turned the characters of the opening – the lovers, the old curmudgeon, and the servant – into Harlequin, Columbine, Pantaloon and Clown. In the third part, the Harlequinade, these stylized figures, deriving from the *commedia dell'arte*, went through their comic routines, and then there

114

was a grand last scene. Elaborate machinery and spectacle – transparencies, magnified dioramas, skating scenes, balloon journeys – increasingly became pantomime's *raison d'être*, and the transformation scenes, with gauzes lifting and banks opening to reveal realms of light, pyramids of divine beings and *femmes suspendues*, exercised the ingenuity of designers and mechanics.

Thackeray had an immense relish for these gaudy fantasias, and he welcomed their annual advent elatedly. 'In a few days come the Pantomimes, huzza', he wrote to Fitzgerald in 1831. The enthusiasm lasted well beyond the period of childhood – indeed, never ceased. Pantomimes were even better than ballet from the viewpoint of allowing one to feel superior to one's entertainment, and their comic sections were largely concerned with food, which perhaps pleased Thackeray. Joseph Grimaldi, greatest of the clowns, who invented most of the tricks that became traditional in the Harlequinade, based much of his humour on thefts of oysters or hams, turning dogs into strings of sausages with patent machines, and suchlike. Being able to laugh at this may have given Thackeray a feeling of release from his own inordinate appetites, just as the clowns he once saw at Astleys, doing an act which involved a schoolmaster flogging boys, seem to have exorcized, for the time being, his mania about flagellation. The act delighted him more, he recalls, than any books he had ever read, though he remained quite unable to perceive the reason: 'Why? What is there so ridiculous in the sight of one miserably rouged man beating another on the breech?'

The clown's effectiveness in exploding anxieties that trouble the depths of consciousness extended, also, to death, and this constituted a sizable part of clowning's allure for Thackeray. He disliked tragedy, as we have seen. Pantomime seemed to him a superior form because the dead came back to life. He admired the way in which persons who had been decapitated by butchers, or put into mangles and brought out eighteen feet long, revived at a quiver of Harlequin's stick, and embraced their foes, while the good fairy uttered her 'magic octosyllabic incantations of reconcilement'. Pantomime's unreality was its strength. It cut loose from the confines of thought and fact. Its creators, Thackeray remarked approvingly, were above 'great blundering realities' or the inculcation of moral apothegms.

But pantomime was, for Thackeray, supremely beautiful as well as therapeutic. He could not, he affirmed, conceive of anything 'more brilliant and magnificent' than the fairy scenes at Drury Lane that had entranced him as a boy – with gauze curtains lifting, and dancing-girls who shimmered in an 'unearthly splendour', and panoramic creations by the young William Clarkson Stanfield, later a famous marine painter and Royal Academician. Stanfield was scene-painter at

Drury Lane from 1826 to 1830, so the experiences Thackeray has in mind belonged to his adolescence, between the ages of fifteen and nineteen. The dawn of manhood, and the desperate wish to be pure that puberty brings, were what these bright extravaganzas and their spiritual, 'unearthly' girls answered to. They 'awakened', as Thackeray puts it, 'an innocent fulness of sensual enjoyment that is given only to boys'. It was sex at its most ardent and idealistic. And since, Thackeray argued, 'the enjoyments of boyish fancy are the most intense and delicious in the world', and since pantomime, especially at Drury Lane, provided 'the realisation of the most intense youthful fancy', it followed that pantomime purveyed the highest aesthetic pleasure vouchsafed to humankind.

Of course, pantomime was sham, too, as Thackeray, being Thackeray, never tired of pointing out. The fairies had dingy cotton stockings with crumpled knees; their complexions were carmine and pearl-powder, and their contours, cotton-wool. As youth passed, these aspects of the enchantment became apparent. Besides, even before the child had learned to see through its magic, pantomime was a sort of *memento mori*, for it always had to come to an end, and leave the child in the grip of the cold world again. The inrush of reality intrigued Thackeray. At the end of his novels – of *Vanity Fair*, of *The Newcomes* – he will shut the 'puppets' up in their box, or dismiss the characters to 'Fable-land', as if that poignant recognition of the falsehood on which our pleasure has been based were an indispensable part of the pleasure. *Rebecca and Rowena* turns, finally, into the last scene of a pantomime, with Thackeray describing the crowning moment of the illusion, and its collapse:

I think I perceive behind that dark scene of the back kitchen (which is just a simple flat, painted stone-colour, that shifts in a minute) bright streaks of light flashing out, as though they were preparing a most brilliant, gorgeous, and altogether dazzling illumination, with effects never before attempted on any stage. Yes, the fairy in the pretty pink tights and spangled muslin is getting into the brilliant revolving chariot of the realms of bliss. – Yes, most of the fiddlers and trumpeters have gone round from the orchestra to join in the grand triumphal procession, where the whole strength of the company is already assembled . . . Mammas are putting the girls' cloaks and boas on; papas have gone out to look for the carriage, and left the box-door swinging open, and letting in the cold air: if there *were* any stage-conversation, you could not hear it, for the scuffling of the people who are leaving the pit. See, the orange-women are preparing to retire. Tomorrow their play bills will be as so much waste-paper.

The speaker Thackeray represents here isn't taken in for a moment, of course, by the pantomime's gorgeous finale, and quite enjoys exposing the shifts actors and management are put to. But the bustle of departure he describes suggests, for all that, crude, blighting realities supervening upon something that belonged, in its fragile way, to another world – 'the realms of bliss'.

Thackeray's phrase is aptly religious. From what has been said, it will be seen that, for him, pantomime served to a marked degree as a substitute for Christianity. It proffered a toy Christianity, which suited him even better than the real thing, since it could be derided at will. Most of the comforts and cautions that Christianity traditionally supplies could be matched in pantomime. It entailed becoming as little children; it overcame death; it taught the vanity and transience of earthly pleasures; it engendered pure love, 'an innocent fulness of sensual enjoyment'; it freed man from his guilty obsessions; it nourished his hunger for the supernatural and the miraculous, and it was, of course, produced to celebrate an annual Christian festival. Moreover, it was Christianity with some of paganism's vitality intact, as Thackeray acknowledges in the *English Humourists*, when he recognizes in Harlequin's splendour and agility (as well as in ballet-dancers and Punch-and-Judy shows) 'the Pagan protest', treading down darkness and morality.

Still, pantomime was a toy as well as a transcendence, and when Thackeray introduces it into his novels and essays and reviews, as he repeatedly does, the two elements vie. What almost unfailingly reminded him of pantomime was foreign parts. Abroad the soldiers were small, the clothes peculiar, and the politics ridiculous, all as in pantomime. The continent of Europe, and for that matter Asia as well, or the bits of it Thackeray visited, were essentially immense theatrical promotions, woefully tatty at times, but kept going by the resident foreigners to regale the British tourist. A degree of insular brashness fostered the formation of this viewpoint, undeniably, and sometimes nothing more was involved than that – witness the haughty account in *The Newcomes* of the priestly pomp Clive encounters in Rome:

my lord the cardinal, in his ramshackle coach, and his two, nay three, footmen behind him! flunkeys that look as if they had been dressed by the costumier of a British pantomime; coach with prodigious emblazonments of hats and coats-of-arms, that seems as if it came out of the pantomime too, and was about to turn into something else.

The sham element of pantomime dominates here. Thackeray brings it in to belittle a religion which he despised. But his theatrical comparisons are more often angled to convey, besides a sort of defensive mockery, the bewitching newness of foreign parts, their unreality and liberating frivolity, and their ability to turn the tourist into a spectator, dumb and functionless. The landing at Vigo in *Cornhill to Grand*

Cairo dazzlingly demonstrates these effects. The whole town seems 'like a dream' or 'a little show got up to amuse us'. The houses are 'curiously small, with arcades and balconies, out of which looked women a great deal too big for the chambers they inhabited'. Troops of the Spanish army, parading in the Plaza del Constitución, appear absurdly diminutive, with uniforms of ginghams, cottons and tinsel, and huge epaulets of sham silver lace, 'like those supplied to the warriors at Astley's, or from still humbler theatrical wardrobes'. At the end of the parade the women and soldiers are 'shut up in their box again', and the tourists rejoin their ship. 'The sun had set by this time, and the moon above was twice as big and bright as our degenerate moons are.' As that last phrase confirms, it is by no means simple derision that Thackeray's conversion of Vigo into a stage-set transmits. The theatrical device registers his joy at the brightness and queer size of things, and at their harmlessness. Even the little soldiers have the charm of playthings.

Germany constituted the biggest pantomime of all. The Germany Thackeray knew was not, of course, the Prussian-led military power of the second half of the century, but the loose confederation of states, thirty-nine in all – sovereignties, petty princedoms and grand duchies – that had been left behind by the Congress of Vienna. That the German courts provided havens for pantomime, playful oases in the steely landscape of politics, is a fantasy that Thackeray can be found drifting fondly back to at every stage in his career. In *The Kickleburys on the Rhine*, for instance, he depicts a little German spa and casino town called Noirburg, which is really Homburg, capital of the landgraviate of Hesse-Homburg, and imagines the Margreave as:

a prince in a Christmas pantomime – a burlesque prince with two-pence-halfpenny for revenue, jolly and irascible, a prime-minister kicking prince, fed upon fabulous plum-puddings and enormous pasteboard joints, by cooks and valets with large heads which never alter their grin.

Thackeray had intended *The Kickleburys* as his Christmas book for 1848. Unluckily, German politics proved themselves less jovial than he had fancied. The February revolution of 1848 in Paris sparked off an uprising in Vienna, and in May Metternich fell. The German princes found themselves powerless in the face of the popular clamour. They could not look to Prussia for support, since the kindly Frederick William had turned out to be quite unequal to the situation, and was soon processing round the streets of Berlin wrapped in the German tricolour. Autocracy collapsed all over Germany, and a national parliament assembled in Frankfurt. Animosity between moderates and democrats flared up, civil war raged in the streets of the city. Meanwhile the Austrian empire looked like falling to pieces, and Vienna was in the hands of the revolutionaries. It was evident that something had gone badly wrong with the pantomime, and Thackeray changed his mind about making *The Kickleburys* his Christmas book.

He still nurtured the idea of Germany's pantomime princedoms, but from now on he located them in the past, as in *The Four Georges*, where he pictures the old court at Brunswick at the end of the eighteenth century as a place where 'pantomime courtiers', with big cardboard heads, were poked about by a monarch with a 'pantomime sceptre'. He stuck to this idyll because it represented a part of his youth. After leaving Cambridge in 1830, he had, as we have seen, sailed up the Rhine from Rotterdam sketching as he went, and had lived for six happy months in Weimar, capital of the Grand Duchy of Saxe-Weimar-Eisenach. 'Dear little Weimar', as he cherishingly remembered it, had been, under the Grand Duke Charles Augustus, the intellectual centre of Germany, the home of culture and liberalism, and also of Schiller and Goethe – the latter of whom, appointed to the privy council by his friend the Grand Duke, had supervised the building of the theatre and the royal palace. Thackeray arrived just after Weimar's golden age. Charles Augustus had died in 1828, and his successor Charles Frederick appeared to Thackeray 'as silly a piece of Royalty as a man may meet'. He occupied himself in drilling his miniature army – 'four hundred men and nearly as many officers' – and boxing with his valet who, as Thackeray wrote of him, 'in duty bound, falls under the vigorous "coups" of his königliche Hoheit'. Charles Augustus's liberalism had been superseded, and press censorship was severe. Still, it was a beautiful, simple, courteous place, where art, music and letters flourished.

Thackeray's fiction preserves the farcical and the elysian sides of Weimar by transmuting it into a pantomime realm. Pantomime comic foodstuffs supply its name, Kalbsbraten-Pumpernickel, and the names of its stage-properties, such as its literary journal, the Kartoffeln-kranz. It measures four miles across, but abounds in ludicrous dignitaries, like the celebrated Speck in the *Fitzboodle Papers*, who is Oberhofarchitect and Kunst-und-Bau-Inspektor, responsible for the design of the Grand-Ducal sentry boxes. It sends three and a half men to the army of the German Confederation, and the statuary of the great Pump in its central square shows Peace routing the god of war.

When Thackeray came to write his greatest novel, he used this peaceful, pantomime duchy to crown its structure. It is the Eden to which Amelia and Dobbin are swept off, as love and happiness begin to well up through the vicissitudes of the plot. Warfare, bereavement and realism give way, like gauze curtains being lifted, and we enter a land of toy soldiers and comic food, where the fountains run with beer

119

and 'uncommonly sour wine', and people climb poles for 'prize sausages hung with pink ribbon', and the army consists of 'a magnificent band', which also does duty on the stage of the Pumpernickel theatre, 'in Turkish dresses with rouge on and wooden scimitars'. Politics are no problem: everyone enjoys despotism, and the elective assembly has never been known to sit (in July 1848, when this part of *Vanity Fair* appeared, that would have had, for author and audience alike, a particularly nostalgic ring). True, Thackeray nowhere states, as he did at the end of *Rebecca and Rowena*, that we have shifted into pantomime. But from what we have seen of his developing imagination, it's clear that the light and laughter of the closing scenes derive, at least in part, from that source – as also, of course, from opera, since it is in Pumpernickel that 'a new world of love and beauty' bursts upon Amelia, when she first hears the operas of Mozart and Cimarosa.

How typical of Thackeray, his detractors may feel, to reduce the Athens of Germany, the home of Goethe and Schiller, to a pantomime scenario – a toytown of comic foodstuffs. It's typical, though, only because being like a pantomime was an advantage in his view. We've seen him arguing that pantomime enshrined innocent love, and the highest aesthetic pleasure. Making Weimar into Pumpernickel meant purging its culture of the grandiose elements, that always stuck in Thackeray's throat when he contemplated art, but redoubling its delight. Thus the opera-house where Amelia experiences her maturing ecstasy has the unpretentiousness of pantomime about it – one of those 'snug, unassuming, dear old' German operas, Thackeray relates, where the audience 'sits and cries and knits stockings'.

But if pantomime Germany gave Thackeray the climax of *Vanity Fair*, it was France, it seems, that fitted in best with his urge to see foreign parts as stage-shows, and we must return to France, where so much of his theatrical infatuation began, to complete our picture. On the one hand, Thackeray's contempt for the French nation was so extreme as to be almost self-parodying. 'I can hardly bring to mind that anything is serious in France', he remarks in *The Paris Sketch-Book*, 'it seems to be all rant, tinsel, and stage-play.' The French were incorrigibly given to fanfaronade and braggadocio; sham liberty, sham glory and knocking down omnibuses were the measure of their politics; they were sentimental, hypocritical, vain and four-feet high; and they hated the English. On the other hand, they were exciting, even at their most tawdry. Indeed, their tawdriness was a positive incentive to Thackeray's imagination. He loved writing about it. It stimulated some of his finest irony, and it allowed him to revel in the poetry of sham, exposing the paint and pasteboard beneath the grandeur, the dingy details in the masquerade. With the French, at their fêtes and carnivals, theatre tipped out onto the streets, garishly blending the real and the fantastic, like those backstage goings-on that so powerfully attracted him. In *Shrove Tuesday in Paris*, where he recounts his meeting with the ex-governess Mlle Pauline, one of the models for Becky, the carnival-time scene is tumultuously theatrical, with revellers dressed as 'Spanish grandees, Turkish agas, Roman senators', troops of actors from Franconi's in their stage-costumes, and 'triumphal cars, adorned with tinsel and filled with musicians'. Mlle Pauline herself seems to be wearing remnants from a theatre wardrobe – 'dressed like a man, in a blouse and a pair of very dirty-white trousers . . . an oilskin hat with a huge quantity of various-coloured ribbons, and under it an enormous wig with three tails'. As usual when Thackeray gets onto such subjects, the writing has a frustrating doubleness. The artist and Bohemian in him, plainly aroused, keep struggling with a prissy conformist and Francophobe. Thus when he calls on Mlle Pauline a few days later (merely, he reassures his readers, to get some shirts mended), he finds her 'eating soup in a foul porter's lodge, from which she conducted me up a damp, mouldy staircase to her own apartment, on the seventh floor'. The insanitary adjectives are dropped into the account so as to publicize Thackeray's fastidious aloofness to the whole nasty affair even as he mounts the staircase, but they do not prevent us from seeing that what happened at the top, could Thackeray only be constrained upon to portray it, would be much more intriguing than the flabby reflections on the differences between French and English morals, which we have to make do with in the event. As with his backstage glimpses, the door shuts too quickly for us to catch more than a fleeting impression of the dinginess and beauty beyond.

His divided impulses clash even more in another description of the carnival's wild theatricality (it was a subject he repeatedly came back to) – this time from *The Paris Sketch-Book*. The occasion was a rather special one, for it had been given out that a condemned man, Fieschi, was to be guillotined that morning, and Thackeray was eager to view the execution:

A friend, who accompanied me, came many miles, through the mud and dark, in order to be in at the death. We set out before light, floundering in the muddy Champs Elysées; where, besides, were many other persons floundering, and all bent upon the same errand. We passed by the Concert of Musard, then held in the Rue St. Honoré; and round this, in the wet, a number of coaches were collected. The ball was just up, and a crowd of people, in hideous masquerade, drunk, tired, dirty, dressed in horrible old frippery, and daubed with filthy rouge, were trooping out of the place: tipsy women and men, shrieking, jabbering, gesticulating, as the French will do; parties swaggering, staggering forwards, arm in arm, reeling to and fro across the street, and yelling songs in chorus: hundreds of these were bound for the show and we thought ourselves lucky in finding a vehicle to the execution place, at the Barrière d'Enfer. As we crossed the river, and entered the Enfer street, crowds of students, black workmen, and more drunken devils from more carnival balls, were filling it; and on the grand place there were thousands of these assembled looking out for Fieschi and his cortège. We waited and waited; but alas! no fun for us that morning: no throat-cutting; no august spectacle of satisfied justice; and the eager spectators were obliged to return, disappointed of their expected breakfast of blood. It would have been a fine scene, that execution, could it but have taken place in the midst of the mad mountebanks and tipsy strumpets who had flocked so far to witness it, wishing to wind up the delights of their carnival by a *bonne-bouche* of murder.

The opposed parts of Thackeray's personality come apart so resoundingly here that he seems to speak in two different voices. 'Alas! no fun for us that morning' and 'It would have been a fine scene, that execution' are perfectly appropriate remarks for someone who has floundered a considerable distance through mud and darkness to secure a good view of the decapitation. Set against these are the indignant sarcasms about an 'august spectacle of satisfied justice', and the disdainful comments on the mob's conduct, colour and appetite for blood, which make us feel that we are in the company of an altogether more principled observer. Thackeray does not wish to mix with the cast, so to speak, but his keenness to see a man have his head cut off in the midst of a rouged, costumed multitude – 'a fine scene' – is undisguised, and it reveals him as an admirer of the Theatre of Cruelty, some hundred years before Artaud invented it. It is not an unexpected development, for, as we have seen, the forms of theatre that confounded reason, such as ballet and pantomime, had always enthralled him, and he had acknowledged that the thrill of watching a dancer like Fanny Elssler was rather like the thrill of a public execution. In the Theatre of Cruelty lust, madness and perversion escape entirely from the constraints of rational conduct, as in the decorous surroundings of the ballet or pantomime they are never quite able to do. The mind experiences a release. 'There is something singularly pleasing, both in the amusement of execution-seeing, and in the results', as Thackeray puts it. 'The mind, which has been wound up painfully until now, becomes quite complacent and easy.' Of course, seated beside Thackeray the advanced play-goer, there is always the other Thackeray, feeling thoroughly disgusted, and earnestly exhorting his twin to remember that he's British. This straitlaced Thackeray can be a bore, and in the execution-carnival we feel we should enjoy ourselves better without him. But elsewhere it was his presence that allowed Thackeray's characteristic irony to evolve. For the ironist needs to be able to stand witheringly apart from his subject, as well as to feel its seductive undertow.

Thackeray's most sustained ironic treatment of the French gift for bringing theatre onto the streets is *The Second Funeral of Napoleon*, which he wrote in December 1840, and was still talking about as his best book three years later. He wasn't far wrong, because although the early pages are marred by self-preening banter of a sort he was always prone to, it develops into an extraordinarily acute and vivid satire, laughable, but with the decaying corpse of Napoleon grotesquely enthroned at its centre ('The nostril and the tube of the nose appear to have undergone some slight alteration . . .'). His genius for crowd scenes, drawing a city's pageantry and concourse into a few pages, with no sense of shrinkage, and his ability to keep his writing fresh by the naturalness with which he lets his attention fritter itself away on odd incidents, were never more finely evidenced.

The occasion was the transportation of Napoleon's remains from St. Helena to Les Invalides, amid scenes of national glorying. For much of the time Thackeray simply quotes from French newspapers and official sources, culling the most bloated paragraphs, so that the farcical, bespangled death-masque is tottering under its own weight even before he lets his prose loose upon it. What he fixes on with most relish and derision in his own account is the scenery – the gilt paper eagles, the striped calico flags, the plaster-of-Paris urns, the Archbishop's mitre of 'consecrated pasteboard' and spangled tassels, and the two hundred goddesses along the Champs Elysées, painted to look like marble and standing on wood and canvas bases that wag in the wind. His absorption in theatrical sham turns here into a hilarious elegy on human grandeur, epitomized by the bust of Lafayette that has to be moved out of the procession's way:

In the middle of the Invalides Avenue, there used to stand, on a kind of shabby fountain or pump, a bust of Lafayette, crowned with some dirty wreaths of 'immortals', and looking down at the little streamlet which occasionally dribbled below him. The spot of ground was now clear, and Lafayette and the pump had been consigned to some cellar, to make way for the mighty procession that was to pass over the place of their habitation.

This miserable casualty, and the throng of people solemnly bearing a rotting cadaver along an avenue of wooden statues, provide a comment on human futility which, if Thackeray's account stopped there, would prefigure the Theatre of the Absurd almost as clearly as his execution-carnival anticipates the Theatre of Cruelty. But in fact the *Second Funeral* passes on to the waiting crowd inside Les Invalides, chattering and laughing, and a more familiar kind of theatre develops. Fat National Guardsmen lay down their muskets, hop about to keep warm, and produce ham and other eatables from their cartridge cases. A woman in a pink bonnet keeps sitting in the reserved seats, and being turned out by ushers, to the delight of the congregation; and to describe her effect Thackeray brings the subject round to pantomime, which the comic soldiers and their food had already set one thinking of:

Did you ever see a chicken escape from a clown in a pantomime, and hop over into the pit, or amongst the fiddlers? and have you not heard the shrieks of enthusiastic laughter that the wondrous incident occasions? We had our chicken.

So we are back in the welcoming absurdity from which Pumpernickel was created. Thackeray's impulse to fit foreigners into a theatrical mould, or rather to see them as busily fitting themselves into it, has once more prevailed.

Theatre provided Thackeray, then, with an alternative world, which suited his restless purposes admirably, because it could so quickly be turned inside out. The bright side enchanted him, and transcended his reason and scepticism. But the shabby side, the patent sham, remained available for reason and scepticism to play upon. He was not a man who could remain happy long unless he was criticizing something, so his ideal pleasures had both to disarm and invite criticism. Backstage-life lured his imagination, since he felt that there the reality behind the sham might be discovered, but also because it remained a mystery to him, dropping down into social levels that he could not plumb, and offering a way out of narrow Victorian mores which part of him, but only a part, longed to follow. This escape from English middle-class norms was also offered by foreign cultures, which is why Thackeray habitually translates them into theatre. Yet that act of translation itself implies a sense of their unreality and impermanence. It's evident, we might add, that what initially attracted him to the eighteenth century was its theatrical look. He imagines it, in *The Four Georges*, as a period when London society swarmed with 'singing-women and dancing-women' from the continental operas, and 'all fashionable female Europe' had its face 'plastered with white and raddled with red' ('like Scaramouch's in the pantomime', as Lambert, in *The Virginians*, observes). One of his earliest reviews had likened the early eighteenth century to a stage-set, on which the 'glittering pageant' was rendered bewitching only by 'gas and distance'; the knights, seen more closely, turned out to be 'dirty dwarves in tin foil', and the ladies 'painted hags with cracked feathers and soiled trains'. Viewed like this, the theatre of the past would have been a promising field for his destructive genius (and is so in *Barry Lyndon*). But one of the disappointments of *Henry Esmond* and *The Virginians* is that the dirty dwarves and hags fail to appear. The overlay of gentility, stateliness and social decorum attracts Thackeray too much, by this time, for him to wish to tear it away.

]6[

Time

Time plagued Thackeray. He kept at the subject like a moth at a lamp. It produced much of his saddest, but also much of his most scathing writing. For, as a satirist, he tended to ally himself protectively with time, and deride the brief stay of love and beauty. He saw time as a destroyer. As ripener, or renewer, he scarcely gave it a glance. Nor did time's vaster havoc concern him, as it did, for example, Tennyson. The gradual shift of continents, the cooling of the sun, mankind's eventual extinction – these matters, if they occurred to Thackeray at all, would have seemed well outside the range of his individual worries. He worked at a starker level, dwelling on remembrance of things past. His master theme, the vanity of worldly pleasures, did not represent for him a religious proposition. Worldly pleasure was not wicked, it simply vanished.

His own life had confirmed this. As a child, he lost his father, was separated from his mother, and pitched out of princely India into a squalid English school. As a rich young man, enjoying his fortune, he was suddenly deprived of it. His wife was taken from him in a peculiarly horrible way, because, though still present physically, she had become another person, unable to recognize husband or children, and caring for nothing, as Thackeray wrote to Jane Brookfield, 'but her dinner and her glass of porter'. He feared for the sanity of his younger daughter as well. The temporariness of human personality haunted him. It reflects in the portrait of Lord George Gaunt in *Vanity Fair*, 'the brilliant dandy diplomatist of the Congress of Vienna', whom his mother finds, on her visits to the asylum, 'dragging about a child's toy, or nursing the keeper's baby doll'. Quite early in life, Thackeray began to think of himself as old. The years had taken away more than they would bring again. Even in 1835, still in his mid-twenties, he described himself to Isabella as a 'sulky grey-headed old fellow'. He had never bothered to keep his body fit or active: it soon repaid him with pain and inconvenience.

His feelings of transience gathered round a set of seemingly un-related topics, to which he kept returning. One was food, or more specifically the remains of a meal after the guests had left. This was a common emblem for mortality among Dutch still-life painters of the seventeenth century. They used pieces of broken bread, or an over-turned wineglass, to catch the ephemeral nature of human things. Perhaps Thackeray got the idea from them. But it seems, too, to have been rooted in his own experience. An undergraduate letter talks about his attendance at college wine-parties; and *The Book of Snobs*, twenty years later, describes these occasions and the hangovers that followed them. 'A parcel of lads' would:

sit down to pineapples and ices at each other's rooms, and fuddle them-selves with champagne and claret . . . Milk punch – smoking – ghastly headache – frightful spectacle of dessert-table next morning.

Precisely the same 'frightful spectacle', complete with pineapple and ice, makes its haggard presence felt in *Pendennis*, when Harry Foker, giving a dinner at Richmond for some ballet girls and equestriennes from the French hippodrome, feels suddenly sickened by the painted, cigar-puffing females around him, and sits 'lost in thought' at the head of the table:

amidst melting ices and cut pineapples, and bottles full and empty, and cigar-ashes scattered on fruit, and the ruins of a dessert which had no pleasure for him.

Why pineapple and melted ice should have stuck in Thackeray's mind, it's impossible to say. But the ashy fruit and collapsing dainties provide a vivid focus for young Foker's mood, an embodiment of jaded revel, and fleetingly recall the end of one of Flaubert's most brilliant tableaux – the fancy dress ball in *Sentimental Education* – when the morning light streams in on Frédéric Moreau and the raddled theatre girls, and 'the sticky patches of punch and syrup' staining the tables.

Similar soiled provender is sighted in *The Newcomes*, the morning after the party at which Clive throws his wine in Barnes's face:

the tables were still covered with the relics of yesterday's feast – the emptied bottles, the blank lamps, the scattered ashes and fruits, the wretched heel-taps that have been lying exposed all night to the air.

The ensuing scene is a failure (a poor attempt to re-do Rawdon Crawley's arrival at Sir Pitt's after the Steyne débâcle). The human characters enter, uttering the noble sentiments customary in *The Newcomes*, and the fictional level plummets. But in the leftover food and drink Thackeray's imagination, and his time-sense, find, for the moment, something they can make bleak and telling.

In a letter of 1856, to Mrs. Procter, consoling her for the death of her mother, the spoiled feast becomes openly an emblem for life's ultimate let-down. Thackeray touches first on the agony of losing a child (one of the accustomed agonies that shaped the Victorian character):

Little children step off this earth into the Infinite and we tear our hearts out over their sweet cold hands and smiling faces that drop indifferent when you cease holding them and smile as the lid is closing over them.

Compared to this, the death of the aged is scarcely to be deplored at all:

Where's the pleasure of staying when the feast is over and the flowers withered and the guests gone. Isn't it better to blow the light out than to sit on among the broken meats, and collapsed jellies, and vapid heeltaps?

In any other writer, death and collapsed jellies might seem un-dignified partners, and the association of Mrs. Procter's deceased mother with a hearty meal, somehow indelicate. Yet it is so true to Thackeray's imaginative habits that the conjunction is managed with entire tact and profundity; and the jellies acquire a special aptness in the neighbourhood of the wanly smiling children, whose deaths Thackeray imaged at the start.

The deathly mixture of food and ashes, which cigars and dessert-fruit intrude into Foker's or Clive Newcome's high-life scenes, stays in Thackeray's mind when he seems to be talking about quite other things. In the *English Humourists* he explains how unfunny he has found Congreve's comedies:

my feelings were rather like those, which I daresay most of us here have had, at Pompeii, looking at Sallust's house and the relics of an orgy: a dried wine-jar or two, a charred supper-table, the breast of a dancing-girl pressed against the ashes.

Despite the historical jump, the 'frightful spectacle' of Thackeray's undergraduate dessert-table can again be detected here, as can his interest in ballet-dancers. His imaginative involvement at once makes the writing more subtle. Death apes life. Fire has 'dried' the wine-jars, as throats did, and the girl's breast presses, as if lovingly, ashes. The result, though brief, is a great deal more worth having than anything Thackeray had to say about Congreve or the English humourists.

But the ruined dessert is only a sideline, if a fruitful one. Thackeray has bigger materials for figuring time's wrack. Among these, altera-tions undergone by places and buildings were a constant spur to his creative powers. This was natural, for the two cities he knew best, Paris and London, changed drastically during his lifetime. He saw old haunts swept away, and strange façades rise in their place. The trans-formation of Paris had been started under Napoleon I, and landmarks like the Arc de Triomphe, the Carrousel arch, and the Madeleine were of his planning, but the Second Empire vastly accelerated the process, 'pulling down and building up as eagerly as New York', as Thackeray remarked. The sumptuous new buildings and wide thoroughfares impressed him, especially the Rue de Rivoli, and he would certainly have approved of their ulterior purpose, which was to make the construction of barricades more difficult. But the Paris of his boyhood had vanished. In the windy spaces of the new Place de la Concorde, with its heaps of statuary and its obelisk, imported from Luxor in 1836, he felt lost and bitter. As for London, it oppressed him with a sense of meaningless reduplication. It was to the west and south that the great wen was bulging in the early decades of the century. The building of three new bridges at Vauxhall, Waterloo and Southwark between 1816 and 1819 eased the southward growth. Lines of terraced housing filled up Lambeth and Camberwell, both of which doubled their populations in the 1820s. Estates of 'semis' sprouted in Brixton and Peckham, while, further south still, the wealthier classes were erecting their detached villas at Denmark Hill, Tulse Hill and Brixton Hill. To the west of the City, in Tyburnia, a new fashionable residential area came into being around Portman Square, as S. P. Cockerell's plans for spacious crescents and terraces attracted the professional and the better-off commercial classes. Thackeray, writing in 1848, expressed wonder at the speed with which stucco and sameness were invading this region:

where, as you wandered yesterday, you saw a green strip of meadow, with a washerwoman's cottage and a teagarden; and today you look up, and lo! you see a portly row of whitey-brown bow-windowed houses, with plate-glass windows, through the clear panes of which you may see bald-headed comfortable old fogies reading the *Morning Post*.

Titmarsh, in *Our Street*, inhabits a district which is in the process of being taken over by the developers. When he moved in his lodgings were in the country, but he now finds that they have been absorbed into Sir Thomas Gibbs Pocklington's 'new white-stuccoed Doric-porticoed genteel Pocklington quarter'. The Ram and Magpie inn, where the market gardeners used to eat, has become the Pocklington Arms, but meanwhile obstinate tenants refuse to sell up, so that a tripe shop and an iron-bedstead warehouse and a barber's with a pole linger on amid the novel splendours. The way the southward march of suburbia swallowed up the old country mansions, burying the lawns and orchards under brick and mortar, also aroused Thackeray's disdain. Sophia Hobson's Clapham mansion in *The Newcomes*, with gardens and hothouses where grapes, peaches and pineapples flourished, disappears beneath Sophia Terrace, Hobson's Buildings, and other populous localities. To the north-west of London, too, the depredation of the outlying villages was in full swing. *Philip*, written in the 1860s, about events some thirty-five years before, records that streets and terraces now cover the site of Mugford's country retreat at Hampstead, with its paddock and Guernsey cow and home-baked bread. The developers' habit of calling the new streets, that had obliterated gardens, Gardens, did not escape Thackeray's ironic attention. 'Gardens', he observes in *Vanity Fair*, 'was a felicitous word not applied to stucco houses with asphalte terraces in front, so early as 1827.'

It would be wrong, of course, to cast him as a precocious conservationist or frustrated town-planner. The keen regret at the destruction of London's countryside, voiced by other Victorians, like Ruskin, he did not echo. He viewed the rash of horrible suburbs with almost pleased resignation. They confirmed his sense of time's vagaries. His historical perspective stretched back to the time when, as he said in *Catherine*, Albion Street was a desert, and 'fragrant walls of snowy hawthorn blossoms' edged the Edgware Road. His London differed from Dickens's because it had more ghosts in it. Whereas Dickens habitually fixes on the engaging variety of human life, and the sanitary conditions, Thackeray attends to the shades from the past that flit along the pavements and up the stairs. Once-fashionable districts, fallen into decrepitude, offer a favourite playground for these historical fancies. He likes reminding his readers that Soho was sought after by 'the lords and ladies of William's time', until Bloomsbury put it out of fashion, and that in Queen Anne's reign Great Russell Street became 'the pink of the mode':

Fashion has deserted Soho, and left her in her gaunt, lonely old age. The houses have a vast, dingy, mouldy, dowager look. No more beaux, in mighty periwigs, ride by in gilded clattering coaches; no more lackeys accompany them, bearing torches and shouting for precedence.

The gilt, torches, coaches and lackeys are standard components of this Thackerayan mood, re-emerging again and again in his perambulations of the London streets. The figures run, ride, and carry torches, like figures in a dream. They are never stilled or recognized. They simply run, ride and carry torches, and so embody the endless hurry of time, the generations treading one another down:

Why shall not one moralize over London, as over Rome, or Baalbec, or Troy town? I like to walk among the Hebrews of Wardour Street, and fancy the place, as it once was, crowded with chairs and gilt chariots, and torches flashing in the hands of the running footmen.

Though the details are standardized, the eighteenth century came to him more vividly in these backward flashes than when he tried to urge its characters onto the stage in full-dress fictions. With a few swift phrases he could make the lights flicker across its surface, the coaches rattle and the footmen run, but when he tried to plump it out with incident and dialogue, it drooped. The feeling of rapid transience, vital to his genius, got encumbered and mislaid in the routines of costume drama. Hence his success in essays, sketches, and odd paragraphs that swerve away from the business of his novels and dart into the past.

Time-stricken streets and buildings repeatedly provide an excuse for this in the novels. Thus in *Philip*, soon after the Wardour Street meditation quoted above, the two young men retire to smoke their cigars to an outbuilding:

In that building there were stables once, doubtless occupied by great Flemish horses and rumbling gold coaches of Walpole's time; but a celebrated surgeon, when he took possession of the house, made a lecture-room of the premises, – 'And this door', says Phil, pointing to one leading into the mews, 'was very convenient for having *the bodies* in and out' – a cheerful reminiscence. Of this kind of furniture there was now very little in the apartment, except a dilapidated skeleton in a corner, a few dusty casts of heads, and bottles of preparations on the top of an old bureau, and some mildewed harness hanging on the walls.

Here we can detect Thackeray diverting the course of his fiction expressly to smuggle into the narrative some favourite accompaniments to his reverie on time. That a previous tenant of Dr. Firmin's house should have converted the stables into an anatomy lecture-room, and should have happened to leave a skeleton behind when he moved out, and that, while using the lecture-room, he should have allowed some bits of early eighteenth-century harness, overlooked by their previous owners, to remain mildewing on the walls, constitutes a set of circumstances not overburdened with likelihood. But skeletons and mildew are extremely important to Thackeray, as are horses to pull the coaches which, as we have seen, constantly dash through his vision of the early eighteenth century. So likelihood has to be relaxed to accommodate these trappings. Once we get inside Dr. Firmin's house, skeletons or fragments of skeletons lurk behind every decoration:

Over the sideboard was the doctor, in a black velvet coat and a fur collar, his hand on a skull, like Hamlet. Skulls of oxen, horned, with wreaths, formed the cheerful ornaments of the cornice. On the side-table glittered a pair of cups, given by grateful patients, looking like receptacles rather for funereal ashes than for festive flowers or wine. Brice, the butler, wore the gravity and costume of an undertaker.

This house, in Old Parr Street, is in fact the last in a line of gaunt, mouldering houses, extending back through Thackeray's fiction to his very earliest days, and accounting for some of his richest imaginative compositions – poetic honeycombs of frayed furniture and super-annuated interior fitments, which close around his characters like molluscs, and allow him to delve into the past down their chill corridors and creaking stairs. He varies and elaborates their senile splendours tirelessly, but obsessive elements recur. Thus the Old Parr Street ox skulls and funeral urns turn up, slightly adapted, in the decor of the house which Colonel Newcome takes at 120 Fitzroy Square:

The house is vast but, it must be owned, melancholy. Not long since it was a ladies' school, in an unprosperous condition. The scar left by Madame Latour's brass plate may still be seen on the tall black door, cheerfully ornamented, in the style of the end of the last century, with a funeral urn in the centre of the entry, and garlands, and the skulls of rams at each corner. . . . The stables were gloomy. Great black passages; cracked conservatory; dilapidated bath-room, with melancholy waters moaning and fizzing from the cistern.

The moaning cistern and scarred front door give the house human sensibilities that inevitably recall Dickens. Thackeray's usual dislike of animated inanimates yields to a more fluid view of the sensed world. He is never more Dickensian than in these architectural fantasies. Madame Latour's face and house coalesce, so that when the house gets a coat of paint it is likened to her rouge, which 'only served to make her care-worn face look more ghastly'.

A still earlier house and woman organically linked, and falling to pieces in tandem, form the imaginative kernel of *Mr. and Mrs. Frank Berry* in *Men's Wives*. The story is planned as a simple essay on the ruins of time. The first part describes the great fight at Slaughter House School between Berry and Biggs, and teems with blood and animal spirits. Years afterwards the narrator, Fitzboodle, meets Berry again in Versailles, and is taken back to the Berry house for dinner, through a garden with a fountain and grotto, and up a mouldy stair:

It was one of the old pavilions that had been built for a pleasure-house in the gay days of Versailles, ornamented with abundance of damp Cupids and cracked gilt cornices, and old mirrors let into the walls, and gilded once, but now painted a dingy French white. The long low windows looked into the court where the fountain played its ceaseless dribble, surrounded by numerous rank creepers and weedy flowers, but in the midst of which the statues stood with their bases quite moist and green.
I hate fountains and statues in dark, confined places: that cheerless, endless plashing of water is the most inhospitable sound ever heard. The stiff grin of those French statues, or ogling Canova Graces, is by no means more happy, I think, than the smile of a skeleton, and not so natural.

The ornate cheerlessness bunches this together with the Old Parr Street and Fitzroy Square houses ('cheerless' and 'ornamented' pick up 'cheerful ornaments' and 'cheerfully ornamented' in those establishments). So do the sense of vanished inhabitants and the bits of skeleton – in this case the skeletal smiles of the statues (Old Parr Street had statues too, with 'broken noses', and dark green moss). But the writing, because this is early Thackeray, is richer and more intense. Age has bleached the gilded mirrors, and sapped the energy of the dribbling fountain. The statues seem locked in – 'confined' – and locked into their grins, performing a wretched mockery of enjoyment, and the moist green deposit forming on them forebodes decomposition. When we meet Mrs. Berry, we understand the meaning of the deathly courtyard. She is 'exceedingly white and lean', her hair is 'rather scarce', and she has 'a small mouth with no lips – a sort of feeble pucker in the face as it were'. She maintains a 'rigid and classical look', like the statues, and wears round her neck a 'miniature of her late father, Sir George Catacomb, apothecary to George III'. The ripe, red Berry, the schoolboy fighter, has been caught by a Catacomb – a lipless, balding approximation to a skeleton. The rest of the tale merely illustrates, through domestic squabbles, the relentless grip this deadly thing has on him.

The conglomeration of statues, skeletons, slime, dribbling water, a dilapidated pleasure-house and blighted lovers seems to relate to a permanent set of associations in Thackeray's mind. It appears again, in an oddly roundabout way, in Chapter XLVII of *The Newcomes*. There Thackeray compares the novelist to the palaeontologist, reconstructing, from a fragment of bone, a prehistoric monster, 'wallowing in primaeval quagmires'. As the scientist 'traces this slimy reptile through the mud', so the novelist probes human personality. From this we pass immediately to the old garden of the Hôtel de Florac, where Clive and Ethel walk along an avenue of lime-trees, and Clive is discovering the hopelessness of his love. The place is full of statues – a moss-eaten Triton 'curling his tail' in a fountain basin, a 'damp Faun', Venus and Cupid 'under the damp little dome of a cracked old temple', and Caracalla, 'frowning over his mouldy shoulder' at Nerva, on whose head the château roofs have for years been 'dribbling'. Here the de Florac ancestors 'disported in hoops and powder': it was a pleasure-house, like the Berrys' Versailles pavilion. Two blighted couples now wander in it – Clive with Ethel, and Madame de Florac with her husband in his wheelchair.

The same compulsion has, once more, grouped statues, skeleton and dribbling water – as if no other set of objects will do to voice Thackeray's fears about the disappointments time and women inflict. And the moist, green bases of the Berry statues, along with the moss-eaten

Triton's curling tail at the de Floracs, connect up with another of Thackeray's odd associations – that of the passage of time with mouldy fish. We find this, for instance, in *The Virginians*, where 'two old monsters of carp' have been in a pond at Castlewood for centuries, according to tradition, and have their backs 'all covered with a hideous grey mould', to prove it; and the carp at Sans Souci, which Frederick the Great used to feed, and which are there still, 'with great humps of blue mould on their old backs', provide Thackeray with an essay on mutability in the *Roundabout Papers*. He likens the Sans Souci carp to the toothless, palsied crones in the St. Lazarus workhouse – 'that dismal harem'. So, by way of fish, we come round again to the decaying woman of Frank Berry's tale. Fish, women and a Triton's curling tail also recall, of course, Thackeray's trauma about fish-tailed women: we see two regions of his imagination merging.

Before we leave Thackeray's crumbling houses, a couple of others deserve a glance both from the early work, and among his most brilliant creations: Sir George and Lady Thrum's in *The Ravenswing*, and Castle Carabas in *Snobs*. The Thrums live in 'an old, tall, dingy house, furnished in the reign of George III' with 'funereal' horse-hair chairs, mouldy carpets and 'little, cracked sticking-plaster miniatures of people in *tours*'. The *tours* (knobs of false hair) link the Thrum pictures with Mrs. Berry, who wore a *tour* to hide her baldness; and the 'dismal urns' on the Thrums' sideboard are kin to Dr. Firmin's. But the Thrum house has its own prolific collection of miseries, from the 'queer twisted receptacle for worn-out knives with green handles' to the 'grey gloom' that hangs over the stair carpet, reflecting its inhabitants' physical decline. The upper rooms are the most unwholesome:

There is something awful in the bedroom of a respectable old couple of sixty-five. Think of the old feathers, turbans, bugles, petticoats, pomatum-pots, spencers, white satin shoes, false fronts, the old, flaccid, boneless stays tied up in faded riband, the dusky fans, the old forty-years-old baby-linen . . . All these lie somewhere, damp and squeezed down into glum old presses and wardrobes. At that glass the wife has sat many times these fifty years; in that old morocco bed her children were born. Where are they now?

The jumbled detritus of clothes and commodities, which are what remains of the Thrum marriage, sound disconcertingly organic, as if they might be soiling to the touch. The 'flaccid, boneless stays' suggest unhealthy flesh, softened by time, like the body they have been occupied in propping up. This effect is heightened by the moisture and squashiness which, Thackeray assures us, pervades the whole heap of rubbish – it is all 'damp and squeezed down'. The mention of the bed, and of the births that have taken place in it, naturally edges our thoughts (if, having reached the bedroom, they were not already travelling in that direction) towards the Thrums' physical relations, and in that context the clammy old underwear lying around has an inescapably tainting influence. The passage is a triumph of obliqueness, for though Thackeray tells us nothing about the state of the Thrums' bodies, we are in no doubt by the end that they would be highly unenjoyable to see or handle. We agree that there is 'something awful' in the Thrum bedroom, and have a lively sense of what it is, yet strictly Thackeray has done no more than list items of clothing.

Like Thackeray's other mouldy mansions, the Thrums' is not exactly melancholy to read about. While he busies himself with multiplying the evidences of rot and ruin, we can see that he relishes what he's at. He rummages through the Thrums' things with a disgusted smile, and we share his exuberance at each new nastiness he comes across. As the piles of brick and mortar he constructs grow more elaborate, so the horror and hilarity in his response mingle more wildly. Castle Carabas in *Snobs* is the most bizarre of his time-houses, as well as the deathliest and dampest. The wetness, inseparable in Thackeray's thinking from the lapse of time, here gathers to a head:

A damp green stretch of park spread right and left immeasurably, confined by a chilly grey wall, and a damp long straight road between two huge rows of moist, dismal lime-trees, leads up to the Castle. In the midst of the park is a great black tank or lake, bristling over with rushes, and here and there covered with patches of pea-soup. A shabby temple rises on an island in this delectable lake, which is approached by a rotten barge that lies at roost in a dilapidated boathouse.

Several features are familiar: the lime-tree avenue and shabby temple from the de Florac garden; the slime and ornamental water from the Berrys'. Reading on, we come to the usual memories of gilded coaches and eighteenth-century revellers wearing hoops, and the classical statuary, which we have learnt to expect, appears as soon as the officiating housekeeper starts her guided tour:

The great'all is seventy-two feet in lenth, fifty-six in breath, and thirty-eight feet 'igh. The carvings of the chimlies, representing the buth of Venus, and Ercules, and Eyelash, is by Van Chislum, the most famous sculpture of his hage and country.

And so on. The housekeeper, sweeping house, pictures and statues into her torrent of gibberish, is a symptom of the meaningless grandeur of the place. Its vast galleries and echoing halls are a spatial equivalent of the fearful vistas of time which shrivel human significance. They spell madness and death:

I should go mad were I that lonely housekeeper – in those enormous galleries – in that lonely library, filled up with ghastly folios that nobody dares read, with an inkstand on the centre table like the coffin of a baby, and sad portraits staring at you from the bleak walls with their solemn, mouldy eyes.

And yet, as the exceptionally Dickensian baby's-coffin-cum-inkstand reminds us, it is still comic horror, at most, that all these eerie piles and moaning water cisterns and clammy corsets and weird statues and skeletons have been generating. We have been in Dickens-land all along, or an outpost of it colonized by Thackeray, and in Dickens-land even the teeth of time have their droll side.

But when Thackeray turns to depicting the effects of time on people, rather than buildings and furniture, the jollity stops. He shows, more starkly than Dickens, how people sour – women especially. Dickens's young women do not age. His marriages mostly occur at the ends of novels, so that the happy couple can be fancied wandering off into a golden haze, attended by a growing contingent of little ones. Thackeray, on the other hand, writes best about wrecked marriages, and when he essays something cosier (as in the amorous sallies of Laura Pendennis and her husband) the reader is justifiably dismayed. Among his deepest apprehensions about life was that it soiled people – and soiled them first, of course, as children. 'What shall I say to you about our little darling who is gone?' he wrote to his mother, when his daughter Jane died. 'I don't feel sorrow for her, and think of her only as something charming that for a season we were allowed to enjoy . . . and now I would be almost sorry – no, that is not true – but I would not ask to have the dear little Jane back again and subject her to the degradation of life and pain.' Children began to deteriorate very quickly, in his view. He responded to their almost unearthly beauty: one of the most touching moments in *Vanity Fair* is when poor Miss Osborne, steeped in spinsterhood, breaks radiantly to her father the news of her meeting with little George – 'He is as beautiful as an angel'. But Thackeray did not allow the beauty of children to deflect his eye from their greed and callousness. George illustrates these acquirements well. Far from sharing Amelia's agony when she tells him that they must part, he is elated, and goes off to brag to his school-fellows about the carriage and pony he will have when he lives with his grandfather. As we watch the little chap lording it over the Osborne establishment, inviting the ladies to take wine with him, and delighting the servants by his gentlemanlike ways ('How he *du* dam and swear'), we realize that he is becoming a midget version of his father, with his father's talent for attracting undeserved love and esteem.

Children seldom return affection in Thackeray. When John Pen-dennis dies, the last name he tries to articulate is that of his son, Arthur, who has been his pride and glory throughout life. But what

Arthur feels is 'a sort of secret triumph and exultation', for he realizes
that he will not have to go to school any more. The eyes of a Thackerayan child will always dry at the sight of gingerbread or plum cake,
let alone permanent school holidays, however sharp its grief. It is one
of the paradoxes of human relations in his novels that children should
be loved so dearly, yet be largely incapable of love themselves. The
anguish their deaths arouse is in this sense undeserved: 'The death of
an infant which scarce knew you, which a week's absence from you
would have caused to forget you, will strike you down more than the
loss of your closest friend.'

Nor does time improve matters much, from this angle, if the child
is spared. Its capacities for love, as they grow, will draw it away from
those who have lavished devotion on it from the cradle. Thackeray
records this process achingly. Even Colonel Newcome, tiresome old
worthy as he is, and cruelly handicapped by the weight of authorial
approval he has to carry, recovers some credibility when Thackeray
casts him in the role of disappointed parent. The Colonel finds the
views of art bandied about by Clive and his friends utterly bewildering.
He goes secretly to the National Gallery, and stands for hours,
catalogue in hand, before the exhibits that Clive likes, 'desperately
praying to comprehend them'. Just for a moment, in his puzzled
resentment, he seems a human being:

As he thought what vain egotistical hopes he used to form about the
boy when he was away in India – how in his plans for the happy future
Clive was to be always at his side; how they were to read, work, play,
think, be merry together – a sickening and humiliating sense of the
reality came over him.

Yet the Colonel's vanity and egotism were only what we call love.

It follows that children are thoroughly unsafe (though also irresistible) receptacles for one's hopes and affections, and this makes Dobbin's
plight at the end of *Vanity Fair* the more poignant. The last we see of
him, he is snatching up his daughter Janey to keep her from the
contaminating presence of Becky Sharp. Of Janey he is 'fonder than of
anything in the world' – ' "Fonder than he is of me", Emmy thinks,
with a sigh'. Yet Dobbin's little Jane, unlike Thackeray's, will not,
unless she dies too, escape 'the degradation of life and pain'. Thackeray's closing comment – 'Ah! *Vanitas Vanitatum!*' – must include
Dobbin's love for his child, and that final, protective gesture that we
watch him making.

Of course, Dobbin's wife bears the chief responsibility for impressing upon him the vanity of human wishes. Women, not children, are
the real let-down. It is one of the fine strengths of the novel that when
Dobbin gets 'what he has asked for every day and hour for eighteen

years', it should prove a disappointment. There is no melodrama, as in Dickens's failed marriages. Mrs. Dobbin does not flee to France with a pistol, or crawl upstairs reeking of gin, like Mrs. Dombey or Mrs. Blackpool. Dobbin finds love and gratitude in Amelia; she, love and pity in him. 'He never said a word to Amelia that was not kind and gentle, or thought of a want of hers that he did not try to gratify.' 'Try' receives some stress, for he cannot love Amelia as much as he, or she, would wish, and the calm authority of his speech to her, just after she had quarrelled with him in Pumpernickel, remains to colour the end of the novel indelibly: 'No, you are not worthy of the love which I have devoted to you. I knew all along that the prize I had set my life on was not worth the winning.' Coming from Dobbin, it sounds neither smug nor lordly, simply true. For Amelia stands arraigned, eventually, as the kind of girl who could be infatuated by George Osborne. That is what Dobbin wins, and he is sadly cognisant of it, learning, as Thackeray puts it in *Rebecca and Rowena*, that 'it is only hope which is real'.

Unlike the Dobbins', most of Thackeray's unhappy marriages have a resident mother-in-law to help them on their way to ruin, and to keep before our eyes a specimen of time-battered womanhood. Thackeray quite understood that he repeated himself inexcusably in this respect, and he even incorporated complaints about it into his own work. 'Oh, how *stale* this kind of thing is', Laura Pendennis protests in *Philip*. 'You are always attacking mothers-in-law!' But the obsession proved too strong to break. Mrs. Shawe was to blame. She had set herself against her daughter's marriage to Thackeray (as *Philip* recounts), and the vituperation to which she had treated her son-in-law when he arrived in Cork with his raving wife in 1840 left an ineffaceable scar. She regarded herself, not Thackeray or Isabella, as the wronged party, prating, as he reports it, 'of her great merits and sacrifices'. So little could he adjust to this viewpoint that he judged it sheer lunacy. Mrs. Shawe seemed 'really and truly demented' to him: 'I scarcely get a meal at her home but I am obliged to swallow an insult with it.' He was struggling, almost penniless, and saddled with an ill wife, and it was this moment that his enemy chose to sting him with her taunts. He could not get over it. The spectre of a self-righteous domestic tyrant, expert in humiliating meanness, and pursuing her own ends with almost maniacal determination, clung to his fiction from the early years of his marriage until the end of his life. Mrs. Shum in *Yellow-plush*, Mrs. Hoggarty in *The Great Hoggarty Diamond*, Mrs. Gashleigh in *A Little Dinner at Timmins's*, Mrs. Captain Budge in *Hobson's Choice*, Lady Kicklebury in *The Kickleburys on the Rhine*, and Mrs. Baynes in *Philip*, perpetuate the type with more or less virulence: vulgar, insinuating social-climbers, who clamp themselves to the doomed young-marrieds like vampires. Particular instances of pride and folly pass from one to another of them. Mrs. Hoggarty, for instance, insists on setting up a servant in livery, employing for the purpose an undersized sixteen-year-old who follows her on walks bearing a large gold-headed stick; and Mrs. Captain Budge inherits this peculiarity, dressing the knife-boy, Peter Grundsell, in a green suit and a hat with a knob on top 'like a gilt Brussels sprout', and making him carry her prayer-book behind her when she goes to church.

Time did not heal. The mothers-in-law got more nightmarish with the years, more like invaders from a savage world. 'When the Indian prisoners are killed, the squaws always invent the worst tortures', remarks Philip, apropos of Mrs. Baynes. 'You should have seen that fiend and her livid smile, as she was drilling her gimlets into my heart . . . I can see her face now: her cruel yellow face, and her sharp teeth.' Mrs. Shawe has sprouted fangs.

Prominent among these vindictive portraits is Mrs. Mackenzie from *The Newcomes*. She is Thackeray's most powerful mother-in-law because time shapes her. She uncoils only gradually, whereas the others tend to be static uglies. From the early information we get about her, Mrs. Mackenzie might be taken as a winning amalgam of frolicsomeness, dependability and sex-appeal. Pendennis finds her 'a very brisk, plump, pretty little widow'. She has rushed down from Edinburgh to nurse her sick brother. Though thirty-three, she looks twenty-five, has a 'gay and lightsome spirit', and trips round the Newcome house bringing good cheer. A soldier's widow, she is capable as well as decorative, 'active, brisk, jovial and alert', with a 'fine merry humour of her own'. Everyone realizes that she intends her daughter Rosey to marry Clive, and Clive laughs at the jolly situation 'as merrily as the rest'. 'She was', Thackeray assures us, 'a merry little woman.'

The reader who flicked forward at this point to the last few chapters might confidently expect to find Mrs. Mackenzie still merrily trotting, and espoused to Colonel Newcome. But who, he might wonder, is this creature that Clive and his father are shackled to in the closing scenes – a 'boa-constrictor', a 'female tyrant, stupid, obstinate', 'a vulgar, coarse-minded woman' who pursues her wilting menfolk with 'brutal sarcasm and deadly rancour', a monster of 'greed and rapacity' whose wheedling flatteries nauseate Pendennis? It is Mrs. Mackenzie still, but time and its trials have got at her, and eaten away her merry parts. The transformation is quite credible. Even at the start, there were warning signs: her snobbishness, vigour and ambition; the servants' tales of her tantrums and shrewishness with Rosey. Besides, the later Mrs. Mackenzie has a right to be furious. The colonel really has embezzled Rosey's fortune, choosing, as even Pen admits, to conduct business 'in utter ignorance and defiance of the law'. When Mrs. Mackenzie says he is not to be trusted with money, it is no more than the mean truth. Clive, her son-in-law, really is a wastrel. Pendennis and his wife really do despise her, and consider her lower class. Looking back we can see that the praise she got, even early on, reeked of condescension. She was called 'brisk' and 'active', like a servant. Her awareness of these wrongs, and her disappointment, and daily stinting and scraping, have turned her into the thing that sticks its head round the door after the humiliating scuffle with Clive over his little boy's hat:

The door is flung open, and the red-faced Campaigner appears. Her face is mottled with wrath, her bandeaux of hair are disarranged upon her forehead, the ornaments of her cap, cheap, and dirty, and numerous, only give her a wilder appearance. She is in a large and dingy wrapper.

Even here we feel some sympathy with her: the description is so disdainful. But there is no sympathy in the narrative; and if we invent excuses for Mrs. Mackenzie's behaviour, we get no encouragement from Thackeray. He just supplies the facts. His achievement is remarkable, for in Mrs. Mackenzie he presents what he condemned *Madame Bovary* as – 'a heartless, coldblooded study of the downfall and degradation of a woman', and he allows us to see its entire probability. Mrs. Mackenzie is one of time's likelier ruins.

Dennis Haggarty's Wife, written only two or three years after the quarrel with Mrs. Shawe, is less likely – a fantastic unleashing of vengefulness and ferocity on Thackeray's part, certainly his most heartless study of a woman's degradation, and his most bitterly powerful work. It involves a mother-in-law and a wife, but it is for the wife that the more venomous treatment is reserved. The narrator, Fitzboodle, recalls an 'odious Irishwoman', Mrs. Gam, who used to frequent the Royal Hotel at Leamington. Like Mrs. Mackenzie (and Mrs. Shawe) she was a military widow, and similarly occupied in trying to marry off her daughter, a girl with 'excessively bare shoulders' and weak, red eyes which she used to roll at every eligible bachelor. Fitzboodle's friend, Dennis Haggarty, is a suitor for this young lady, and eventually marries her. Ten years later Fitzboodle, strolling on the beach near Dublin, runs into Haggarty, who is evidently in reduced circumstances, and accompanied by ragged children. He takes Fitzboodle home to a wretched cottage, and there, seated beside some bottles of porter and a cold mutton bone, they find the former Miss Gam:

Mrs. Haggarty was not only blind, but it was evident that smallpox had been the cause of her loss of vision. Her eyes were bound with a bandage, her features were entirely swollen, scarred, and distorted by the horrible effects of the malady. She had been knitting in a corner when we entered, and was wrapped in a very dirty bed-gown. Her voice to me was quite different to that in which she addressed her husband. She spoke to Haggarty in broad Irish: she addressed me in that most odious of all languages – Irish-English, endeavouring to the utmost to disguise her brogue, and to speak with the true dawdling *distingué* English air.

What impresses about the ensuing interview is the narrator's lack of compassion. The writing quivers with fury and disgust at the blind woman's accent, her superior airs, her pathetic pretence that the hovel contains a full complement of domestic servants, and her bid to make herself look attractive for her guest:

She left me to indulge my reflections for half-an-hour, at the end of which period she came down stairs dressed in an old yellow satin, with the poor shoulders exposed just as much as ever. She had mounted a tawdry cap, which Haggarty himself must have selected for her. She had all sorts of necklaces, bracelets, and earrings in gold, in garnets, in mother-of-pearl, in ormolu. She brought in a furious savour of musk, which drove the odours of onions and turf-smoke before it; and she waved across her wretched, angular, mean, scarred features, an old cambric handkerchief with a yellow lace-border.

The intensity of the narrator's malevolence is alarming, and curiously unjustified. To denounce Mrs. Haggarty's 'infernal pride, folly, and selfishness' seems extravagant – as if contracting smallpox and going blind were an egotistical whim. This sense of furious irrelevance increases when Thackeray launches into a tirade against the mulish dulness of 'certain people' – 'selfish, stingy, ignorant, passionate, brutal' – of which class we are supposed to recognize blind Mrs. Haggarty as a representative.

The story earned Strindberg's admiration, understandably enough. Its excitement, though, does not issue from any insights into female failings, but from the feeling that we are in the presence of a writer half-crazy with hatred and self-pity, for which the narrative is hardly more than a mask. Haggarty, as Thackeray describes him, finds himself chained to a woman who, because of her mutilation, is 'no longer the same as the woman he loved'. At the end he is deserted and robbed of his money by his wife and mother-in-law. One child dies; they take the others; and his wife, before they drive him out of doors, tells him she never loved him. Like Mrs. Shawe, the mother is a narrow, religious woman, convinced of her own righteousness, secure in 'that wonderful self-complacency with which the fools of this earth are endowed'. The coincidence of much of this with Thackeray's own circumstances is patent – the dead child, the lost money, the estranged wife. But no less striking is the distortion. The robbed, outcast husband – a 'noble heart' flung away upon a 'foul mass of greedy vanity' – is a hysterical travesty of Thackeray; and the ravaged, blinded wife, neither recognizing nor loving the man she married, a fearful caricature of poor Isabella.

The fascination that Thackeray felt at the decay of women's bodies shows up all over his work. The elderly lady in *The Paris Sketch-Book*, who inserts her false teeth with such an upsetting clatter, illustrates it. So does Mrs. Bullock's kiss in *Vanity Fair*, 'like the contact of an oyster', and Mrs. Quiggett in *The Virginians*, who 'strongly resembles' a white cockatoo, and rocks about in her senile mirth 'till all her keys, and, as one may fancy, her old ribs clatter and jingle'. Portraits and statues pander to this gruesome delight, by showing hags as the houris they once were. So Madame Bernstein, whose face reminds George Warrington of the socket of an exploded Roman candle, is positioned before a Kneller depicting her at the age of twenty-four; and Lady Bareacres, toothless and bald, stands beside 'the matchless Dancing Nymph of Canova', for which she sat in her youth; and diabolical old Lady Kew is preserved in her former condition in a portrait by Harlowe, where she is represented painting, in her turn, a miniature of her son Lord Walham, since dead. Time sees to it that portraits are lies before their paint is dry.

The relationship of a portrait to time and change becomes more eerie when, though the human sitter has died, some object included in the painting remains visible near it, and unaltered, as if bringing a particle of the dead person back into the room. Thackeray noticed this effect more than once. In *Lovel*, a 'simpering effigy' of Lovel's dead wife Cecilia, playing a harp, looks down from the wall, while the harp itself stands in a corner beneath a leather cover. The conjunction gives the narrator 'a sort of *crawly* sensation', and when a sparrow happens to fly through the window and perch on the leather case, it strikes him that death has been indecently roused, as if 'all the ghosts in Putney churchyard' had rattled their bones. On the announcement of Lovel's remarriage, a string of the harp, under its 'shroud' of cordovan leather, breaks with a loud report. The occurrence remarkably recalls a moment in Lawrence's early novel, *The Trespasser*:

Siegmund's violin lay in the dark, folded up, as he had placed it for the last time, with hasty, familiar hands, in its red silk shroud. After two dead months the first string had snapped, sharply striking the sensitive body of the instrument. The second string had broken near Christmas, but no one had heard the faint moan of its going. The violin lay mute in the dark, a faint odour of must creeping over the smooth, soft wood. Its twisted, withered strings lay crisped from the anguish of breaking, smothered under the silk folds. The fragrance of Siegmund himself, with which the violin was steeped, slowly changed into an odour of must.

Lawrence delves into the experience more richly, giving sensuous fulness to the instrument's aliveness and gradual death. It is typical of Thackeray that he's half inclined to keep the whole fancy at bay with jokiness (his string breaks with a *'bong'*, as against Lawrence's 'faint moan'). Typical, too, that his harp doesn't come alive as Lawrence's violin does. It remains an object, which the painted woman on the wall is trying to use in order to communicate: she is a 'sickly genteel ghost' who finds that her 'defunct voice' can't be heard. The harp and portrait recur in *Philip*. A painting of Mrs. Firmin, leaning 'with bare arms on a harp', looks down from the wall, and, says the narrator, 'followed us about with wild violet eyes', while the harp stands 'smothered in a leather bag in the corner'. Mrs. Firmin's frantic eye-movements, like those of someone gagged, and her 'smothered' instrument, both suggest unwilling dumbness. The apprehension is of a person trapped in death, rather than, as in Lawrence, of insentient things gaining life. The Berrys' statues, confined in their mouldering well of a garden, belong to the same fear, and, as one might expect, though Mrs. Berry in that story is not yet officially dead 'a harp in a leather case' stands in her room, waiting for her long silence.

Portraits, then, represent for Thackeray frozen bits of the past still shamingly on show, stifled voices still trying to speak. Old letters did the same. They, too, belong to the cluster of objects his thoughts on time kept bringing him up against. But his attitude towards them changes, and in a way that sums up his whole career. The early work handles them scathingly; the late, tearfully. Here is a representative late piece, from *The Newcomes*:

In the faded ink, on the yellow paper that may have crossed and re-crossed oceans, that has lain locked in chests for years, and buried under piles of family archives, while your friends have been dying and your head has grown white – who has not disinterred mementoes like these – from which the past smiles at you so sadly, shimmering out of Hades an instant but to sink back again in the cold shades, perhaps with a faint sound as of a remembered tone – a ghostly echo of a once familiar laughter? I was looking, of late, at a wall in the Naples Museum, whereon a boy of Herculaneum eighteen hundred years ago had scratched with a nail the figure of a soldier. I could fancy the child turning round and smiling on me after having done his etching.

It's affecting, of course. The little phantom turning round to smile and instantly snuffed out by the implacable centuries puts time's terrible way with children in a nutshell. But a large helping of elderly doleful-ness has also gone to make up the passage, and Thackeray's strange assumption, in the first sentence, that his readers will all be white-haired fits in with this. His early work regarded old letters much more savagely. There were 'no better satires' on human inconstancy, he claimed in *Vanity Fair*: 'vows, love, promises, confidences, gratitude, how queerly they read after a while'. Either way, the reader of old letters finds himself alone – with a bundle of ghosts, or a bundle of delusions.

This brings us to Thackeray's preoccupation with loneliness which, as the reader of this chapter will have noticed, keeps mingling with his fear of time. His time-stricken houses are lonely; the mouldy statues that fill their gardens give a solitary air to the human intruders. His empty bottles and scraps of food, deserted by guests; his ephemeral townscapes, with their landmarks torn down; his portraits staring out from the past, all impress on the individual that he is alone. 'A distinct universe', Thackeray observed, 'walks about under your hat and under mine'. Time intensifies loneliness because, being in time, the individual is isolated not only from his fellow men, but from past and future embodiments of himself. He can conceive of himself, at any moment, only as a forlorn digit in a sequence of selves stretching before and after, each insensibly different from the next. It seems to have been this feeling that led Thackeray to associate time and loneliness with mirrors, and especially with mirrors set so that they reduplicate images in an unending series. So we find Miss Osborne in *Vanity Fair* sitting, dreary and alone, in her father's house:

The great glass over the mantelpiece, faced by the other great console glass at the opposite end of the room, increased and multiplied between them the brown holland bag in which the chandelier was hung; until you saw these brown holland bags fading away in endless perspectives, and this apartment of Miss Osborne's seemed the centre of a system of drawing rooms. When she removed the cordovan leather from the grand piano, and ventured to play a few notes on it, it sounded with a mournful sadness, startling the dismal echoes of the house.

The piano's cover links it with Thackeray's shrouded harps, of course. Leather instrument-covers had an unfailingly bereaved look for him, and this one is not watched by a dead portrait, as the others were, only because, as we learn in the next sentence, George's picture, which hung nearby, has been relegated to the lumber-room. The brown holland bag repeats the note of deathly confinement, and the mirrors create an infinity of lonelinesses. In Dr. Firmin's Old Parr Street house in *Philip*, where harp, portrait, and the other signatures of time, cluster, reduplicating mirrors are also found: 'everybody's face seemed scared and pale in the great looking-glasses, which reflected you over and over again into the distance'. The fear instilled by endless, wraith-like repetitions of oneself affects, too, the old Princesse de Mont-contour in *The Newcomes*, who finds herself residing in apartments fitted up in the style of Louis XVI, and containing Thackeray's most unfriendly pair of mirrors:

In her bed is an immense looking-glass, surmounted by stucco Cupids: it is an alcove which some powdered Venus, before the Revolution, might have reposed in. Opposite that looking-glass, between the tall windows, at some forty feet distance, is another huge mirror, so that when the poor Princess is in bed, in her prim old curl-papers, she sees a vista of elderly princesses twinkling away into the dark perspective; and is so frightened that she and Betsy, her Lancashire maid, pin up the jonquil silk curtains over the bed-mirror after the first night; though the Princess can never get it out of her head that her image is still there, behind the jonquil hangings, turning as she turns, waking as she wakes.

The Princess's fear is complicated. Her old face contrasts with the rococo eroticism of the mirror's surround, and by multiplying the contrast the mirrors coarsely insist on this. Like many of Thackeray's mirrors, they hold, too, a sort of unseen historical sediment, consisting of the faces they have, or might have, reflected – in this case a 'powdered Venus' dismayingly unlike the Princess. (When Thackeray visited the Galerie des Glaces at Versailles, he typically set about computing how many courtiers' faces its mirrors had mirrored: a quarter of a million, he reckoned, and 'every one of them lies'.) But the Princess's mirrors intimate the future as well as the past, revealing a 'vista of elderly princesses', gradually diminishing and all lonely. Further, the thing in the mirror seems not just a reflection but a baleful presence, aping the Princess's movements even when hidden behind hangings. Thackeray's imagining here suggests a conspiracy between mirrors and loneliness that is not really susceptible of rational analysis. It is comparable with the curious incident later in *The Newcomes* when James Binnie returns to his lonely house after parting from his favourite niece, Rosey, and looks at the mirror which has so often reflected her face:

the great callous mirror, which now only framed upon its shining sheet the turban, and the ringlets, and the plump person, and the resolute smile of the old Campaigner.

'The Campaigner' is, of course, Mrs. Mackenzie, Rosey's mother and James's sister, who is to nurse him until his death, which soon ensues. The episode could have been written only by someone who found mirrors abnormally worrying. There is no reasonable excuse for Binnie's behaviour with his mirror, or for bringing a mirror in here at all. We don't normally look into mirrors to discover who is absent or present in the house. But, for Binnie, Rosey's loss means that she is missing from, of all places, the mirror. So is he. Moribund, he seems already to have lost his reflection, and finds 'only' his sister in the glass. And she appears framed and gleaming, as if her menacing intentness, as well as her inscrutability, could not be projected save through a mirror-image. In a comparably dejected key, Dobbin, on the morning of George's marriage to Amelia, shelters from the rain in a coffee-room, feeling lonelier than he has ever felt since boyhood, and notices how the passers-by leave their 'long reflections on the shining stone'. Loneliness and mirroring unite again. Dobbin's solitariness finds its natural match in the drear, attenuated world of reflections. Thackeray's curiosity about mirror-effects lies, it's worth noting, near the core of his creativity. When he thought about his greatest book, he thought about a mirror. The title-page of *Vanity Fair* shows a ragged jester gazing glumly into a looking-glass. The self-scrutinizing satirist sees in his mirror vanity, isolation, and the effects of time.

Being extremely conscious of time and its disadvantages, Thackeray increasingly played about with it in the structure of his novels, so as to turn them into time-cheaters. The treatment of age in *Henry Esmond* illustrates this. The book starts in 1691, when Esmond is twelve, and Rachel a married woman with a four-year-old daughter. Although she is supposed to have her beauty destroyed by smallpox in 1694, she gets progressively younger as the story proceeds. In Book II Chapter xv, set in 1709, she is 'almost forty' but, we are told, 'did not look to be within ten years of her age'. A mere two pages later, she has acquired 'the shape and complexion of a girl of twenty'. By Book III Chapter vii she seems younger than her daughter. Meanwhile Esmond puts on years as alarmingly as Rachel casts them off. Though she is persistently referred to as his 'mistress', and speaks to him in 'a mother's sweet plaintive tone', he is already acting as her 'tutor' by the age of sixteen. By Book III Chapter iv he appears 'ten years older' than she does. Another couple of pages, and he is describing himself as an 'old fellow' fit to be her 'grandfather', and after three more chapters he feels 'a hundred years old'. Contemporary reviewers were displeased about Henry's eventual marriage with Rachel. It 'affects us somewhat like a marriage with his own mother', said the *Athenaeum*. That, of course, was the point, or part of it. Thackeray's time-twisting allows Henry to find in Rachel a composite bride, satisfying a whole range of masculine whims. He marries his mother, grand-daughter, pupil and mistress all in one. Thackeray once remarked that when he was sixty he would probably marry 'a girl of eleven or twelve, innocent, barley-sugar-loving, in a pinafore', and with Rachel rejuvenating at such a rate Harry plainly hasn't long to wait for that pleasure.

Thackeray did not try out a dateless couple like Henry and Rachel again. Instead he complicated his later novels with incessant flash-backs and flicks forward, to make time in them seem flexible. In the first two numbers of *The Newcomes*, for instance, we jump from Clive and the Colonel in the Cave of Harmony, back to the history of the Newcome family in George III's reign, forward to the Colonel's childhood and adolescence, forward again to his son's return from India and schooldays, back to the Colonel's marriage, and so on. The reader is jogged about, and the narrative line keeps slipping from his grasp. In the nineteenth century, this aspect of Thackeray's art seemed new and perplexing, 'He goes round and round', complained Mrs. Browning, 'till I'm dizzy, for one, and don't know where I am.' The modern reader is likely to think immediately of Conrad, and since both authors were caught up with the isolation of the individual, as well as with involved time-schemes, it looks a promising comparison.

In fact, it isn't. Whatever else Conrad dislocates time for, it is not to comfort or console the reader. But Thackeray's time-shifts regularly have that as their object. He seems to want us to know, almost from the start, that everything turned out all right. The footnotes and insertions by 'later hands' in the eighteenth-century novels fit in with this purpose. Conrad withholds information. About a third of *Nostromo* elapses, after Decoud's arrival on the Great Isabel, before we learn how he died, and during the interim we are shown tantalizing evidences of his death, such as his memorial tablet. In *The Secret Agent*, news of a terrorist blown to pieces in Greenwich Park arrives, together with a hint that it may be Verloc, considerably before a recognizable bit of scorched overcoat turns up to inform us that it was Stevie. Thackeray, on the other hand, thrusts reassuring tidings of the future upon his audience, even when they would be distinctly untormented if they remained in ignorance. When Alfred, the sick child in *The Newcomes*, is clambering on his uncle's knee, we are apprised that he will one day be 'a jolly young officer in the Guards'. At the start of *The Virginians* Harry arrives in Bristol in 1756 wearing mourning for his brother George, but we already know George can't really be dead, because we have been told that he fought in the American War of Independence. Narrating the second part of the novel, George fills it with maundering allusions to the happy family life he is enjoying at the time of going to press, so we are in no danger of thinking that he perished in the combat. The idea seems to be to dispel anxiety, and induce a sort of fagged-out smile, with soothing murmurs about contentment and ripe old age. 'I protest there is nothing so beautiful as Darby and Joan in the world. I hope Philip and his wife will be Darby and Joan to the end', croons Thackeray, about half-way through *Philip*, and well before the wedding has actually taken place, 'I tell you they are married; and don't want to make any mysteries about the business'. We get the same kind of Sunset-Homes serenity in *Denis Duval*, where Denis hastens to divulge, before his adventures have well begun, that he won Agnes de Saverne in the end, and that she is sitting before him as he writes, with her 'raven locks streaked with silver'. Indeed, by the time of *Denis Duval* Thackeray is explaining his novel's dislocated chronological structure as just another of senility's lovable lapses:

Why do I make zigzag journeys? 'Tis the privilege of old age to be garrulous, and its happiness to remember early days. As I sink back in my arm-chair, safe and sheltered. . . .

And so on. Certainly it is a disappointment to the reader who has watched Thackeray's relentless explorings of time's destructiveness, to come across him doling out these slack-witted consolations at the end of his career. Besides, echoes of that destructiveness persist in the later novels, cheek by jowl with euphoria about the blessings of age. Only a few sentences before the Darby-and-Joan bit in *Philip* we are shown Charlotte and Philip, during their courtship, leaving notes for each other in a clock on the mantelpiece, 'on which was carved the old French allegory, *Le temps fait passer l'amour*', and the couple in *Denis Duval* entrust their love-letters to a similarly depressing post-box – a hole in a tomb in the churchyard, where the narrator, when he revisits it in later life, finds 'only a little mould and 'moss'. Such portents of decay naturally make the atmosphere of hoary-headed contentment look suspect.

The fact is that Thackeray did not believe in the blessings of age, which is why his writing about them goes limp. In his letters he drops the pretence, and stands before us as a tired, sated hedonist, with dulled appetites, waiting for death as he glumly ingorges his beef-steak and claret: 'I can part from them without a very severe pang, and *nota* that we shall get no greater pleasures than these from this to the end of our days. What *is* a greater pleasure? Gratified ambition? accumulation of money? What?' Even lust has petered out, he finds, and refuses to be tickled back to life: 'When one is twenty, yes, but at 47 Venus may rise from the sea, and I for one should hardly put on my spectacles to have a look.'

The circlings of time in Thackeray's later novels, then, though they look like advanced literary structures, mark a retreat from his aware-ness of time's irresistible linear progression. But this is not the whole truth about them. They also allow expression to his sense that the past is present in the present, shaping it, and, through memory, providing most of the contents of what we think of as our consciousness of the present moment. In the early twentieth century the stream-of-consciousness novel and works like Eliot's *Four Quartets* emphasized the same facts. For someone who lived so much among his memories as Thackeray, the idea was inescapable. 'A man can be alive in 1860 and

1830 at the same time', as he argues in the *Roundabout Papers*. 'Bodily I may be in 1860, inert, silent, torpid; but in the spirit I am walking about in 1828, let us say; – in a blue dress-coat and brass buttons.'

The novel in which the time-scheme gets most complicated, and remains most faithful to Thackeray's wry, lucid view of age, without being tempted into balmy consolations, is *Lovel the Widower*. Time here doubles back, nips forward, drifts aside and jolts into place, wandering in the tunnels of memory, and evolving a graphic impression of a mind constantly reformulating its own past in order to create its present. The past's intrusion into the present is the story's whole subject. Lovel's ex-wife looks down from the wall; his mother-in-law lingers on and makes the house miserable; Elizabeth, the governess, finds her past career as a ballet-dancer dragged up and made public; and Batchelor, the narrator, is disturbed by memories of the cowardice – or prudence – that prevented him from marrying Elizabeth when he had – or seemed to have – the chance. The moment when he almost proposed to her remains brightly islanded in his mind. He held the blue spectacles, which he had made her take off – like a fragment of shed time; he heard 'two canaries making a tremendous concert in their cage' and 'two children quarrelling on the lawn' – things which, we realize, Batchelor's mind in the crisis of indecision seized on as emblems of the harmony or disharmony which marriage could bring, which is why he remembers them long afterwards. Before he can overcome his doubts the tableau is shattered by yet another intruder from the past – Elizabeth's scrounging mother, Mrs. Prior, with her 'old familiar cracked voice'. And Batchelor, in the years that follow, can never quite be sure whether he lost or gained. He escaped being related to Mrs. Prior, but he has settled for a diminished, celibate, self-indulgent life in Pump Court, with a snuffy laundress who bullies him. Like Prufrock, he takes refuge in self-disparagement. The defensive unseriousness of the whole narrative is brilliantly lifelike.

Thackeray's growing preoccupation with the past, and his experiments in narrative structure, are, then, like his attachment to the historical novel, efforts to redeem and outmanoeuvre time. His imitations of the styles of earlier periods, as in the *Spectator* essay in *Esmond*, and his habit of making characters live again in book after book, may be seen from the same angle. He liked to fancy that nothing really died, that he would meet his little dead daughter again, and that the notes of the coach-horn he used to hear tootling over Salisbury Plain as a boy were still 'reverberating in endless space'. These fancies and stratagems are themselves oblique testimonies to the menace which time held for him. Its disastrous effects on places and people profoundly engaged his imagination, and prompted some of his greatest work, proliferating into images of statues, skeletons and dribbling water, ashy fruit, dead portraits and shrouded harps, mouldering fish and hags and wildernesses of mirrors, which arise from the levels of consciousness at which poetry is born, and always make us want more.

7[

What Went Wrong

A book which makes claims for Thackeray's earlier as against his later work must say what went wrong with the later. Previous chapters have touched on this point; this chapter will develop it. But to stop it becoming an orgy of blame, the second half will take a look at Thackeray's particular kind of honesty and self-knowledge, and show these qualities surviving to the end of his career.

With *Pendennis*, a disastrous decency and simplicity overtake Thackeray's characters. *Vanity Fair* had been full of tarnished people whom it is hard to make simple judgements about. Rawdon Crawley, for example, as Orwell notes, though from one point of view a 'thick-headed ruffian' who lives by swindling tradesmen, is, according to his own code, not a bad man. He would not desert a friend in a tight corner, and we are in no doubt that he will behave bravely on the field of battle. In the end we almost respect him. Orwell brackets Major Pendennis with Rawdon as a 'comparatively subtle type' – a 'shallow old snob', who yet manages to earn our amused tolerance. That seems a fair description of the Major and his effect. But about no one else in *Pendennis* are we allowed to be in two minds to this extent. Of the women, Blanche Amory is a pouting concoction of weaknesses, hopelessly nobbled from the start. Set against her is spotless Laura with her 'sparkling glance', whom Thackeray festoons in religious phraseology. He bids us 'look with love and wonder' on her 'pure fragrance', categorizing her as one of those happy souls whose 'virgin loving trust' allows them to 'fear no evil because they think none'. This is inept as well as flatulent, for we have already seen Laura thinking evil – registering malice and groundless suspicion on finding Fanny Bolton nursing Pen in his lodgings. But Thackeray's idealizing urge outruns his brain. By the end Laura is so 'heavenly pure' that Pen's affection for her has to be classified as 'almost paternal', lest it should seem irreverently sexy.

Mrs. Pendennis receives similar glorification. 'A high-bred English lady', Thackeray explains, 'is the most complete of all Heaven's subjects in this world', and Mrs. Pendennis belongs to that social group. Before such 'angelical natures' as hers, 'the wildest and fiercest of us must fall down and humble ourselves, in admiration of that

150

adorable purity which never seems to think or do wrong'. As a representative of the 'sacred mystery' of maternal love, she follows Pen around with 'sainted benedictions', whispers the *Christian Year* to him, and opens his mail to save him from a lower-class match with Fanny Bolton. This subterfuge might seem unworthy of an angelical nature, but Thackeray justifies it. When Pen confronts his mother over the purloined letters, the gallant Warrington, conveniently on the spot, volunteers the story of his own unfortunate marriage with a 'boor' who could not, he found, share his intellectual interests, and to whom he has accordingly been obliged to pay an annuity on condition that she and her children 'hide themselves away'. The upshot of this moral tale is that Mrs. Pendennis is seen to have saved her son from a fateful and perhaps costly step by breaking off the affair with Fanny. The Pendennis family is reunited, amid tears and kisses, Pen himself falling down at his mother's 'sacred knees' and sobbing out the Lord's Prayer. And lest there should be any further questioning of her authority, Mrs. Pendennis dies within a quarter of an hour.

Thackeray quite approved of her tactics over Pen's mail. 'My mother would have acted in just such a way if I had run away with a naughty woman', he wrote, 'that is I hope she would.' Pen's mother was modelled on Mrs. Carmichael-Smyth, of course. 'Mrs. Pendennis is living with me (she is my mother)', Thackeray told Clough. But the portrait is idealized and simplified. We should hardly guess from it that Thackeray found his mother intolerably dull and humourless, yet this is so. 'The dear old Mater Dolorosa gloomifies me', he confided to a friend, 'I would rather die than make a joke to her.' Her 'favourite propensity' was 'to be miserable'. Perhaps he stressed her angelic side in the novel to allay qualms of filial guilt. But Helen Pendennis becomes a flatter creature than his mother by consequence. Tamer, too. She is allowed none of Mrs. Carmichael-Smyth's intelligence – her republicanism and radicalism and fierce combativeness on points of Christian Doctrine, all of which aggravated Thackeray.

Pen also suffers from being put through Thackeray's hygienic novel-making machinery. He is the young Thackeray, cleaned up, fitted with manly motives, and perfectly lifeless. His peccadilloes are not meant to lower him in our esteem, and, lest they should, Thackeray pelts us with bluff plaudits. Pen is 'genuine' and 'hearty', an 'honest, brave lad, impetuous and full of good'. His 'frank and brave' manner, annoying to inferiors, befits a 'high-spirited youth'. True, he overspends at college, but this 'insatiable appetite for pleasure' is but a sign of his 'fiery constitution'. It follows that his critics are 'yelping curs'. Pen's faults are necessarily of a rather ungrown-up kind, like buying pretty clothes or over-indulging himself with food and drink, because Thackeray dare not allow him to be sexually impure, as he had been in his own youth. It is firmly enunciated early on that Pen was a clean-liver and, as a gentleman, 'polite to every woman high and low'.

It is partly this effort on Thackeray's part to fabricate something wild yet innocuous that makes Pen's high-jinks with Warrington such a farce. Swigging their 'pot of ale' in 'queer London haunts', roaring jovial ditties, or going for 'a pull on the river', the pair appear to have embarked on an extremely inexpert imitation of masculine pleasures, and the more Thackeray assures us of its entire jollity and robustness, the feebler it seems. Warrington, with his high soul, pipe, and 'rough yet tender' laugh, is probably Thackeray's most fatuous creation, the most catastrophic result of his resolution to be cordial, upright and good-hearted as the Victorians wished. His manly endearments ('I like you, old boy', 'Go in and win, young 'un', and so forth) make even the well-disposed reader blush.

Through Warrington, Thackeray encourages some of his audience's sillier prejudices. He shows him greeting Pen, after months apart, with a handshake and a few gruff words, and contrasts this with the way in which, he says, two Frenchmen would have rushed shrieking into each other's arms, or two Germans covered each other with Havanna-scented kisses. Britons, we are meant to see, really have deeper feelings of friendship than Fritzes and Frogs, but conceal them behind a manly reserve. Again, Pen and Warrington, indulging their 'natural appetite for pleasure and joviality', are favourably compared with their fellow-student Paley. For Paley is a swot, and his unremitting labour, we are told, makes him unappreciative of love, 'sweet song' and 'the beautiful world of God'. Thus gentlemanly idleness is seen to be more meritorious than hard work. Warrington is, indeed, the perfect middle-class answer to the working class. A baronet's son, he can match the working class at their natural accomplishments of fisticuffs and boozing, while remaining ineffably superior to them in every other respect. He drinks beer 'like a coalheaver', yet 'you couldn't but perceive that he was a gentleman', and at Oxford he was known as Stunning Warrington for his facility in beating bargemen. In *Vanity Fair* it was the preposterous Jim Crawley, awash with port, who held forth about his highborn undergraduate friends, and their bashing of bargemen, and what a mark of 'old blood' it was in them – 'I'm none of your radicals. I know what it is to be a gentleman, dammy'. In *Pendennis* we are asked to take such views seriously.

The life Warrington and Pen lead at the Inns of Court, with its domestic inconveniences, gives Thackeray an opportunity to pander to another superstition of the comfortably-off, which one can still hear voiced today, to the effect that gentlemen care less about material comfort than the workers, and can put up with tougher conditions, as is proved by the Spartan accommodation in the public schools and older universities:

> The poorest mechanic in Spitalfields has a cistern and an unbounded supply of water at his command; but the gentlemen of the inns of court, and the gentlemen of the universities, have their supply of this cosmetic fetched in jugs by the laundresses and bedmakers, and live in abodes which were erected long before the custom of cleanliness and decency obtained among us.

It's hard to say whether Thackeray's notion of the Spitalfields mechanic with his cistern of water is just a lie, intended to entrench the propertied class in their complacency, or whether it is the result of simple ignorance. Probably a bit of both. At all events, the truth of the matter was somewhat different, and it's worth taking a minute or two to examine it. The curious choice of Spitalfields, the centre of London's depressed silk-weaving industry, as an example of working-class comfort was probably dictated by the fact that the Metropolitan Association for Improving the Dwellings of the Industrious Classes had, by 1850, rehoused 216 families in three blocks of 'model' tenements, two of them in Spitalfields. But Thackeray must surely have known that this had done comparatively little to alleviate human suffering in one of London's most hideously overcrowded districts, and the impression he evidently wishes to give of a metropolitan working class plenteously supplied with water will not stand scrutiny.

The history of London's water-supply during the first half of the nineteenth century is a tortuous tale of dedicated reformers, notably Chadwick and Southwood-Smith, being thwarted by the forces of greed and conservatism. There was no central organization. Metropolitan drainage was administered by eight independent Commissions of Sewers, all discharging waste into the Thames, from which the eight independent water companies drew their supplies. The water companies were joint stock ventures, whose activities had become increasingly profitable in the early part of the century with the manufacture of cheap metal water pipes and improved methods of steam pumping. They were under no obligation to provide a piped supply in the houses of the poor, and there was no financial inducement to do so. The Royal Commission Report of 1850 records that in the area supplied by the East London Company, which included Spitalfields, over 500 households had to fetch their water from common tanks, while a further 3,297 were dependent on common outdoor standcocks which were kept running for two hours or less each day. The company drew its supplies from the River Lea, into which the effluents of dye-works, distilleries, chemical works and sewers ran. As a result, by the time the water reached the consumer, it was, the Commission learned, 'very much discoloured, thick, muddy', contained 'organic matters', and had a 'peculiar smell'. When collected from the standpipes it had to be carried home in open vessels and was, as Dr. Hector Gavin, Lecturer on Forensic Medicine at Charing Cross Hospital, told the Commission, used over and over again until it became 'horribly offensive'. It was frequently putrid by the time it was used for cookery or drinking. Gavin's remarks were based on his experiences in 'the cholera districts', in which category he listed Spitalfields. Disease was the inevitable outcome of such conditions, and in the working-class areas the mortality rate was always high. 'The chances of life of the labouring classes of Spitalfields are amongst the lowest I have met with', wrote Chadwick in his 1842 Report on the Sanitary Conditions of the Labouring Classes.

A Select Committee of the House of Commons had looked into the matter as far back as 1821, but there was no general legislation until the Metropolitan Water Act of 1852. This required the water companies to filter their water 'effectually' and to stop drawing supplies from the Thames below Teddington. In all other respects, however, the Act was a sell-out to vested interests: there were a hundred water-company shareholders in the House of Commons. Nor were its requirements complied with. In 1866 another cholera outbreak killed more than 4,000 people in the East End, after which it transpired that the East London Company had continued to supply unfiltered water from the Lea. So much for Thackeray's happy mechanic with his cistern.

It would not perhaps be worth making such a song and dance about Thackeray's remark on the water-supply if it were not, first, a fair specimen of his trustworthiness as a commentator on the labouring classes – on what went on in those back alleys where, as he says in *Our Street*, 'only the parson and typhus fever visit' – and, second, a representative instance of the bland and shallow idealizing that dominates the later work and pervades, as we have seen, the characterization of *Pendennis*. This idealizing is stepped up in *Henry Esmond*, as Thackeray planned it should be. He wanted the book to be full of 'good lofty and generous people', and told his mother that Henry was 'a handsome likeness of an ugly son of yours'. Henry's college career roughly follows Thackeray's own, and through it he promulgates the same refined contempt for hard work that we found in *Pendennis*. Henry, we are given to understand, is a truly cultured person simply as a result of breeding, and doesn't need to study, whereas mean, servile Tom Tusher, who comes of baser stock, mugs up his classical texts with 'dogged perseverance' and wins a fellowship, though he has 'no more turn for poetry than a ploughboy'.

Henry is, of course, a gentleman, and frequently says so, though as narrator of the novel he drops into the third person for the purpose.

'There was that in Esmond's manner that showed he was a gentleman', Esmond reports, in the scene where he outfaces bold, bad Lord McIun. Indeed, so complete a gentleman is he that he needs no higher title, and in this sense he represents the middle-class answer to the aristocracy just as Warrington was the middle-class answer to the workers. For the plot of the novel hinges on the fact that Henry could be an aristocrat too if he claimed his rights, but has secretly renounced them out of consideration for Rachel, her son Frank, and daughter Beatrix, who believe that the title of Viscount Castlewood belongs in their family, rather than, as is the case, to Henry. His self-denial gives him a 'glow of righteous happiness', and entitles him besides to gratifying displays of humility and esteem from the lords and ladies when they discover the truth. 'Let me kneel – let me kneel, and – and worship you', falters Lady Castlewood, and the Duke of Hamilton, Beatrix's betrothed, who has been rather frosty towards plain Colonel Esmond, grandly apologizes once he realizes that he is dealing with a voluntary ex-Viscount.

Thackeray's readers were evidently expected to derive satisfaction from these courtly capers, and feel themselves to be in elevated company – which is one of the customary satisfactions of the historical novel. Throughout the book people kneel and bow to each other, and make dignified speeches. There's a ceremony at which the three Castlewood ladies dub Henry 'our knight', and another where the Chevalier de St. George, who has been philandering with Beatrix, deigns to cross swords with the angry Esmond, leaving him (quite seriously, it seems) 'extremely touched by this immense mark of condescension and repentance'. Though almost a king, and over in England to claim his crown, the Chevalier proves to be a lecherous, Frenchified youth. 'He seems to sneer at everything. He is not like a king', young Frank tells Henry, 'You are like a king.' So plain Colonel Esmond is shown, in the long run, to be superior not only to aristocrats but to royalty.

In its treatment of women, *Esmond* offers the same crudely contrasted types as *Pendennis*. Rachel takes over from Helen as angel; Beatrix from Blanche as spoiled minx. Henry first tumbles to Rachel's 'pure devotion' in a scene, once much admired by Thackeray critics, set in Winchester Cathedral, and entirely composed of pseudo-religious flummery. Henry calls Rachel his 'dearest saint', she wants him to visit her in the 'holy Advent season', and regrets the closure of nunneries as she feels like entering one. As for Beatrix, with her moues and kittenishness, we are assured that Esmond had never set eyes on a woman 'so arch, so brilliant, and so beautiful'. But when we listen to her conversation with her mother ('your little Trix is a naughty little Trix, and she leaves undone those things which she ought to have done' etc.), we begin to wonder at Thackeray's notion of a brilliant woman, and realize that Beatrix is the product of an age that demanded its females retarded.

Her brother Frank, that 'charming young scapegrace' as Thackeray calls him, is put across as a winsome handful of high spirits, utterly captivating Esmond, and everyone else he encounters, with 'his laugh, his prattle, his noble beauty'. It was 'impossible not to love him', Esmond enthuses. Not loving Frank is, however, something the modern reader finds all too easy. A boastful young drunk, he seems more despicable the more we learn of him. He lords it over the village boys and canes them when playing soldiers with a 'fine imperious spirit', and is sent down from Cambridge for trying to set fire to his college. He takes it as his undoubted right to live off the labour of others: 'Tell Mr. Finch, my agent, to press the people for their rents, and send me the *ryno* anyhow', he writes home on the occasion of his marriage. But we are not meant to find Frank odious. His vagaries are set forth to win our indulgent smiles. Esmond attests to his universal popularity, even among those his class lives by exploiting:

I remember at Ramillies, when he was hit and fell, a great big red-haired Scotch sergeant flung his halbert down, burst out a-crying like a woman, seizing him up as if he had been an infant and carrying him out of the fire.

This contrast between the boy officer and the burly other-ranker had always been a standby with Thackeray. But the turn he gives it here is quite new, and illustrates his drift towards complacent approval of social injustice. Back in 1844, writing *Barry Lyndon*, he had introduced the episode where Lyndon is threatened with a caning by young Ensign Fakenham, fresh from Eton, as an instance of the absurdities of privilege. In *Fraser's*, the following year, he developed the point in connection with the memorial to the fallen in the church at Waterloo, demanding why the names of common soldiers should not be inscribed there as well as those of officers, and alluding to the fatuity of putting young ensigns of fifteen, fresh from preparatory school, in charge of grizzled veterans. He returned to the attack in *The Book of Snobs* with his remarks about the beardless cornet:

I have always admired that dispensation of rank in our country, which sets up this last-named little creature (who was flogged only last week because he could not spell) to command great whiskered warriors, who have faced all dangers of climate and battle; which, because he has money to lodge at the agent's, will place him over the heads of men who have a thousand times more experience and desert; and which, in the course of time, will bring him all the honours of his profession, when the veteran soldier he commanded has got no other reward for his bravery than a berth in the Chelsea Hospital.

In *Esmond*, on the other hand, we are asked to believe that the veteran soldiers really love to be led by these gallant little fellows, and would sacrifice their lives for them.

It was partly the wish to be gentlemanly and elevated, observable in *Esmond*'s characterization, that led Thackeray to set his novel, and *The Virginians*, in the eighteenth century, or rather in an emasculated Victorian replica of that period. As we can gather from the letters and the *English Humourists* lectures, there was a good deal in eighteenth-century culture that failed to satisfy the later Thackeray's requirement of manly purity. Congreve's comedies were, he considered, no more fit to be presented to a polite audience than 'the dialogue of a witty bargeman and a brilliant fishwoman exchanging compliments at Billingsgate'; Swift was 'an awful, evil spirit'; Sterne, 'impure' – 'a foul Satyr'; Richardson, a 'puny cockney bookseller, pouring out end-less volumes of sentimental twaddle'; Fielding's plays, 'irretrievably immoral'; *Joseph Andrews*, 'coarse'; *Peregrine Pickle*, 'atrocious vul-garity'; and Rowlandson's drawings, 'hideous distortions'. It might seem odd that, holding these opinions, he bothered to write about the century at all. But he was greatly attracted by the class distinction and the gambling. A compulsive gambler himself, he naturally felt the appeal of a time when, as he reminds us in *Esmond*, a man of fashion would often spend 'a quarter of his day at cards'. He enjoys describing the highbred composure with which his characters lose their money, and returns to the topic often. But unfortunately he had – or felt he ought to have – moral qualms too, inserts homilies about the wasteful-ness involved, and never, except in the early *Barry Lyndon*, where Barry and his uncle tour the European capitals running a faro bank, makes the gambler's life seem remotely exciting.

Class distinction was an enthusiasm he felt less chary about owning up to, and his eighteenth-century novels are full of celebrations of it. He seems quite concerned to decide when the best time for class-distinction was:

A rich young English peer in the reign of George the Second; a wealthy patrician in the age of Augustus; which would you rather have been? There is a question for any young gentlemen's debating clubs of the present day.

Anything more sickening than a set of privileged youngsters chewing over their chances of being even more privileged in some alternative historical era would, you'd think, be hard to conceive. Yet Thackeray intends it as an alluring prospect. 'A hundred years ago a gentleman was a gentleman', he observes in *The Virginians*. Inferiors like trades-men and artists knew their place, and were treated with a proper dis-dain. George Warrington coolly ticks Garrick off for presuming to address a gentleman familiarly, and later, when he is obliged to write for his living, writhes at the 'insolent patronage' of the 'low hucksters' in the book trade who pay him for his work. This reflects the humiliation Thackeray felt in his early days when he had to truckle to 'low literary men' like Fraser, and also the contempt with which members of his own profession for the most part continued to fill him. The Garrick Club row blew up while he was writing *The Virginians*, and he incorporated into the novel a sneering allusion to 'young Grub-street' (i.e. Yates), and his guttersnipe propensity for reproducing 'the conversation of gentlemen' in threepenny papers. Even the eighteenth-century men of letters whom Thackeray admired receive condescending treatment when they get into the novels, in keeping with the social tone. 'Dick' Steele is an amiable sot, married to a dolt; Johnson, a lovable old eccentric. Very likely Thackeray would have been unequal to the task of portraying Johnson's formidable intellect, even had he wished to do so. But in any case it is not part of his purpose. Gentlemanliness, not genius, is at a premium. Thackeray's Johnson functions as a celebrated public amusement, guaranteed to elicit genial smirks from the initiated.

Above all, the eighteenth century is applauded in these later novels as a high time for etiquette, and Thackeray draws disparaging comparisons with his own day. Thus George, in *The Virginians*, makes 'low and respectful bows' on entering his mother's room:

Nowadays, a young man walks into his mother's room with hob-nailed high-lows, and a wide-awake on his head; and instead of making a bow, puffs a cigar into her face.

This peevish conservatism is far removed from anything the younger Thackeray felt about the eighteenth century. During the 1840s he thought of it primarily as 'the period in all history when society was the least natural, and perhaps the most dissolute'. As we've seen, a few images of vanished glamour habitually flashed across his mind when the subject came up – hoops, patches, periwigs, red heels, coaches. But the brutality and corruption of the age also weighed heavily with him – the cruel punishments, and the armies of degraded men flogged around the continent of Europe, their heads plastered in flour and candle grease, slaughtering one another on campaigns which meant nothing to them, and could bring them no conceivable benefit. This is the scenario for *Barry Lyndon*, a novel which presents a far more compelling view of the past than the watery confection dispensed in *Esmond* or *The Virginians*.

Indeed, these two novels when compared with *Barry Lyndon*, appear not so much novels at all as elongated synopses – novels which never got themselves fully written. The way battle is described demonstrates this. Barry, giving his account of the Battle of Minden, admits that he is quite in the dark as to the overall strategy, and saw nothing of the generals or high-ranking officers. His recollections are disconnected and personal. He killed a French Colonel of the Cravates with his bayonet:

and finished off a poor little ensign, so young, slender, and small, that a blow from my pig-tail would have despatched him, I think, in place of the butt of my musket, with which I clubbed him down. I killed, besides, four more officers and men, and in the poor ensign's pocket found a purse of fourteen louis-d'or, and a silver box of sugar plums; of which the former present was very agreeable to me. If people would tell their stories of battle in this simple way, I think the cause of truth would not suffer by it. All I know of this famous fight of Minden (except from books) is told here above. The ensign's silver *bon-bon* box and his purse of gold; the livid face of the poor fellow as he fell.

These are, Barry acknowledges, 'not very dignified details', and their power to bring the past into focus depends precisely on this. They have the accidental quality of lived experience (the sugar-plums satisfying, of course, Thackeray's urge to use food imaginatively). But in *Henry Esmond*, though the hero spends much of his time on Marlborough's campaigns, the accounts of the fighting are wearisomely unspecific. We are given history-book outlines of the strategy and conduct of the generals, while the action vanishes beneath strings of platitudes and euphemisms. At Ramillies there was 'frightful slaughter' and 'dreadful carnage'; at Blenheim the French artillery did 'severe damage among our horse', the plundering English put 'all around them to fire and sword', and so forth. Nothing gets hurt, except a few abstract nouns, and the reader, far from seeing any undignified details, feels blindfolded by the decorousness of the writing. Frequently Esmond, the narrator, assumes that we shall know all he has to say already, and offers that as a reason for not bothering. Of Oudenarde 'there is little need to speak, as it hath been narrated in every Gazette'; of Malplaquet, 'the gazeteers . . . have given accounts sufficient'. This fudging clashes absurdly with Esmond's own pleas for more realistic accounts of warfare. 'Why does the stately Muse of History', he demands, leave out the 'brutal, mean and degrading' side of battle? And when he argues with Addison about his poem 'The Campaign', he maintains that literature ought to make warfare look 'hideous bloody and barbarous', as it really is.

Addison's reply – that in 'our polished days' the Muse can't 'begrime her hands' with such realistic stuff – provides the key, of course, to Esmond's stultifying narrative method. The reticence about battle is quite deliberate. From the outset he warns his readers that he is going to show a 'laudable reserve' by not dwelling on his military exploits, 'which were in truth not very different from those of a thousand other gentlemen'. The trouble with such a disclaimer is that we start wondering why we should read him at all if he hasn't the sense to realize that anyone's experience, accurately seen, is distinct and individual. And by the time we finish the book we know that our misgivings were well founded. Pursuing his ideal of eighteenth-century gentlemanliness, Thackeray sacrifices precision at every turn. Only once, in all the novel's military comings and goings, do we get a glimpse of anything as vivid as Barry Lyndon's sugar-plum ensign (it is, in fact, patently a rewriting of that episode), when Frank, whose youth and boastfulness exempt him from Esmond's reserve, describes how he killed a big mosquetaire at Ramillies, and found sixty-five Louis and a flask of Hungary-water in his holsters.

Vapid, generalized treatment of warfare persists in *The Virginians*. Thackeray explains that he hasn't the 'skill' to portray 'the details of the life military', though his story calls for them, so the reader must supply them 'out of his experience and imagination'. This process of leaving the novel unwritten extends to other areas of subject matter also. It is acknowledged, in both *Esmond* and *The Virginians*, that a lot of eighteenth-century conversation and conduct would be too coarse for Victorians to abide. 'Things were done which we would screech now to hear mentioned', admonishes Thackeray, and doesn't mention them. His is a bowdlerized eighteenth century, robbed of its humour. Lord Castlewood tells 'boisterous stories', but we don't hear them; Sampson entertains the ladies with 'lively jokes', but Thackeray assures 'fair readers of the present day' that he has no intention of outraging their 'sweet modesties' by letting us share the laugh; Madam Bernstein retails scandal about Maria, but Thackeray does not 'choose to record' it. This sort of thing contributes to the feeling that one is reading a tiresomely deficient secondhand account of a novel, rather than a novel. So does the bad language, or lack of it. Thackeray keeps reminding us that his characters are garnishing their speeches 'with many oaths needless to reprint'. And the negligent, gentlemanly tone which will not stoop to specification pervades the narrative even when Victorian delicacy would not have been in the least offended by greater detail. The banquet set before Madam Bernstein at Castlewood was 'a very good one'; Madam Esmond sends 'large and handsome presents' for General Braddock's staff; George and Harry go to Ranelagh and hear 'a piece of Mr. Handel's satisfactorily performed'. What food? What gifts? What music? Thackeray declines to be circumstantial. The feebleness of the phrasing astonishes us when we recall how the young Thackeray would particularize about just these subjects.

The excuses he gives for not writing his novel vary from chapter to chapter in *The Virginians*. He won't reproduce Theo's love-letters, because that would reveal 'tender secrets' to the 'public gaze'; he won't give an account of Theo's and Harry's farewell, because he feels 'averse to all ideas and descriptions of parting'; he can't say what happened in the row between Beatrix and Lydia, because his narrator was out of the house at the time; he won't go into the love-affair of Maria and Henry, because love-affairs in fiction are too 'stale'. He feels like throwing the whole thing up – 'I cannot write this part of the story' – and the reader would seemingly be well advised to do the same: 'The incidents of life, and love-making especially, I believe to resemble each other so much, that I am surprised, gentlemen and ladies, you read novels any more.' All this blasé disinclination for his task, though tiresome, is purposeful. Thackeray aims to convey the air of an eighteenth-century gentleman, and in his version of the period the eighteenth-century gentleman's characteristic function was lolling languidly, often with a cup of chocolate for historical colour. Lord Castlewood, for instance, appears 'languid in his bedgown' over break-fast chocolate; and Henry, intent on gentlemanliness, 'lolled at ease and sipped his chocolate' of a morning. The negligent narrative method in *The Virginians* is an attempt to transfer this well-bred inertia into a fictional mode: a literary equivalent of lolling. The effort, or lack of effort, was, of course, entirely congenial to the older Thackeray's fatigue and hauteur.

The Newcomes, written between *Esmond* and *The Virginians*, is infinitely superior to them at its best (as in the decline of Mrs. Mackenzie, or Colonel Newcome's desperate hours in the National Gallery). Set in the nineteenth century, it doesn't subject us to the lordly reticences with which Thackeray tries to authenticate his forays into the past. But his resolve to make his main characters high-souled and lovable burdens it grievously, as it does the other novels under discussion. Only when he allows some disreputable people in does the writing liven up. Thus the whole digression about the Duchesse d'Ivry and her shady entourage seems about to break off and become a different and better novel, more like *Vanity Fair*. The Duchess's cultural fads are dashingly documented – her ultra-Philippism and Catholicism and Pantheism and boredom and mischief-making; her eastern travel book, *Footprints of the Gazelles*; her craze for Dumas and Hugo and de Musset; her friendship with M. de Castillonnes, absinthe-drinking dandy son of a family of Bordeaux grocers, whose lyrics, *Les Râles d'un Asphyxié*, cause a sensation in the Latin Quarter. Fished out of the Sacré Cœur convent at sixteen to be married to a nobleman of sixty who snores over the classics in his dreary mansion off the Faubourg St. Germain, the Duchess has some claim on the reader's sympathies, and watching her at the roulette tables with her 'beautiful agate bonbonnière full of gold pieces' is a welcome relief from the company of Clive and his father. She has links with Becky. Her little daughter pathetically avers that mamma kisses her only in public, as does Rawdon; and her gambling friends, she maliciously informs Lady Kew, used to hang around at Gaunt House when *la sémillante Becki* was queening it there. However, Thackeray has renounced the demi-monde, and after this glance at its attractions he bundles the Duchess and her cronies out of the novel.

Of the characters with a more permanent stake in the book, Clive and his young pals, who are supposed to provide the gaiety and animation, prolong the unhappy example set by Pen and Warrington in *Pendennis* – indeed, Pen and Warrington both turn up here, to join jovial Fred Bayham and the other wags. Clean-limbed young fellows, their spirits high and their hearts in the right place, they are exceedingly shallowly conceived and Thackeray's patent infatuation with them rapidly becomes wearing. Clive's laughter 'cheered one like wine', we are advised; his 'gaiety and frankness' were 'delightful and winning'. It is hard to believe. Clive's manner of expressing himself, particularly about art, makes the reader wince – 'Wasn't Reynolds a clipper! that's all! and wasn't Rubens a brick!' It is a crashingly unsuccessful attempt, on the part of an ageing novelist, to simulate the speech of the young. And the values Clive gives voice to in his art criticism are not ones from which Thackeray maintains an ironic distance, but closely resemble his own. When Clive enthuses about Vandyke, 'I'm sure he must have been as fine a gentleman as any he painted', he is prizing exactly the kind of thing his creator prized, at any rate in his dotage. 'You see he must have been at a good public school', pronounced Thackeray of John Leech's drawings in a *Quarterly Review* article of 1854. He uses Clive as an agent for promulgating other of his snobbish and sectional prejudices. Clive's Britishness receives emphasis. Being a 'well-bred English lad', we learn, he has a purer mind than the youth of other nations. He is meant to illustrate, too, the entirely delightful results of the unequal distribution of wealth. 'His money was plenty, and he spent it like a young king', cheers Thackeray; 'few sights are more pleasant' than to watch a 'manly English youth' exercising his 'noble privilege to be happy' in this fashion. 'Why', we are asked, 'should not this young fellow wear smart clothes' and 'take his pleasure'? The answer, we feel, might well have something to do with the Spitalfields mechanic. But the level of Thackeray's cogitations does not really merit an answer. Vapouring on about the days of his youth, he coddles himself in a sentimental conservatism which, only ten years back, he would have been the first to get his knife into. He sighs for the high old times when young noblemen squandered fortunes on horses, and kept alive the 'fine manly old English custom' of knocking down their social inferiors.

He wags his head over the present spirit of the age which tends to 'equalise all ranks'.

A concomitant of this is his scarcely-disguised contempt for intellectual and artistic achievement. We are left in no doubt that Clive, though a failure as an artist, is a finer fellow and a truer gentleman than those who succeed. Clive's studio companions are likeable enough, but low, and could do with more soap. Thackeray seems unable to respond to anything but the superficialities of the art student's life – the long hair, velvet waistcoats, 'innocent gaiety' and 'jovial suppers on threadbare cloths'. It is a hackneyed, bloodless and patronizing picture. That the artist is engaged on anything serious or passionate never, so far as we can tell, enters his head. J. J., allegedly the genius of the bunch, is a footling milksop, who succeeds by dint of a minute accuracy – reproducing 'every leaf' in the trees he paints. There can be few less credible portraits of genius. As for the intelligentsia who assemble in Mrs. Newcome's Bryanstone Square drawing-room, they include, we are told, an eminent oboe-player, a Royal Academician, a celebrated Italian baritone, two noted geologists from Germany, a political economist, and other representatives of the learned professions. But they are introduced into the novel only to be scoffed at for wearing beards, or eating ice-creams quickly, or having funny names. We do not hear their conversation, and feel pretty sure that Thackeray would not have the necessary resources to present it. He counts on his readers despising these people because they have brains and talents, and because they do not move in the society to which Clive and his friends have the entrée.

The Colonel, of course, is another of the book's high-souled drawbacks. He was deliberately manufactured as an improvement on life, so Thackeray could only blame himself for the reader's impression that the Colonel has somehow lost his stuffing, and been artificially stiffened to remedy it. Thackeray based him chiefly on his stepfather, but explained that it was necessary to 'angelicize' Major Carmichael-Smyth for the purpose. His private opinion of the Major was that he was a 'simple honest old bore' who weighed down his wife with his 'dulness' and kept whatever company he was in 'mum and dismal'. 'I don't want to live to be 76, if 76 is to be no better fun than that', he remarked on contemplating Colonel Newcome's prototype. The reduced circumstances in which the Carmichael-Smyths lived, and their humble circle of friends, aroused Thackeray's scorn: 'the undignified dignity, the twopenny toadies, the twaddling society'. Actually, from what one hears of the Major, Thackeray's fictional portrait seems to have left out some of his more appealing traits, in the interests of dignity. He was an extreme radical, like his wife, and an amateur inventor, with a room stuffed full of chemical junk, and an unhealthy interest in medicaments. A design for a steam carriage was among his projects. He lived in Paris, and greatly enjoyed annoying the French, calling his dog 'Waterloo' so that he could have a justification for shouting that word when out walking. None of this varied and suggestive material gets into the Colonel, who bored even Thackeray in the end. He was glad to get rid of him for a while by packing him off to India. 'The story seems to breathe freely after the departure of the dear old boy', he confessed in a letter.

However, the dear old boy had to come back, and Thackeray arranged for him a touching end among the Poor Brothers of the Charterhouse. In this role the Colonel behaves humbly and gratefully, and retains his dignity, which distinguishes him from a Poor Brother we have heard of earlier, an ex-butler of Lord Todmorden, who continually grumbles about his food, the number of chapels he has to attend, the gown he has to wear and the Master's treatment of him, and generally shows himself an 'odious, querulous, graceless, stupid and snuffy old man'. The difference is class. The Colonel, 'a gentleman, every inch of him', feels thankful for what he gets, while the lower orders whine and agitate. Thackeray was contributing to a current controversy. Dickens's magazine, *Household Words*, had devoted a piece to the Charterhouse charity in 1852, remarking that it seemed to be run for the benefit of the officials who administered it. The Master had £800 a year and a sumptuous residence of thirty-three rooms, and his colleagues were provided for on a similar scale, while the ostensible beneficiaries, the eighty Poor Brothers, received a bare cell each and £25 a year, and had to tolerate humiliating regulations, inadequate nursing, scanty food, and the evident contempt of the gentlemen who were so handsomely paid for looking after them. The appearance of *The Newcomes* aroused *Household Words*, in December 1855, to a fuller treatment of the subject.

The charity had been founded, it pointed out, in the seventeenth century, to provide free education for forty poor boys and sustenance for eighty old gentlemen. Though a lay foundation, it had been taken over by the Church, and turned into a school for the sons of the rich. Boys were nominated to the forty free places from the great families of the land. It was thus a perfectly respectable school, but had 'cast out, as uncongenial, the element of charity'. The case of the Poor Brothers was different and worse. They were frankly regarded as an encumbrance, and housed in cramped, verminous accommodation, less well-appointed than that available in gaols. When the officials were not in residence, no meals were cooked for the Poor Brothers. Any complaints were dictatorially punished. One Poor Brother had been expelled for the offence of requesting that the daily services, which Poor Brothers had to attend, might be conducted reverently, rather than scrambled through, as was the custom. Contrary to the terms of the charity, the Master, the Rev. W. H. Hale, was a pluralist, Vicar of St. Giles's, Cripplegate, Archdeacon of London, and Resident Canon of St. Paul's, earning in all about £4,000 a year. His salary as Master had increased sixteen-fold since the foundation of the Hospital; the Poor Brother's stipend, four-fold. When the Poor Brothers drew up a statement of their grievances for the Governors, the Master replied with a pamphlet in which he was sarcastic about their claims to be treated as gentlemen, and dismissed their other points unargued. Thackeray, *Household Words* concluded, had presented in Colonel Newcome 'what a Poor Brother of Charterhouse should be in theory, and is in fiction'.

It seems pretty clear that Thackeray was, in reality, under no illusions about the matter, and that the conclusion of his novel attributes dignity and honourable poverty to a set of men that he knew to be generally rather scoffed at, and scoffed at himself. At Charterhouse the Poor Brothers were known as 'Codds' (short for Codgers), and J. W. Irvine recalls that when he was a boy there in 1855 Thackeray came up to him one day and asked 'Do you know any of the old Codds?', adding, with a dig in the ribs, 'Colonel Newcome is going to be a Codd'. As a real Codd he might have made an intriguing fictional subject, but Thackeray, trying to sound as if he would never dream of digging anyone in the ribs, converts the end of his book into cant. His drift into complacency can be measured if we compare Charterhouse in *Pendennis* with Charterhouse in *Vanity Fair*. It is at Charterhouse ('Whitefriars') that Lord Steyne procures a place for young Rawdon Crawley, so that the coast may be clear for that munificent nobleman to debauch Rawdon's mother. Thackeray supplies an acid sketch of the institution's history. Originally a Cistercian Convent, it was, he recounts, seized upon by Henry VIII, 'the Defender of the Faith', who hanged and tortured those of the monks 'who could not accommodate themselves to the pace of his reform'. Transformed to a school, it was 'originally intended for the sons of poor and deserving clerics and laics', but the opportunity of getting an education for nothing proved too much for the greed of its noble governors, who accordingly, 'with an enlarged and rather capricious benevolence', sent their own sons, and those of their relations and sycophants, 'to profit by the chance'.

From *Pendennis* on, then, we may say that Thackeray acceded to a wish, his public's and his own, to make people appear finer, nobler, purer than reality. When he borrowed them from life, he spruced them up first, brushing off quirks and imperfections. He viewed social institutions, especially British ones, through a rosy lens. The poor, it appeared, had nothing to complain about; the rich, little to disquiet their consciences. By dint of suppression and misrepresentation, he squeezed himself into the guise of a kindly, decorous, warm-hearted nineteenth-century gentleman, basking in memories of youthful sunshine, or alternatively a kindly, decorous, warm-hearted eighteenth-century gentleman, similarly basking, but in period costume. If we turn, now, to two representative early works, the *Journey from Cornhill to Grand Cairo* and *The Irish Sketch-Book*, we shall see how much of Thackeray this transmogrification killed.

What strikes you first about the *Journey* is its honesty. Thackeray eschews rapture, and gives the renowned tourist-attractions a cool look.

I do not think much of the mosque of St. Sophia. I suppose I lack appreciation. We will let it go at that. It is the rustiest old barn in heathendom . . . a colossal church, thirteen or fourteen hundred years old, and unsightly enough to be very, very much older. Its immense dome is said to be more wonderful than St. Peter's, but its dirt is much more wonderful than its dome, though they never mention it.

Thackeray? No, Mark Twain in *The Innocents Abroad*. But the unbuttoned self-confidence might easily be mistaken for the Thackeray of the *Journey*, and reading either book it's constantly a temptation to flick across to the other, for the bits where their paths cross, to see how Twain's impressions, twenty years later, compare. Thackeray lacks Twain's American insularities ('Como? Pshaw! See Lake Tahoe'), but he equals him in freshness and disrespect. He is frankly bored by the interminable churches and palaces, all more or less large and splendid, and adorned with more or less large and splendid allegories in distemper, which it is the tourist's job to trudge through. When he finds one locked, it's a relief. In Lisbon, for instance:

First we went to the Church of St. Roch, to see a famous piece of mosaic-work there. It is a famous work of art, and was bought by I don't know what king for I don't know how much money. All this information may be perfectly relied on, though the fact is, we did not see the mosaic-work: the sacristan, who guards it, was yet in bed; and it was veiled from our eyes in a side-chapel by great dirty damask curtains, which could not be removed, except when the sacristan's toilet was done, and at the price of a dollar. So we were spared this mosaic exhibition; and I think I always feel relieved when such an event occurs. I feel I have done my duty in coming.

While ostensibly talking about what he didn't see, Thackeray conveys the fusty, ornate atmosphere of the church, and the pace of Lisbon life, much more vividly than the minutest account of the coloured pieces of marble behind the curtain could have done. The details which make you feel what it was like to be there accrue casually, round the edges of what seems the main subject. Likewise with the Roman aqueduct that

Thackeray missed seeing outside Lisbon. 'A dismal excursion of three hours' over 'diabolical clattering roads, up and down dreary parched hills, on which grew a few grey olive trees and many aloes', brings the party to a locked gate, where they are informed that the aqueduct has been shut because a local brigand had made a practice of pitching unwary travellers from its arches into the ravines below, and robbing their corpses. So they return to the ship. The expedition has drawn a blank, and the reader never gets even a secondhand report on the aqueduct. But he picks up by the way a graphic impression of the land's wildness and desolation, its colours, contours, terrain and vegetation, without Thackeray's seeming to have pointed them out at all.

Even when the tourist-attractions aren't actually closed he mostly finds them disappointing, and instead of giving a proper account of them wanders off into private grumbles. Athens, for instance, prompts him to a disparaging assessment of classical literature (which people only pretend to like, he suspects, because it's 'proper and respectable'), and to some jibes at the expense of Byron and Greek liberty. 'Think of "filling high a cup of Samian wine"; small beer is nectar compared to it, and Byron himself always drank gin.' But while the antiquities are skimped, things a guide-book would leave out – the way the light falls, colours, incidentals, four Greeks 'lolling over greasy cards', women with skin like 'coarse whitey-brown paper' – get caught up in his thought and come out bright and sharp. You live the journey through Thackeray's mind and sensations. What he personally touches, tastes, notices, bulks much larger than the public monuments. The Turkish bath he took in Constantinople occupies ten times as much space as the Acropolis (though he quite liked the Acropolis), and well over a hundred times the space allocated to St. Sophia, which, unlike Twain, he didn't get inside as it was shut for Ramadan. He is adept at observing what gives foreign places their foreignness – always mundane things, like the coins in Jaffa 'made of a greasy pewtery sort of tin', which the natives seemed so curiously fierce to possess. Eyes catch his attention. In Turkey the Negro children are 'queer little things in night-gowns of yellow dimity, with great flowers, and pink, red, or yellow shawls, with great eyes glistening underneath'; in Alexandria he sees children sitting in doorways, their eyes completely closed up with a 'green sickening sore, and the flies feeding on them'; in the Arab quarter of Cairo he finds an old friend who has gone oriental, and has a courtyard full of 'camels, gazelles, and other beautiful-eyed things'. They dine together, of course, off 'delicate cucumbers stuffed with forced-meats' and 'yellow smoking pilaffs' and 'ruby pomegranates, pulled to pieces, deliciously cool', and drink water freshened in 'porous little pots of grey clay'.

This intent response to food, drink and their accessories – the glimpse of the pomegranate's glistering inside, the feel of the little clay pot – spreads, as we might expect, through the whole work. It forms a rich reservoir of sweetnesses, stickinesses, toothsome exoticisms, to flood and captivate the reader's senses. But more than that, it rivets the work to the everyday. We keep flopping into a café to escape the palaces and artworks, and find there the real life of the country unspectacularly going on. This, for instance, from Thackeray's stay in Smyrna:

There was, under the plane-trees, a little coffee-house, shaded by a trellis-work, covered over with a vine, and ornamented with many rows of shining pots and water-pipes, for which there was no use at noonday now, in the time of Ramazan. Hard by the coffee-house was a garden and a bubbling marble fountain, and over the stream was a broken summer-house, to which the amateurs may ascend, for the purpose of examining the river; and all round the plane-trees plenty of stools for those who were inclined to sit and drink sweet thick coffee, or cool lemonade made of fresh green citrons. The master of the house, dressed in a white turban and light blue pelisse, lolled under the coffee-house awning; the slave in white with a crimson striped jacket, his face as black as ebony, brought us pipes and lemonade again, and returned to his station at the coffee-house, where he curled his black legs together, and began singing out of his flat nose to the thrumming of a long guitar with wire strings. The instrument was not bigger than a soup-ladle, with a long straight handle, but its music pleased the performer; for his eyes rolled shining about, and his head wagged, and he grinned with an innocent intensity of enjoyment that did one good to look at. And there was a friend to share his pleasure: a Turk dressed in scarlet, and covered all over with daggers and pistols, sat leaning forward on his little stool, rocking about, and grinning quite as eagerly as the black minstrel. As he sang and we listened, figures of women bearing pitchers went passing over the Roman bridge, which we saw between the large trunks of the planes; or grey forms of camels were seen stalking across it, the string preceded by the little donkey, who is always here their long-eared conductor.

It is a whole quality of life that this passage, in its quiet way, manages to inveigle the reader into appreciating; a humble but dignified leisureliness, skilled at making elegant pleasures out of the materials that come to hand, like the shade of trees and running water. The style, objective, unemphatic, but treasuring ordinary things such as empty pots and the colour of clothes, precisely fits the intent. At the same time, a good deal of information about the Turkish character and Turkish society is obliquely conveyed: slavery, strict religious observance, the subjugation of women, male ferocity combined with a love of sweet things, industrial backwardness (the Roman bridge still in use), inertia. Baldly put, they sound an uninviting lot: but Thackeray,

avoiding such peremptory formulations, blends the elements back
into a living scene, a civilization.

That the insistence on food in the *Journey* amounts to a remedial
assertion about the priorities usually considered seemly in life and
guide-books emerges particularly from Thackeray's visit to the
pyramids. The party travels up the Nile in a steamer, and gathers on
the deck before dawn, eager to catch its first glimpse of the mighty
edifices. And when the pyramids – or three of them – come into sight,
Thackeray finds that all he can think is – 'two big ones and a little one':

Several of us tried to be impressed; but breakfast supervening, a rush
was made at the coffee and cold pies, and the sentiment of awe was
lost in the scramble for victuals.

Practically all we hear of the pyramids is what the party had for breakfast. Neither he nor anyone else, Thackeray is vexed to discover, is at
all moved by the 'exaggeration of bricks' lying 'rosy and solemn in
the distance'. As an account of a visit to the pyramids, this might seem
seriously deficient, but it is really quite the opposite. It yields a
brilliant impression, not of the pyramids, but of seeing the pyramids –
so vast, simple and dead that the human spectator is at a loss to know
how to respond, and finds himself scuttling, almost defensively, for
food. Thackeray leaves a pyramid-shaped blank in the reader's mind,
but the blank is more expressive than any routine account of a pyramid.

It seems worth clarifying a few of the methods of the *Journey* in this
way, because Thackeray has been suspected of mindless debunking
in it. Its honesty is in fact the product of a mind unusually alive, and
wary of received opinion. The national and cultural prejudices that the
later Thackeray falls over himself to condone, are here questioned. He
describes Gibraltar, for instance, as a 'great British depot for smuggling
goods into the Peninsula', and, while giving due credit to the gallantry
of its capture, insists that it is a piece of land 'seized out of the hands of
its natural owners' – as much a transgression of justice as it would be
for the Spaniards to establish themselves off Land's End and fortify
St. Michael's Mount. Of the Crusades, he admits that his sympathies
have always been with the Turks:

They seem to me the best Christians of the two; more humane, less
brutally presumptuous about their own merits, and more generous in
esteeming their neighbours. As far as I can get at the authentic story,
Saladin is a pearl of refinement compared to the brutal beef-eating
Richard – about whom Sir Walter Scott has led all the world astray.

True, Thackeray is trying to annoy, but at least it comes from a mind
prepared to think and doubt, which distinguishes it from the stale
religiosities of the later novels.

The honesty in *The Irish Sketch-Book* has a less immediately appealing ring, but is honesty for all that. Thackeray was in Ireland in 1842. Between 1831 and 1842 six potato harvests had failed. In the next ten years hundreds of thousands of people died of starvation, and the exodus to America began. Thackeray was on the brink of the Great Hunger. He arrived in Dublin in June: the worst time. June, July and August were always the famine months, because one crop was eaten, and the next not ready to dig. He saw beggary and wretchedness all around. His reactions were natural and unforgivable, and no one who has spent any time in a country swarming with beggars will be surprised by them. The 'hideous, leering flattery' on every hand filled him with contempt and rage. He felt disgust when he managed to resist giving money, and resentment when he did not. The people couldn't, he told himself, be as destitute as they seemed, and if they were they had no right to be. He had, so he says, not the 'slightest sentiment of compassion':

They come crawling round you with lying prayers and loathsome compliments that make the stomach turn; they do not even disguise that they are lies; for, refuse them, and the wretches turn off with a laugh and a joke, a miserable grinning cynicism.

Had he thought, he might have recognized in the laugh a spurned human creature trying to retrieve its dignity. But fury at the way he is being treated obliterates thought, and that enhances the work's genuineness. His unreasonableness is almost comic at times. Outside Carlow cathedral a 'wretched tottering hag' starts 'whining the Lord's Prayer as a proof of her sincerity', but forgets it half-way through, which leaves Thackeray 'thoroughly disgusted'. Withholding charity on such grounds has a rich satiric potential that, on cooler consideration, he could hardly have missed. But he records his immediate responses faithfully, and makes no retrospective claim to Christian feeling. In the market at Limerick , he asks the price of pears, and is outraged to be told that they are twopence each, when he can see 'two little ragged beggars standing by, who were munching the fruit'. Evidently there is one price for him and another for the children; and this is all that registers with him. That the children and the saleswoman face starvation, and he doesn't, isn't a factor his indignation can take into account. He is incensed when beggars cringe, and when they don't. The 'wheedling servility' of the women in Limerick makes him want to hit them, but he thinks it monstrous when the youths in Ballintoy start calling for money 'in a fierce manner, as if it was their right'. The endless physical and mental deformity sickens him:

the epileptic idiot holding piteously out his empty tin snuff-box; the brutal idiot, in an old soldier's coat, proffering his money-box and grinning and clattering the single halfpenny it contained; the old man with no eyelids, calling upon you in the name of the Lord; the woman with a child at her hideous, wrinkled breast.

He feels it 'a shame' that such horrible figures should be 'allowed to appear in public'. He gives one 'hideous wretch', his face 'half eaten away with disease', money to go away, and is scandalized when the sufferer declines to go. In the beauty spots the beggars spoil the scenery. Even at the Giant's Causeway he finds two, 'howling for money', and 'no oaths, threats, entreaties would drive these vermin away'. Thackeray speculates that, if the Irish are to attract tourism, they will have to post policemen on the rocks to discourage beggars or 'fling them in the water when they appear'.

To condemn his revulsion would be footling and hypocritical. What else could he do but feel repelled? The poverty was quite beyond his power to relieve. If he gave what money he had away, he and his family were as likely to starve, in early nineteenth-century England, as the Irish. The beggars did not regard him as a human being, but as a prey. Their every action degraded him. No doubt his anger was sometimes unreasonable, but it gave a vent to his feelings, and what good would remaining reasonable have done? The vibrant hatred has an irresistible sincerity, which no amount of pious lament could have supplied. Its directness is a great deal more decent and respectable than the smug falsities about the comfort of the poor that we have seen the late Thackeray purveying. As with Lawrence's outbursts against the filthy peasants in *Sea and Sardinia*, the fury is felt by the reader as a liberating thing, eclipsing morals. Lawrence, cursing the villagers as 'dirty, disgusting swine' because, having no indoor toilets, they are obliged to use the fields, is no more rational than Thackeray. 'Quite unreasonable', he admits, but he is 'towering with fury' all the same. Thackeray makes it equally clear that he sees how intolerant and unjust he is being in his outcries about the beggars. Everywhere one goes, he remarks, 'ragged amateurs' start from the bushes, offering to carry your umbrella, or perform any other service:

And all the while they look wistfully in your face, saying, 'Give me sixpence!' as clear as looks can speak. The unconscionable rogues! how dare they, for the sake of a little starvation or so, interrupt gentlefolks in their pleasure!

The sarcasm is now directed against himself, and the issue is at last humanely seen; though that doesn't discredit the former fury, or Thackeray's honesty in recording it.

His faculty for observing himself impartially, as here, provided the foundation for what people refer to as his cynicism – that is, of all that is most pungent and healthful in his work. His letters often show him hacking his own motives and behaviour to pieces, as when he writes to his mother, in 1839, about a friend called Salt who was dying of consumption:

would you believe it? the monster and his family are starving and have the impertinence to send to us every second day, the impolite rogues, what do they mean by plaguing a gentleman thus? I thought myself a very fine fellow tother day (Friday) when I gave him a shoulder of mutton minus three slices, a loaf and a bottle of wine and a brace of shillings – but now am most cruelly plagued by the poor wretch's importunity, and begin gravely to say 'We can't be always giving'. Heavens what a lie! If I fancy a bottle of wine or a dinner at the Garrick I can always find a reason why it should be not only pardonable but necessary – and so the world wags.

Impatience, and impatience at his own impatience, mingle cleansingly here. Self-criticism of the most unsparing sort (what could be more honest than to admit that you are meanly treating a dying friend?), yields him, as the last words indicate, a firmer conviction of other people's hypocrisies. It was always so. He didn't like himself over-much; that's partly what makes him so likeable. He felt that his enemies were very probably justified: 'I often think', he remarked, that 'the party who hates you, and he who loves you, are both right.' At the same time, he was too balanced to indulge in self-abasement. He didn't imagine, or pretend, that he was much worse than most. Hence his confidence in reading the nastiness he detected in himself into his observation of others:

When I hear of bad luck happening to people, I am glad, that's the fact, and I am sure that the generosity or kindness with which one endeavours sometimes to relieve a man that has fallen into misfortune is often the result of one's personal good spirits and gratification at the contrast between the sufferer and oneself.

Plainly Thackeray is admitting to nothing singular. A consideration of the kind of stuff that people daily pay to read in newspapers will quickly inform one that pleasure at others' hurt is a universal human trait, and that one need not be especially ashamed, therefore, at always having felt it oneself. The stimulating factor in Thackeray's thinking is that he presses on from a confession of his own *schadenfreude* to a general suspiciousness about philanthropy.

The epigrams which result from such insights, and which are re-current up to and in *Vanity Fair* (but hurriedly switched off after-wards), often take money as their subject, since Thackeray, having lost a lot of it, was an expert on the way it altered people's regard for you. 'To part with money is a sacrifice beyond almost all men endowed with a sense of order'; 'What love, what fidelity, what constancy is there equal to that of a nurse with good wages?'; 'What a dignity it gives an old lady, that balance at the banker's.' These are typical. Like all clever, ill-natured things, they instantly appeal. But the pleasure they give worries some critics. Don't they, it is asked, encourage a slick contempt for our fellow humans? Certainly Thackeray is capable of contempt, as any honest person must be. In *The Artists*, for instance, he argues contemptuously that vanity, the commonest human failing, is an 'inestimable blessing' in its way, for the world is full of half-wits, especially half-witted votaries of the arts, and if some malevolent spirit were to take the vanity from their brains and replace it with self-knowledge, they would walk off Waterloo Bridge in despair. Vanity prevents the suicide rate from getting out of control, and it follows that we should thank God for it.

But the epigrams are seldom just expressions of contempt. He saw himself, and through himself others, too fully for this. The one about men endowed with a sense of order being unable to part with money, for example (applied in *Vanity Fair* to Pitt Crawley), sounds like a sneer at mean, conventional people, but isn't. Thackeray goes on to question the motives behind generosity, and suggests that it is a form of thriftlessness, 'a lazy delight in spending'. The thriftless man gives five pounds to a beggar, and thinks well of himself, though he is merely indulging his weakness. The thrifty man drives beggars away, and denies himself every pleasure – including the pleasure of giving to beggars – so that he may live within his means and ruin no one by his debts. He is 'good, wise and just'. Seen in this way, open-handedness is more selfish than meanness. The epigram Thackeray started out from has turned on its head. His own experience of driving beggars away no doubt aided thoughtfulness here. It is another instance of his fruitful self-scrutiny. So is his crack about a nurse with good wages. He really means it: a well-paid nurse *is* more faithful even than near relations. He proceeds to a serious consideration of what nurses have to put up with, and points out what hypocrites we are when we complain about them, since we would not stick their jobs ourselves at any price: 'What man's love is there that would stand a year's nursing of the object of his affection? Whereas a nurse will stand by you for ten pounds a quarter, and we think her too highly paid.' Thackeray knew what he was talking about. He had tried nursing his wife, and soon got sick of her drooling inanities. And the third of the quoted epigrams, about the dignity a bank balance gives to an old lady – here, too, Thackeray did not exclude himself, or us, from the implied criticism. He knew how much money meant to him; and he challenged his readers to deny its influence on them. Which of them, he asked, if told that the man seated next to them at dinner had half a million, would not regard him with increased interest?

It was claimed at the start of this chapter that the gift for seeing himself objectively, which is the ground of his satire, never died out, but survived to the end of his career. So it did, spasmodically. The letters are the best place to look for it. In them, he picks himself to pieces with perfect candour, always ready to admit that he is 'just as great a humbug' as his neighbours. But the letters are not honesty's only repository. Even in such a self-indulgent setting as the *Roundabout Papers* can be found, stranded among the banter and garrulity, pieces like *On a Pear Tree*, which take an ironic look at the reactions of a respectable, property-owning citizen, as observed by the late Thackeray in himself. The essay reports the theft of some pears from his London garden, and his subsequent feelings. He addresses dire warnings to the unknown marauders, and plans fearsome counter-measures. Next time they will find themselves impaled in a ditch, or writhing in a man-trap, or blasted from the tree by gunfire. He imagines the newspaper headlines that will proclaim his successful coup: 'Daring Attempt at Burglary – Heroic Victory over the Villains'. He muses on the unfairness of life: if he himself were to rob an orchard a guard-dog would be sure to fasten upon him before he had laid hands on the smallest pippin; yet other folk carry off whole bushels of fruit with impunity. He finds that he suspects everyone he sees of complicity in the theft, and refrains from going to church because he knows that he would be wondering all the time which of the worshippers came over his wall. His peace of mind is gone. The world is a poisoned place:

How can I hold out the hand of friendship in this condition, when my first impression is, 'My good sir, I strongly suspect that you were up my pear-tree last night?' It is a dreadful state of mind. The core is black; the death-stricken fruit drops on the bough, and a great worm is within – fattening, and festering, and wriggling!

The self-deriding hyperbole puts the affair into perspective. At the same time an extremely accurate account has been presented of the agitation which a robbed person feels: agitation dependent on his not being able to get his loss into what an unrobbed person would call perspective. Self-inspection yields Thackeray a balanced view of unbalance.

What he asked in general wasn't that people should be virtuous – given human make-up that was hardly feasible – but that they should be conscious: see themselves, and see through themselves. Being conscious, in his terminology, was the opposite of self-confidence and self-esteem. People who thought the world would be poorer for their leaving it, or who imagined that they were engaged on enterprises of momentous significance, were in particular need of a dose of consciousness. Being conscious meant not being satisfied or happy. *Vanity Fair* was planned as an aid to consciousness: 'I want to leave everybody',

Thackeray explained to Robert Bell, 'dissatisfied and unhappy at the end of the story. We ought all to be with our own and all other stories.' Consciousness was, he realized, extremely rare among human beings – perhaps non-existent. 'Who is conscious?' he inquired, despairingly, in a letter to his mother. The occasion of this question was Mary Graham, Thackeray's mother's niece, who had been brought up at Ottery St. Mary almost as his sister – Laura to his Pendennis. Unlike Pendennis, though, Thackeray heartily detested his Laura, holding that she was 'crazy with vanity', and Mary seems to have felt the same about him. When they met, they were effusively affectionate: 'How we did kiss and smack away at each other!' Thackeray recalls grimly, 'But what a lie it was!' And typically it occurs to him that his dislike of her may be rooted in his own pride: 'Perhaps I am trying to run her down because of the £500.' The £500 was a loan Mary had obliged him with back in 1841, when things were going badly. Intent on being conscious, he analyses himself, and finds that this good turn has left him with a burden of resentment which he is impelled to ease by vilifying his benefactress. Self-knowledge of this sort persuaded him that benefits were generally difficult to forgive – more difficult than injuries – and he expresses this belief in, for instance, *Vanity Fair*, when at old Sedley's bankruptcy his most determined and obstinate opponent turns out to be John Osborne, whom Sedley had set up in life and generously aided, thus supplying ample motive, Thackeray insists, for Osborne's rancour:

When one man has been under very remarkable obligations to another, with whom he subsequently quarrels, a common sense of decency, as it were, makes of the former a much severer enemy than a mere stranger would be. To account for your own hardheartedness and ingratitude in such a case, you are bound to prove the other party's crime. . . . From a mere sense of consistency, a persecutor is bound to show that the fallen man is a villain – otherwise he, the persecutor, is a wretch himself.

Insights of this quality, as limpid as water and as hard as granite, form one of the foundations of *Vanity Fair*'s greatness, and they are the harvest of, in Thackeray's terms, consciousness.

If we ask what went wrong with Thackeray after *Vanity Fair*, then, the relaxation of his effort to be conscious must come high on the list of answers. In private, the effort intermittently continued, but he kept it from his books. Their job was now to make people complacent, not dissatisfied or unhappy. The leading characters acquire noble hearts, which pump high-grade syrup around their frames. Meanwhile the vituperative honesty of *The Irish Sketch-Book*, and the scorn for uplift which animates the *Journey from Cornhill to Grand Cairo*, are smuggled out through a side door. 'I have done my best to work as an artist telling the truth', wrote Thackeray in September 1847, as he looked back over his career to date, 'and, morbidly perhaps, eschewing humbug.' He could not have said that ten years later.

Vanity Fair

One of the aims of the foregoing chapters has been to show that *Vanity Fair* is not as splendidly isolated from the rest of Thackeray's output as it might seem. Imaginative obsessions, ways of looking, principles of style knit it in with his previous and (less securely) with his subsequent writing. For all that, it is incomparably greater than anything else in his *œuvre*, and a study of Thackeray can't shirk the task of trying to expound that greatness – though, as with all supreme works of literature, the critical effort is bound to look bald and halting beside the original. By any sane reckoning, it is one of the major works of art of the nineteenth century; and it is the only English novel of that period which, in theme and range, challenges comparison with *War and Peace*. The pros and cons of the Tolstoyan parallel will be discussed a bit later, but first we need to decide what kind of mastery lies at the heart of the novel, and propels it so spectacularly beyond the things Thackeray occupied himself with before and after.

When one sets about answering this question, two factors at once stand out: the characterization, and the massive apparatus of authentication, the bombardment of specification and realistic allusion, against and within which the characters move. The success of the characterization is the biggest surprise for a reader of Thackeray's previous stuff, since in that, despite the imaginative and ironic brilliance, the characters are usually too scathingly or condescendingly depicted to leave a deep impression. Thackeray moves them around, but he doesn't seem involved in them. In *Vanity Fair*, he soon found himself regarding them as fellow human beings. 'How curious it is! I believe perfectly in all those people, and feel quite an interest in the Inn in which they lived', he wrote in a letter of 1848, announcing that he was off to see the Hôtel de la Terrasse in Brussels, where Becky had stayed. Consequently, judging even quite minor figures in *Vanity Fair* is like judging real people. Qualifications, mitigations, counter-arguments quickly arise. The solid ground of condemnation or approval dissolves. We are forced to weigh circumstances, and to distrust our own standpoint. There is scarcely a one-sided character in the book. Thackeray compounds this effect by occasionally making firm pronouncements about his personages which we, because of what he shows us elsewhere, are inclined to dispute. His own attitude towards his creatures was not stationary but organic, growing as the book grew.

This is most evident in the basic contrast between Amelia and Becky. At the start, when the two are taking their leave of Miss Pinkerton's academy, the difference between them is perfectly clear-cut and dull. Becky 'never was known to have done a good action in behalf of anybody', while Amelia is 'one of the best and dearest creatures that ever lived' (or so it stood in the first edition: later Thackeray modified it to make Amelia just 'a dear little creature'). There's no denying that the tritely moralistic segment of Thackeray's personality which initiated this contrast continues to put its oar in from time to time throughout the book, reminding us how wicked Becky is, and what a bad effect it has on her complexion. She looks 'haggard, weary and terrible' in unguarded moments, we're notified. Dobbin, here employed by Thackeray as a sort of spiritual Geiger-counter, shrinks from her with 'instinctive repulsion'. But the more we learn about her, the more inclined we are to defend her against her creator's primmer assessments. Her sin, simply, is that she does everything in her power to escape from poverty, and from the contempt that, she has found, it brings. As a penniless girl at Miss Pinkerton's, employed to teach French in exchange for her keep and a few guineas a year, she has to put up with constant slights and humiliations. She looks stunted beside the well-fed lady pupils, and is treated as a natural inferior, though in intellect, courage and will to learn she far excels them. Already an expert linguist, she turns herself by hard work into a highly competent musician, only to be required by Miss Pinkerton to employ her new talent in giving unpaid piano lessons to the junior pupils. Commendably, Becky refuses. As a mere employee she is not thought a fit recipient of the two-and-ninepenny dictionary handed out as a standard leaving present to the other girls, and when well-meaning Miss Jemima makes the insult more apparent by clumsily thrusting a copy upon her at the last moment, Becky understandably flings it out of the window. When she goes home with Amelia, her tattered luggage attracts the grins and sneers of the Sedley servants. Mrs. Blenkinsop, the housekeeper, despises her because she is poor and educated. ' "I don't trust them governesses, Pinner", she remarked to the maid. "They give themselves the hairs and hupstarts of ladies, and their wages is no better than you nor me." ' The groom who accompanies her when she goes to take up her new job at Sir Pitt's house insults her about the old dresses which, as all the servants know, Amelia has looked out for her on parting: 'I hope you've forgot nothink? Miss 'Melia's gownds – have you got them – as the lady's-maid was to have 'ad?' Encouraged thus, it is no wonder that Becky learns to conceal her feelings, and commits herself to a course of self-interest and ambition. Generosity and honesty are, as she sees it, luxuries which only the rich can afford. Watching the nice, privileged ladies at Queen's Crawley, she observes that she too could be virtuous and dole out gifts to the poor if only she had £5,000 a year. 'And', comments Thackeray:

who knows but Rebecca was right in her speculations – and that it was only a question of money and fortune which made the difference between her and an honest woman? If you take temptations into account, who is to say that he is better than his neighbour? A comfortable career of prosperity, if it does not make people honest, at least keeps them so. An alderman coming from a turtle feast will not step out of his carriage to steal a leg of mutton; but put him to starve, and see if he will not purloin a loaf.

This account of the narrow divide between themselves and criminals caused some indignation among Victorian readers, but Thackeray stuck to his guns. To G. H. Lewes who, writing in the *Chronicle*, had deplored the suggestion that vice grew from poverty, he replied stoutly, 'If Becky had had 5,000 a year I have no doubt in my mind that she would have been respectable.' That he found Becky's opinion convincing is not really a surprise, for he had simply put his own view of the matter into her mouth. When he was experiencing poverty himself for the first time in 1839, he had written to his mother about a moneyed acquaintance, whom he described as 'good, sober and religious, a fine English squire', and had added Beckyishly 'if I had 3,000 a year I think I'd be so too'.

Becky acts as Thackeray's representative in other respects as well. Of the major characters she is the only one intelligent enough to embody his satirical wit. The sparkling, derisive accounts of country life which she sends back to Amelia from Sir Pitt's house are an early indication of this. Thackeray jocularly disowns them, and assures his readers that Becky, not he, is sneering at Sir Pitt and his household. But in fact Becky's letters patently derive from Thackeray's malicious description, in *The Book of Snobs*, of the tedious rural routines at Major Ponto's. Again, the revenge Becky takes upon the Bareacres family is plainly an outlet for Thackeray's own hatred of aristocratic insolence. Lady Bareacres has treated Amelia with insulting hauteur when asked to dinner by the Osbornes, and it is Becky who has the job of righting the wrong. She refuses to sell her horses to Lady Bareacres, when a French occupation of Brussels is expected, and amuses herself by walking round the immobilized Bareacres carriage making loud remarks about the jewels which the conquering troops will find concealed in its upholstery, until her noble adversary is half dead with rage and terror. It is a marvellous vengeance and Becky has

readers and author firmly behind her as she inflicts it. Though captivated by snobbish aspirations herself for a while, she finds fashionable
London a fearful drag in the end, and longs for something livelier: 'O
how much gayer it would be to wear spangles and trousers, and dance
before a booth at a fair.' Here, too, she speaks for the young Thackeray
who, not yet the hanger-on of lords and ladies, was concerned to paint
high society in unappealing colours. He loved to talk of himself as a
Bohemian, and he makes Becky one. The boisterous, vagabond
existence in cheap hotels and gaming houses greatly appeals to her.
She enjoys herself in her tatty garret at Pumpernickel, hobnobbing
with the German students, and in portraying this life Thackeray
drew on his happiest youthful memories.

All this is not to deny, of course, that Becky is detestable, but she is
not merely detestable. Thackeray himself observes, during the
Waterloo episode, and quite seriously it seems, that she is of a 'good-
natured and obliging disposition'. If this is so, she is remarkably
successful in concealing it at times, but even her blackest acts find
extenuation if we look hard enough. Her ill-treatment of little Rawdon
is the failing which makes the heart bleed most, especially the brutal
scene in which she boxes his ears for creeping downstairs to listen to
her singing, while Lord Steyne, whom she has been entertaining,
laughs. Becky's deed is horrible, but not simply heartless. Thackeray
shrewdly shows us that she is most violent where she feels most guilty.
Her neglected child is 'a reproach and a pain to her'. She hates little
Rawdon for what she has done to him.

Sadly for Becky, she cannot find any maternal affection in her heart.
Children bore her. It does not take much imagination to relate this
inadequacy to her early experiences at Miss Pinkerton's, and as a
governess. People began thrusting unwanted children into her charge
before she had ceased being a child herself. Thackeray does not leave
us to work out the effect of this for ourselves: as the two girls leave
Miss Pinkerton's at the start of the novel, Amelia voices her own
realization that Becky must have had enough of children. Events prove
her right. It also helps Becky's case that little Rawdon, despite her
misuse, turns out well. If we heard him howling for his mama very
often, we should find it hard to excuse her, however much we reminded ourselves of the bad time she had in her formative years. But
in fact Thackeray trims the balance of his novel by making Rawdon
develop into a cheerful, plucky little fellow, 'generous and soft in
heart', whereas George Osborne junior, who has had endless maternal
affection lavished upon him, becomes a spoiled, selfish, imperious brat,
and cowardly to boot. As little Rawdon informs his papa, George
blubs when his pony canters, whereas he, Rawdon, does not. To judge
by results, Becky is a more successful mother than Amelia.

She is also a more successful wife. Amelia cannot retain George's affections for more than a couple of weeks after their wedding, and she has not the feeblest shadow of an idea about how to assist him in his financial troubles. Becky, on the other hand, successfully settles with Rawdon's creditors on very favourable terms, secures the Governorship of Coventry Island for him, and makes him into a proud, happy husband, quite transformed and redeemed by his devotion to her. 'When she sang, every note thrilled in his dull soul, and tingled through his huge frame. When she spoke, he brought all the force of his brains to listen and wonder.' Rawdon is immensely improved and ennobled after his marriage. George deteriorates during his, though it lasts only a few weeks.

Becky is always worth watching because her resourcefulness and vitality, and the interplay between her hypocrisy and her genuine feelings, make her unpredictable. Our realization that she is a free agent helps to make the novel alive. 'The greatness of a novelist like Tolstoy', Cyril Connolly has it in *Enemies of Promise* ,'is that he creates characters who being real creations are able to think and behave unlike themselves, to be false to type. Proust also had some of this greatness, and in English, Thackeray.' Outside of *Vanity Fair*, Thackeray doesn't qualify for the compliment very signally; but in that novel Becky, at any rate, conspicuously merits it. She keeps evading our categories. When we think we have grasped her principles, she twists out of our defining clutch. As she listens outside the door, for instance, to Dobbin's stormy interview with Amelia in the next-to-last chapter, she admires him, even though he has just been vilifying her – ' "Ah!" she thought, "if I could have had such a husband as that – a man with a heart and brains too!" ' – and she writes a note trying to get Dobbin to stay in Pumpernickel. When, despite this, he leaves, she ensures his success with Amelia by producing the note which poor infatuated George had written to her on the night before Waterloo, and forcing Amelia to read it. None of this is in her interest. The selfish, reasonable course would have been to keep Dobbin and Amelia apart, and fleece Amelia at leisure. Yet the course she actually takes is, when we consider it, perfectly convincing. She is able to express profound contempt by taking it upon herself to manage Amelia's fate. Except by rescuing the 'little pink-faced chit', she could not demonstrate her final and complete superiority. Moreover, by producing George's love-letter she ensures that her helping hand will give Amelia, in passing, a smack in the face, so she has the rare pleasure of being simultaneously virtuous and vindictive. To seduce George was one thing: but to be able to prove to his wife, who has mourned for him for years, that she seduced him is, for Becky, the cream of malicious enjoyment. And Becky's instant reference to self as she eavesdrops on Dobbin – thinking what a wife *she* would have made him – is likewise credible. So her seeming altruism doesn't make us feel she is being improperly sugared to ensure a happy ending. She plays false to type, not false to character.

The same goes for the famous thrill of animal excitement she experiences at the novel's climax when Rawdon, escaping unbeknown to her from the sponging-house, surprises her, aglitter with guilt and diamonds, in Steyne's company, and flings the nobleman bleeding to the ground. At a blow, Becky's schemes lie in ruins. Years of hard work and hypocrisy are cancelled in an instant. She might justifiably feel both aghast and aggrieved. But in fact she watches Rawdon, quivering with something like adoration, and something like desire. 'She admired her husband, strong, brave and victorious.' 'When I wrote the sentence', Thackeray told Hannay, 'I slapped my fist on the table, and said *"that* is a touch of genius!".' It was, because it strikes through to other kinds of life going on in Becky than plot and 'characterization' demand. It frees her from the reader's and author's knowingness. But, again, when we think back, we aren't incredulous about it. The earliest glimmering Becky had of Rawdon's existence was when she saw two pictures in her room on her first night in Sir Pitt's house – 'two little family pictures of young lads, one in a college gown, and the other in a red jacket like a soldier. When she went to sleep, Rebecca chose that one to dream about'. It is recognizably the same Becky that stands before Rawdon at the catastrophe. Her active temper responds to the glamour of a fight. Besides, for a woman usually obliged to be so masterful, to feel helpless before a man's physical strength is a luxury. And watching Lord Steyne floored and gashed satisfies her impatience with the restraints of civilized life – like flinging a dictionary out of the window, or sticking a knife in her husband, as in the Gaunt House charades. Steyne has regularly treated her with bantering contempt, calling her a 'poor little earthenware pipkin', and so forth. Now she has her revenge. Thackeray's touch of genius is not stuck on. It comes up from the depths of his novel, so that the more we think about it, the more we see that it would have been impossible for Becky to respond in any other way.

Another thing that adds to our esteem for Becky, besides our acknowledgement of her as a living creature, is that the people who malign her – like Mrs. Bute or silly, snobbish George – are generally people for whom we have by no means unqualified respect. *Vanity Fair* is a novel in which the opinions expressed by characters about other characters are extremely important and extremely untrustworthy, often rebounding on those who venture them. When George remarks that he doesn't want a governess for a sister-in-law, and reminds Becky of her 'place', we feel shame for him and solidarity with her. Likewise, when Rawdon refers to George, whom we have come to look on as rather a dandy, as a 'young flat' who is habitually rooked at billiards, we suddenly see poor George from the superior elevation of a smart cavalry regiment, and feel some sympathy for him, instead of despising him as Rawdon would have us. Thus the puppets are not set separately on the stage, but with their strings intertwined. A pull at one jerks those around it. The contrasts set up between adjacent characters illustrate this too. Becky would look less excusable in a novel that did not contain Amelia. Amelia's weakness recommends Becky's strength. Amelia displays a selfishness just as persistent as Becky's, and the more insidious because it is disguised as love. 'Grow green again, tender little parasite', the injunction with which Thackeray dismisses Amelia, has more scorn in its very indulgence than anything Becky could merit.

Yet Amelia can't be cursorily disposed of, any more than Becky. True, Thackeray keeps giving us cause to despise her. Her 'usual mood' is one of 'selfish brooding'; her letters to Dobbin are all 'cold' and 'selfish'; in her love for George she is 'absorbed in one selfish, tender thought' which stops her noticing other people's misery, even her parents'. What prevents her for years from admitting that the real George wasn't the superb young hero she imagined isn't love but, Thackeray insists, 'pride'. It would wound her vanity too much to acknowledge that she had worshipped a sham. Her notion of manliness is vulgar: she thinks meanly of Dobbin because he lisps. Worse, she keeps him on a string, with no care for his happiness, so that she can both feel she has an admirer and preen herself on being an inconsolable widow. In this she resembles Jane Brookfield, who was ready to flirt with Thackeray, but remained exasperatingly faithful to her husband. Thackeray told Brookfield that he had Jane in mind when he created Amelia. Of course Amelia is not conscious of her own duplicity. She knows herself no better than she understands other people. Thackeray calls her 'our simpleton', and shows her habitually taking refuge from self-examination in tears, or, as he puts it, 'recourse to the water-works'. Despite all this, there are plenty of directives from Thackeray to indicate that Amelia occupies a higher spiritual plane than any other woman in the novel, and that her creator intends us to find her, like a toddler or a favourite dog, the more appealing because she is not intellectually very sharp. We may resist this pressure, but a sense of Amelia's fundamental innocence remains. Besides, who would not rather marry Amelia than Becky? A little dogginess is preferable to being murdered for one's insurance policy.

The male characters, too, are hedged about with conflicting considerations. As we marshal them for praise or blame, we find ourselves hesitating, and questioning our own and the author's assessments. Rawdon Crawley is an oaf and a killer, with savage little eyes.

He is also a swindler, and would gladly put a bullet into anyone who told him so. Yet through his devotion to his little son, and his love for Rebecca and his sister-in-law, Lady Jane, he genuinely matures and deepens. He becomes one of the few convincing repentant sinners in Victorian fiction – the more convincing because he is redeemed not by religion but by fatherhood and female attachment. In his conversion he does not accede to any set of beliefs, but merely to love for people who he believes have more inner beauty than he. Hence he cannot find words to tell Lady Jane about his rebirth. ' "Oh," said he, in his rude, artless way, "you – you don't know how I'm changed since I've known you, and – and little Rawdy. I – I'd like to change somehow. You see I want – I want – to be – ".' He wants to be like her. But for a dragoon with great whiskers it seems a fatuous thing to say, so the speech tails off. 'He did not finish the sentence, but she could interpret it.' The situation is made more Thackerayan by our being able to perceive that Lady Jane is, in reality, no paragon. She un-Christianly insists, in conversation with her husband, that Becky, as a sinner, is 'not worthy to sit down with Christian people', and must be forbidden the house – an effect of her sexual jealousy and incipient love for Rawdon that Thackeray means us not to miss. Rawdon's idol, like all Vanity Fair idols, has a crack.

Just as religious language is avoided in the account of Rawdon's conversion, so his ageing and betterment are shown by Thackeray with typical and brilliant obliqueness. It is the decline of his clothes that we most notice. When 'the famous dandy of Windsor and Hyde Park' rides off to Waterloo in 'his oldest and shabbiest uniform and epaulets', so that, if he is killed, Becky will be able to turn his smarter outfits into cash, it provides a more striking comment on his growing self-lessness and her rapacity than anything either of them could say. Later, when Becky is presented at Court, wearing her magnificent brocade (purloined from Queen's Crawley), and Rawdon follows 'in his old Guards' uniform, which had grown wofully shabby, and was much too tight', it comes upon us, quite suddenly, how useless and tame the dashing warrior has become. Then, after his detention in Moss's sponging-house and the brawl with Steyne, Rawdon rushes round London – to Sir Pitt's, to Gaunt House, to Knightsbridge Barracks – in the crumpled evening dress which he has worn for two days, stared at by passers-by, isolated by his clothes like someone in a bad dream, and unable to get any new ones because the servants at Curzon Street refuse to send his portmanteau. This image of a distraught man, trapped in broad daylight in evening dress, externalizes Rawdon's shame, aloneness and bewilderment. We suffer for him through his clothes.

George Osborne is harder to like than Rawdon, but easier to feel ashamed for. Thackeray is adept at giving him speeches so callow and transparent that they cause us almost physical discomfort, as if an acquaintance were making a fool of himself before an audience. When, on his wedding day, he shouts 'Get out of the way, you little devils', to the damp urchins hanging around outside the church; or growls 'Damn the shillings and halfpence, sir', when drawing out the last of his money, in hopes of impressing the clerk; or boasts offhandedly about the restaurant dinner he gave to the Bareacres, 'Rather a nice thing'; or demands of Amelia at the Brussels opera 'Why didn't you have a bouquet?', while he admiringly eyes one Becky is carrying, we shiver with embarrassment, because Thackeray has caught the lad's style with such malicious accuracy. We feel, too, that these gaffes are understandable, even excusable. George is young (unlike Dobbin, who seems grey-headed even at school), and, by his own standards, hard-up; and he so desperately wants to seem a man of the world and be proud of his wife. The fact that he ought to have bought her a bouquet himself only makes her lack of one the more riling for him. He has some of youth's virtues, as well as youth's faults. He is brave and impetuous and passionately admired in his regiment. On the morning of battle he bounds downstairs, his sword under his arm, to the square where his troops are mustering, flushed with eagerness and anticipation, and devoutly thankful that the weepy parting from Amelia is over. And when, much later, we hear how he died, we recognize the same ardour and fearlessness. The English line, after a day of defensive action, was ordered to advance, and George 'hurraying and rushing down the hill waving his sword, received a shot and fell dead'.

His marriage with Amelia is to his credit, even if it was done half to defy his father. We are shown him looking back over their courtship, and comparing her conduct with his: 'he blushed with remorse and shame, as the remembrance of his own selfishness and indifference contrasted with that perfect purity'. This generous capacity for penitence is part of his youthful appeal. When news of the French advance comes, he sits down in the early hours and, with his heart full of remorse and tenderness ('and', Thackeray can't resist adding, 'selfish regret'), writes to his father, kissing the letter afterwards, and remembering the 'thousand kindnesses' the old man has done him. Then he goes and looks at his wife asleep, and feels 'heart-stained and shame-stricken'. At these moments he is not the sort of character an intelligent reader will feel superior to. So that when Thackeray dismisses him as a 'whiskered prig', and Becky, after he is safely dead, denounces him as 'that selfish humbug, that low-bred cockney dandy, that padded booby, who had neither wit, nor manners, not heart', we know that an injustice is being done, and want to come to the dead boy's defence.

What we know of George's father naturally inclines us to excuse the son, too. Old Osborne – snob, bully, dullard – is one of Thackeray's most fearsome and penetrating portraits. Of his study, we are reminded 'George as a boy had been horsewhipped in this room many times; his mother sitting sick on the stair, listening to the cuts of the whip'. To Osborne George is a possession, to be trained and shown off. The study contains all the boy's copy-books and drawing-books and letters from school, 'marked and docketed and tied with red tape'. After George has defied his father, and married Amelia, old Osborne goes into this sanctum, takes down the family bible, on the flyleaf of which the births of his children are recorded, and, as if setting right an account, 'carefully obliterated George's name from the page; and when the leaf was quite dry, restored the volume to the place from which he had moved it'. The tidiness – waiting for the ink to dry, so as not to spoil the facing page – lays bare Osborne's respect for possessions rather than people. Thackeray reveals the man's essential character in a single gesture, as Tolstoy does when he shows Berg walking across a room to kiss his wife and stopping on the way to straighten a corner of the carpet which is rucked up. But Thackeray does not allow us any easy contempt for Osborne. He has been a generous father. 'Anything that money could buy had been his son's'; and if he found the things money could not buy harder to manage, yet love for his son was an integral part of his being, and as he tries to wrench it out his torment, as well as his venomous fury, is compellingly conveyed. The scenes in which he gets news of George's death, and his last letter, and visits his grave and the battlefield, are magnificent achievements of psychological fiction. Rage and tenderness, grief for his son and a passionate longing to be revenged on him for his disobedience, inextricably mesh in Osborne's heart:

He strove to think that a judgement was on the boy for his disobedience. He dared not own that the severity of the sentence frightened him, and that its fulfilment had come too soon upon his curses. Sometimes a shuddering terror struck him, as if he had been the author of the doom that he had called down upon his son. There was a chance before of reconciliation. The boy's wife might have died; or he might have come back and said, Father, I have sinned. But there was no hope now. He stood on the other side of the gulf impassable, haunting his parent with sad eyes. He remembered them once before so in a fever, when everyone thought the lad was dying, and he lay on his bed speechless, and gazing with a dreadful gloom. Good God! how the father clung to the doctor then; and with what a sickening anxiety he followed him: what a weight of grief was off his mind when, after the crisis of the fever, the lad recovered, and looked at his father once more with eyes that recognized him. But now there was no help or cure, or chance of reconcilement: above all, there were no humble words to soothe vanity outraged and furious, or bring to its natural flow the poisoned, angry blood. And it is hard to say which pang it was that tore the proud father's heart most keenly – that his son should have gone out of the reach of his forgiveness, or that the apology which his own pride expected should have escaped him.

The relentless honesty, the rigorous eye with which Osborne's condition is viewed, gives the prose a bracing, styptic feel which utterly disappears from Thackeray's later work. Full credit is given to Osborne's emotional upheavals, but there is no answering influx of softness from the writer to smudge the diagnosis. An almost biological precision is maintained, congruent with the images of venomous creatures that Osborne's passion gives rise to. At the same time, we are warned against simply looking down on the man. It is a vital (morally, *the* vital) part of Thackeray's purpose to bring us to see that we are like him, and to make us take account of the self-concern entwined about our own affections. 'Which of us is there can tell how much vanity lurks in our warmest regard for others, and how selfish our love is?' It is the absence of precisely such self-examination (of, in Thackeray's sense, 'consciousness') that has turned Osborne from a potentially strong and generous father into something monstrous:

Old Osborne did not speculate much on the mingled nature of his feelings, and how his instinct and selfishness were combating together. He firmly believed that everything he did was right, that he ought on all occasions to have his own way – and like the sting of a wasp or serpent his hatred rushed out armed and poisonous against anything like opposition. He was proud of his hatred as of everything else. Always to be right, always to trample forward, and never to doubt, are not these the great qualities with which dulness takes the lead in the world?

With such a parent to shape him, George was unlikely to turn into a loving or a humble man. We think more kindly of the son as we survey the father.

Dobbin is old Osborne's antithesis. The contrast between them is one of the cross-beams in the book's structure. In their confrontations, blind, maddened arrogance faces cool self-scrutiny, as when they meet after Waterloo:

'Pray have you any commands for me, Captain Dobbin, or, I beg your pardon, I should say *Major* Dobbin, since better men than you are dead, and you step into their *shoes?*' said Mr. Osborne, in that sarcastic tone which he was sometimes pleased to assume.

'Better men *are* dead', Dobbin replied. 'I want to speak to you about one of them.'

Such crude insults slide off Dobbin. He knows himself. True, he is not faultless, and would not be in *Vanity Fair* if he were. As we have seen, he loves an imaginary replica of Amelia – a tailor's dummy – not the breathing, faulty girl. But we learn that he has always been aware of this self-deception, though it was too sweet to vanquish. 'I knew all along that the prize I had set my life on was not worth the winning', he tells Amelia at the end. He is in the habit of pondering his own selfish motives, even where an outsider would be far from accusing him of selfishness. Thus he wonders whether, when he brought about the marriage between George and Amelia, which would not have taken place without his interference, it was 'because he loved her so much that he could not bear to see her unhappy: or because his own sufferings of suspense were so unendurable that he was glad to crush them at once'. Such speculations make him the novel's one 'conscious' character. But his self-doubt also results in his prizing other people too highly, or so some critics complain. George is 'fanatically admired' by Dobbin, and that this should be so is, in Mr. J. I. M. Stewart's opinion, 'nonsense – or only credible if we write him off (in Saintsbury's round phrase) as a fool'. The interaction between characters in *Vanity Fair* is too intricate, however, for round phrases. George – handsome, dashing, athletic – has precisely the qualities Dobbin lacks, so Dobbin, being of a generous and self-suspicious disposition, is inevitably drawn to admire him. Besides, admiring George through thick and thin ('fanatically') is the one means of keeping jealousy at bay, for George has won the girl Dobbin loves. Dobbin would distrust his own motives if he were to dislike George. It is natural for Dobbin to respect George's soldierly virtues, moreover, because soldiering has limited his imagination somewhat – how else can we explain his turning up with 'a wooden horse, a drum, a trumpet, and other warlike toys' for a child whose father has recently been killed in battle? For all that, he has a more delicate moral sense, and can bring us closer to a Tolstoyan state of mind, than any other figure in the book. Like Pierre, whom he resembles in physical awkwardness, he is capable of experiencing shame at the sight of other people's shameful behaviour, though it is in no way his fault. The spectacle of old Sedley, humbled and bankrupt, and calling Dobbin, whom he had often tipped at school, 'Sir', disturbs him in this fashion:

A feeling of shame and remorse took possession of William Dobbin as the broken old man so received and addressed him, as if he himself had been somehow guilty of the misfortunes which had brought Sedley so low.

Dobbin, in his shuffling, tongue-tied way, takes the sins of the world upon himself, and to call him a fool is to miss his spiritual depth.

Coming to the wider issue of how Thackeray's masterpiece compares with Tolstoy's, it's obvious, to begin with, that *Vanity Fair* is at best *War and Peace* without the war. Tolstoy's accounts of military action – Schön Graben, Austerlitz, the slaughter on the Augest dam, the bombardment of Smolensk, Borodino, the retreat from Moscow, and the blood-stained exhibitions that accompany them, the executions, lynching and looting, Rostov's visit to the military hospital, the amputation of Anatole's leg – find no parallel in Thackeray. He would have felt a sham trying to write them. 'There is one fact I must remind myself of as often as possible', wrote Tolstoy, setting out on his literary career, 'at thirty, Thackeray was just preparing to write his first book'. Beginning late, amassing experience of life before taking up one's pen, were, he deduced, the surest paths to literary greatness. But his own experience of life was much more violent and primitive than Thackeray's. He had fought in the Caucasus and at Sevastopol. Thackeray had never soldiered; had hardly so much as held a gun. When his stepfather tried to teach him to shoot, he proved too short-sighted to see the target. No doubt he could have made *Vanity Fair* more sensational with imaginary impressions of the Waterloo fighting, seen through the eyes of Dobbin or George or Rawdon. He even seems to have contemplated doing so. He wrote to Murray for a copy of G. R. Gleig's *Story of the Battle of Waterloo*, so that he could glean some relevant facts, and remarked wryly 'Titmarsh at Waterloo will be a very remarkable and brilliant performance, doubtless'. As the tone of this denotes, he felt bogus and miscast. In the event, there is no first-hand account of the fighting. *Vanity Fair* is built round a thunderous void. The cannon are heard in the streets of Brussels; waggonloads of wounded creak back into the city; fugitives bring confused rumours. Later, scraps of reminiscence filter through: how in the first day's action of Quatre Bras George had cut down the French lancer who had speared young Ensign Stubble, and was grappling with him for the colours; how Major O'Dowd's horse had been shot under him when the regiment charged, and the survivors, riding back, found him seated on Pyramus's carcase, refreshing himself from a case-bottle; how George and Dobbin had stood together in the rain on the morning of Waterloo, watching the black masses of French on the heights opposite. Months afterwards, we travel to the continent with old Osborne, find Brussels swarming with maimed soldiery, are conducted over the battlefield, and have pointed out to us the road where the regiment marched into action on the sixteenth, the place where they repulsed the French cavalry, the bank under which they bivouacked that night, and the hillside down which George ran to his death. We know, in the end, what happened, but we don't see it. While the battle is raging, we are diverted with a comic sequence about a frightened fat man. That Tolstoy can take us into the chaos and carnage endows his novel with a hugely superior grasp on life.

But Thackeray's reasons for depleting his novel deserve respect. The idea of sedentary, pacific readers getting titillation from fictional bloodbaths had always struck him as absurd and indecent. In one of his earliest pieces of journalism, he had criticized the lurid pleasures which the French public seemed to demand from its authors: 'you must dilate on the clotted blood, rejoice over the scattered brains, particularize the sores and bruises, the quivering muscles, the gaping wounds.' For his part, he refused. Living in our own day, he would have been attracted by, for instance, John D. MacDonald's viewpoint on TV violence (as quoted by John Fraser in *Violence in the Arts*): 'the gutsy dramas on the mass media tend to make us forget that the average urban male is so unaccustomed to sudden pain that if you mash his nose flat, he'll be nauseated for hours, spend two days in bed, and be shaky for the rest of the week.' Thackeray (who had not forgotten having his nose mashed flat) would have gone along with this, insofar as it applied to literature. Taking trips into gory glory via one's reading matter was, he considered, puerile and self-deluding.

But, it will be objected, Tolstoy doesn't pander (or doesn't pander much) to this kind of appetite. Following Stendhal's example, he aimed to describe battle realistically. His warriors are vulnerable, and aghast to find how much it hurts to be wounded. He shows us excited young men, who expect warfare to be glorious, and discover that it is merely a collection of average urban males with blood pouring out of them. The ordinariness of the people on the battlefield is what he constantly makes us see. Nikolai Rostov's experience when he unhorses a French dragoon is typical of Tolstoy's method:

Rostov reined in, and his eyes sought his foe to see what sort of man he had vanquished. The French officer was hopping with one foot on the ground and the other caught in the stirrup. With eyes screwed up with fear, as though expecting another blow at any moment, he glanced up at Rostov in shrinking terror. His pale mudstained face – fair-haired, boyish, with a dimple in the chin and clear blue eyes – was not at all warlike or suited to the battlefield, but a most ordinary homely countenance.

The dimple, the foot caught in the stirrup, are earnests of the man's common humanity, and Rostov feels moral nausea to think that he has just struck him with a sword.

A defence of Tolstoy's battle scenes along these lines would, of course, be justified, and, as we have seen, in the early *Barry Lyndon* Thackeray offered a similarly low-key, factual account of battle, plus a justification of it. We may feel it a pity he didn't develop this in *Vanity Fair*, but what we must notice is that, though the novel contains no direct description of fighting, it does not fob us off with the courtly reticences habitual in *Esmond* and *The Virginians*. Rather, it manages to convey the same truths about war as Tolstoy, and forces similar contrasts upon its readers. We watch a young ensign buying equipment shortly before the regiment's embarkation – trying on a new bearskin, 'under which he looked savage beyond his years', and writing a letter full of 'pluck and bad spelling' to his anxious parents, while the tears trickle down his nose and drip onto the paper – for he is only seventeen, and is thinking that he may never see his mother again. Later this same ensign turns up, speared in the leg, in one of the waggons of wounded that roll past the Sedley lodgings. In his fever and delirium he has been imagining himself back at his father's parsonage. Catching sight of Jos Sedley, he holds out a 'hot and feeble hand' and begs him to take him in, and 'give the man two Napoleons: my mother will pay you'. This wounded soldier is not, as he would be in Tolstoy, a detail at the edge of a vast panorama. Of all the casualties carried back from Waterloo, he is the only one we get a glimpse of. Thackeray lets him stand for thousands of others, whom he does not bother to draw in. He provides a sketch; Tolstoy, a mural. But the essential features are the same. The youth and innocence of the combatants, the agony in the jolting casualty carts, the desperation of maimed men pleading to be taken in, these are facts impressed upon us in Tolstoy as we follow Nikolai Rostov's fortunes, watch him trundled back to camp on Tushin's gun-carriage, or witness the arrival of the ambulance vans from Borodino outside the Rostovs' Moscow house. The warrior turning back into a boy crying for his mother is what we see when the swaggering Dolohov is shot: 'My mother. My mother, my angel, my adored angel of a mother', he weeps, as he clings to Rostov's hand. Even the way a boyish face is changed by military headgear is something that both Thackeray and Tolstoy have noted: Pierre observes how alien his friendly French guards seem when they appear in buttoned-up chin-straps and shakos.

As we should expect from our look at Thackeray's imaginative interests, he is especially skilled at using food and commodities to make the ordinariness of soldiers vivid to us. The young Belgian hussar beloved by the Sedleys' cook, Pauline, leaves for battle 'with pockets and holsters crammed full of good things from the larder', and after the undignified flight of the Belgian contingent we find him back in her kitchen, stuffing himself with meat and beer, while he invents tales about the prodigies of courage performed by himself and his companions. We watch Mrs. Major O'Dowd superintending her husband's gear, storing his best epaulets away in a tea canister for the trip to Belgium, and, on the morning of battle, placing in the pockets of his military cloak 'a light package of portable refreshments, and a wicker covered flask or pocket pistol', containing brandy, from which, as we have seen, the Major is found calmly drinking, seated on his dead charger, when his troops return from the attack. The homely details transform the fighting men into individuals – husbands, fathers – setting off with their comforts and possessions neatly pouched and pocketed, and it is the disaster that overtakes these cherished commodities that Thackeray uses to bring home the havoc of war to us, rather than anything we see happening to the men themselves. Relichunters scream round old Osborne when he visits the battlefield, 'offering for sale all sorts of mementoes of the fight, crosses, and epaulets, and shattered cuirasses, and eagles'. The obscenity strikes us the more because we have been shown something of the care with which such objects are tended. Likewise when Rawdon sends home to Miss Crawley at Brighton a box containing a pair of French epaulets, a Cross of the Legion of Honour and the hilt of a shattered sword, with a letter telling her that he stripped these spoils from enemy soldiers, we are given a sense of the chaotic, dissevering effects of war, that can, out of the blue, dump martial trophies in the lap of an elderly English spinster. It makes things worse when we discover, a page or two later, that in reality Becky bought the relics for a few francs from a pedlar in Brussels. The objects seem even more irretrievably adrift and dishonoured. In Thackeray it is not the patients in a military hospital, for we never see inside one, but bereaved commodities that carry the lesson of war.

A single bereaved woman, too, of course. Thackeray uses Amelia to stand for all the war-widows, as Ensign Stubble for all the wounded, of the Napoleonic campaign. It is typical of his fastidious, indirect art that we are not allowed to be present when she receives the news of her husband's death. That supreme shock of grief is, like the fighting, left to our imagination, though the effect of shock is not passed over. Thackeray transmits the suddenness and casualness of death in war by killing George off in a relative clause, which catches the reader unawares: '. . . and Amelia was praying for George, who was lying on his face, dead, with a bullet through his heart'. It is one of the quickest exits in English fiction. George, as a major character, might justifiably have expected something more elaborate, but the impact is stunning. Bids by later novelists to imitate its nonchalance sound, by comparison, either affected or incredible (Virginia Woolf's 'Mrs. Ramsay having died rather suddenly the night before', for instance, or Forster's 'Gerald died that afternoon. He was broken up in the football match' are no more than arty contrivances). George dies believably and with fearful speed.

His death is the last in a series of incidents, breaking in upon the narrative like drumbeats, muffled at first, but growing louder, which Thackeray employs to record war's incursion into the lives of a peaceful family. This is a key theme of the novel, as of *War and Peace*. Through it we come to regard the grand movements of European history as disasters, sending out waves of suffering to engulf innocent and obscure hearts. The first hint of doom is almost a joke. Becky, to shock Amelia, shouts *'Vive Bonaparte!'* as the two girls drive away from Miss Pinkerton's. A little later, when Amelia, Becky and their escorts go to Vauxhall, we learn that the entertainments include a panorama of Moscow, and Mrs. Salmon performing 'The Battle of Borodino', 'a savage cantata against the Corsican upstart'. War is still a long way off – just a theme for songs. And Dobbin laughs at himself when, trying to hum Mrs. Salmon's cantata afterwards, he finds that he is humming the tune Amelia sang when she came running downstairs into the drawing-room, and he first set eyes on her. It's a gentle moment, but sinister too. War and peace move a little closer together, though only in Dobbin's confused and worried thoughts. Then, with Napoleon's escape from Elba, Thackeray brings the girl and the European catastrophe into open conjunction, in one of those superb, offhand panoramas with which he evokes and authenticates the spaces looming behind his figures:

When the eagles of Napoleon Bonaparte, the Corsican upstart, were flying from Provence, where they perched after a brief sojourn in Elba, and from steeple to steeple until they reached the towers of Notre Dame, I wonder whether the Imperial birds had any eye for a little corner of the parish of Bloomsbury, London, which you might have thought so quiet, that even the whirring and flapping of those mighty wings would pass unobserved there?

'Napoleon has landed at Cannes'. Such news might create a panic at Vienna, and cause Russia to drop his cards, and take Prussia into a corner, and Talleyrand and Metternich to wag their heads together, while Prince Hardenberg, and even the present Marquis of Londonderry, were puzzled; but how was this intelligence to affect a young lady in Russell Square, before whose doors the watchman sang the hours when she was asleep: who, if she strolled in the square, was guarded there by the railings and the beadle: who, if she walked ever so short a distance to buy a ribbon in Southampton Row, was followed by black Sambo, with an enormous cane: who was always cared for, dressed, put to bed, and watched over by ever so many guardian angels, with and without wages? *Bon Dieu*, I say, is it not hard that the fateful rush of the great Imperial struggle can't take place without affecting a poor little harmless girl of eighteen, who is occupied in billing and cooing, or working muslin collars in Russell Square?

'Billing and cooing.' Amelia is dove to Napoleon's eagles, though they have no eye for her, of course. They shatter her life without noticing. Europe panics, the funds fall, and old Jos Sedley is ruined. Nor is her prosperity all that will perish. As Dobbin stands in the darkened street in Chatham, watching the light in Amelia's bedroom window, where she is alone with George, he hears cheering from the ships on the river where the transports are taking troops aboard. It is another of the drumbeats. War reaches towards Amelia's love. A few chapters more, and the noises-off have become clamorous. When George returns to his lodgings in Brussels, to find Amelia in bed, he bends over her pillow, her arms close tenderly round his neck, and:

At that moment a bugle from the Place of Arms began sounding clearly, and was taken up through the town; and amidst the drums of the infantry, and the shrill pipes of the Scotch, the whole city awoke.

Through jokes, songs, distant noises, then, Thackeray maps war's gradual approach. And the alarms, muffled or strident, find people pursuing their harmless pleasures – loitering at Vauxhall, making love, or, of course, eating and drinking. The most dramatic collision of war and peace, the moment which sets the whole action aflame, comes when Dobbin finds George, glass in hand, at the buffet table at the Duchess of Richmond's ball, and delivers his terse message: ' "The enemy has passed the Sambre," William said, "and our left is already engaged. Come away. We are to march in three hours." '

Thus Thackeray brings battle to the dining-room door and, as we have seen, highlights facts about it that Tolstoy also makes us conscious of. True, their attitudes diverge in some respects. Thackeray's pulse does not thrill to the splendour of war, as Tolstoy's does even as he portrays its horror. Nor does his heart swell, like Tolstoy's, with national pride. His estimate of his countrymen is less than flattering. They belong to 'the most squeamish if not the most moral of societies', and can be distinguished, when abroad, by the 'happy swagger and insolence of demeanour' with which they swindle landlords and pass dud cheques. It was an achievement for Thackeray to shackle his chauvinism to this degree, for in less guarded moods he was capable of the most abandoned patriotic rant, and would maintain that Englishmen were by nature French-beating animals, superior in body, spirit and eating-habits to the braggartly midgets across the Channel. When he brought his mind to bear on the matter, though, he soon grew ashamed of himself, as in the *Journey from Cornhill to Grand Cairo*, where he observes how he and his compatriots strut about the deck at the sight of a British warship, and impugns the 'wretched, vapouring stuff' of which their patriotism is made.

Unlike Tolstoy, too, he does not vilify Napoleon, or try to render him ridiculous. We are spared any counterpart in *Vanity Fair* to the rambling and unlikely historico-philosophical speculations, tacked onto *War and Peace*, in which Tolstoy labours to explain away the fact that an individual in Tolstoy's judgement so insignificant and talentless, so without psychological intuition or military genius, managed to rally thousands to his banner and spread massacre throughout Europe. For Thackeray there was less of a problem. He was not foolish enough to imagine Napoleon without gifts, and he was more prepared than Tolstoy to believe that envy, hatred and ambition are deeply rooted in quite ordinary people, so that the ruthless self-interest that Napoleon represented was able to find an echo in the breasts of innumerable less dynamic mortals (including, as it happened, himself: a speech in praise of Napoleon had been young Thackeray's one bid to make a hit at the Cambridge Union). With typical economy he indicates this alternative view of the reason for Napoleon's popularity in a couple of words, when he makes Becky shout *'Vive Bonaparte!'*. In her small way, we are meant to see, she contributes to the selfishness that convulses continents. So, in his even smaller way, does little George, that prodigiously narcissistic infant, who, with stunning blindness to his own condition, pens a school essay on Selfishness:

Of all the vices which degrade the human character, Selfishness is the most odious and contemptible. An undue love of Self leads to the most monstrous crimes; and occasions the greatest misfortunes both in *States and Families*. ... The selfishness of the late Napoleon Bonaparte occasioned innumerable wars in Europe, and caused him to perish, himself, in a miserable island – that of Saint Helena in the Atlantic Ocean.

'States and Families'. Thackeray makes little George underline the very point which he ought to, but doesn't, catch – that Napoleon and he, in their different spheres, are of a kind. By these means Thackeray avoids fostering the popular and comfortable falsehood (rather encouraged by Dickens) that the iniquities of those in power are chiefly responsible for mankind's regrettable condition, and that things would be a great deal better if they were left to lowly folk like ourselves.

Selfishness is Thackeray's quarry in *Vanity Fair*. He is out to track it through its sinuous ways, to show it coiled within the most harmless-looking motives. What sets him irretrievably apart from Tolstoy is his view of peace, not his view of war. He did not believe in the basic goodness of mankind left to his own devices. Tolstoy's masterpiece is a hymn to life, finding ultimate reality in wonder and joy and breathless sledge-rides. Thackeray's is hard, sceptical, embittered. Could he have known about Tolstoy's life and work, he would have seen it as a mass of temporary enthusiasms and hypocrisies – the apostle of love embroiling his family and followers in venomous bickering; the apostle of non-violence protected by armed guards; the foe of private property adding acres to his estate; the champion of absolute chastity whose wife was about to bear their thirteenth child;

the champion of the poor, who ravished peasant women, and set his own illegitimate son to work as a groom in his stables. Thackeray has shown us his opinion of such aristocratic idealists in his portrait of Miss Crawley, whom we overhear expounding her egalitarian principles to her new toy, Becky:

You have more brains than half the shire – if merit had its reward you ought to be a duchess – no, there ought to be no duchesses at all – but you ought to have no superior, and I consider you, my love, as my equal in every respect; and – will you put some coals on the fire, my dear.

Miss Crawley's ultra-liberal opinions are repeatedly punctured by Thackeray in this manner. 'I adore all imprudent matches', she roguishly ventures, shortly before working herself into screaming hysterics at the news that Rawdon and Rebecca have wed. The inability of people in *Vanity Fair* to see themselves reaches something of a pinnacle when Jos Sedley, half out of his mind with terror in menaced Brussels, and intent on saving his skin at all costs, refers to the French soldiery as 'dastardly cowards'.

Self-regard and hypocrisy, in these instances, explode in the culprit's face. The stout parties collapse, and little harm is done. But Thackeray is much too serious to leave it at that level. His most trenchant writing comes when he shows selfishness, allied to want and the souring power of time, gathering like poison in the soul. The history of Amelia's parents is a masterly exhibition of this, meticulously recording every shift and indignity. The Sedleys are genial folk at the outset. The chintz marquee of a bed in which the couple mull over their family fortunes and snore the nights away is put across as a veritable hive of bourgeois good sense and cosiness. When Sedley breaks the news of his financial ruin, it brings out the best in his wife. She soothes the broken man with 'incoherent love and tenderness', and the one thought she can spare from him is for her daughter: 'My God, my God, it will break Emmy's heart'. They take shelter in the Clapps' little cottage, and begin, quite happily at first, to decay. Old Sedley trots round with his bundles of greasy documents, and his dreams of money. Mrs. Sedley, still a great person to her landlady Mrs. Clapp, enjoys her colloquies with the greengrocer about pennorths of turnips, and her visitations to the butcher 'who sold hundreds of oxen very likely with less ado than was made about Mrs. Sedley's loin of mutton'. And there Dickens, had he been telling the story, might have left it, with a few words about the blessedness of the humble, and some rib-tickling portrayals of Mr. and Mrs. Clapp's lower-class speech-habits. Not so Thackeray. He refuses to let the forces he has set to work dribble away in improbable good-heartedness. When Dobbin pays his

visit to Sedley, we see what evil passions have been rankling within
the pathetic old wretch. The veins bulge in his forehead as he raves
about his losses, and denounces Bonaparte in senile fury: ' "Give him
no quarter. Bring back the villain's head, sir. Shoot the coward down,
sir," Sedley roared.' He will not hear of his daughter's marriage to
George, thinking nothing of her happiness so long as he can glut his
craving for revenge on the Osborne family.

Mrs. Sedley's descent is slower and meaner. She resents her
daughter's maternal possessiveness. Emmy's unfortunate assertion
that Daffy's Elixir, with which Mrs. Sedley has dosed the baby, is
poison, is turned to account 'with female ingenuity and perseverance',
and furnishes Mrs. Sedley with opportunities for innumerable taunts
and sarcastic self-accusations as the years pass. As Sedley squanders
more and more of the family income on fruitless speculations, penury
bites, the rent is unpaid, Mrs. Clapp turns nasty, the tradesmen are
insolent, and Mrs. Sedley flies at Emmy with spiteful reproaches
whenever she treats her child to some small luxury. There are tears
and sordid rows – always a Thackerayan speciality – and Amelia's
mother shrinks to a peevish scold:

The bitterness of poverty has poisoned the life of the once cheerful and
kindly woman. She is thankless for Amelia's constant and gentle
bearing towards her; carps at her for her efforts at kindness or service:
rails at her for her silly pride in her child, and her neglect of her
parents.

It is horribly believable, as are the insidious pressures that Mrs.
Sedley brings to bear on her daughter to make her part with little
George – for his and the family's good. Help comes at last, of course,
though too late for Mrs. Sedley, who takes her grudges to the grave.
Emmy, restored to fortune, finds Mrs. Clapp servile and fulsome once
more:

But in the vulgar sycophant who now paid court to her, Emmy always
remembered the coarse tyrant who had made her miserable many a
time, to whom she had been forced to put up petitions for time, when
the rent was overdue; who cried out at her extravagance if she bought
delicacies for her ailing mother or father; who had seen her humble and
trampled on her.

The gritty, relentless indictment exhilarates, as vituperation always
does. We feel that charitable humbug has been ripped away, leaving
clean air for the truth to be told in. It is a standard gratification of
Thackeray's satiric period.

But despising all the Mrs. Clapps in Christendom could not make
the reader uneasy about his own selfishness, and Thackeray's finer
strokes in the book are angled to this end. The Self's craftier circlings

are unwound. Its entanglement in fatherly love we noticed with old
Osborne; and Amelia's love for little George is repeatedly recognized
as selfish, despite the holy awe in which Thackeray shrouds it. His
duplicity on the point presents us with a dilemma. We feel unnatural
if we blame Amelia for clinging to her child, yet we come to see,
through her behaviour, that parental love is largely effortless self-
indulgence – a way of giving priority to one's own possessions and
accounting it a virtue. Amelia pores over her miniature of dead George
in the same self-solacing spirit as she cossets the boy, also a miniature
of George. But is she right, eventually, to let little George go? 'No
angel has intervened. The child is sacrificed and offered up to fate',
remarks Thackeray, as Osborne junior departs for Russell Square.
The Biblical allusion seems to Amelia's credit. She is like faithful
Abraham. But the situation in which Abraham and Isaac have previously figured in the story is not reassuring. When we watched old
Osborne deleting his son's name from the family Bible, 'there was a
frontispiece to the volume, representing Abraham sacrificing Isaac'.
As a leaf out of old Osborne's book, child sacrifice doesn't seem such
a good idea. Amelia is brought to it only by famine – 'starved out',
as old Osborne sneers, and that doesn't recommend it much either.
Perhaps she should have clung to her son. Our indecision is instructive.
If we condemn Amelia's selfishness, and praise her unselfish renunciation, we feel that we're crushing something innately human. But
the other course is to condone selfishness.

Not only mother love, but what we think of as sympathy with other
people is, on Thackeray's reading, a species of self-concern – can't,
indeed, be otherwise. We sympathize only where we recognize, or
imagine, some analogy to our own situation. Thus Polly Clapp, an
entirely likeable character, feels really sorry that Amelia should have a
dead husband, and we are shown that her compassion, though perfectly
genuine, is just a fantasy-projection of her own hopes and vanities:

Poor Polly sighed: she thought what she should do if young Mr.
Tomkins, at the surgery, who always looked at her so at church, and
who, by those mere aggressive glances had put her timorous little
heart into such a flutter that she was ready to surrender at once – what
she should do if he were to die? She knew he was consumptive, his
cheeks were so red, and he was so uncommon thin in the waist.

Polly's grief for Amelia comes down to a reverie on Tomkins's waist
measurement. Compassion is self-interest plus a little imagination.

Vanity Fair, then, seethes with selfishness, covert or otherwise, and
it presents, too, a world in which you can hardly stir without wounding
someone else. Unintentional hurts amount to one of the novel's main
subjects, binding together its public and private sectors. Napoleon

advances his eagles, and thousands of Amelia Sedleys mourn, though their suffering was no part of the great man's design. Lesser figures, likewise, pursue their own ends, striking down victims they have never known. For twenty years before the book opens, men have been fighting in Europe 'not by thousands but by millions; each one of whom as he struck his enemy wounded horribly some other innocent heart far away'. So, to descend to civil matters, Becky and Rawdon do not plan Raggles's ruin, or that of his wife and children. They merely wish to live elegantly without an income, and they bear the Raggleses no ill will. Yet because of their heedlessness Raggles is driven to the Fleet Prison and his children are flung on the streets. Even relatively benevolent characters deal woe involuntarily as they go about their business. Dobbin visits the Osborne house to plead that George should be forgiven for marrying Amelia. But Miss Osborne believes that he has come to propose to her, and as he steers the conversation round to marriage the poor spinster's excitement mounts. 'The tick-tock of the Sacrifice of Iphigenia clock on the mantelpiece became quite rudely audible', interjects Thackeray, to keep our minds on the harmless victim. And when she divines Dobbin's true errand, her pain is so evident that her sister and Miss Wirt, listening on the other side of the door, cannot contain their laughter. Dobbin, in his turn, is tormented by Amelia's love for her baby, since he perceives that it shuts him out. As he takes his farewell of mother and child in the nursery, before rejoining his regiment, the atmosphere is sharp with unmeant callousness:

The little pink hands of the child closed mechanically round the honest soldier's finger, and Amelia looked up in his face with bright maternal pleasure. The cruellest looks could not have wounded him more than that glance of hopeless kindness. He bent over the child and mother. He could not speak for a moment. And it was only with all his strength that he could force himself to say a God bless you. 'God bless you', said Amelia, and held up her face and kissed him.

'Hush! Don't wake Georgy!' she added, as William Dobbin went to the door with heavy steps. She did not hear the noise of his cab-wheels as he drove away: she was looking at the child, who was laughing in his sleep.

That the child should laugh seems wickedly cruel, as if he, or some malicious remnant of his father in him, were deriding the defeated suitor. But his cruelty, like his mother's, or like Napoleon's cruelty to her, is quite innocent. He is so far from meaning harm that he is not even awake.

It's curious, finally, that a novel so attuned to the selfishness and pain behind every face should transmit such an exuberant sense of life. It does so partly by having main characters who, as we've seen, are full of angles, so won't drop into fictional holes. They seem inexhaustible, like people, as we appreciate if we contrast them with the typed characters who occupy the first four or five places on the cast-list in most Dickens novels. Thackeray does have Dickensian characters – Sir Pitt, routing in his straw at Queen's Crawley like an ancient hog; wicked Lord Steyne, with his great bald head and his buck teeth glistening savagely – but their colouring looks bold and simple as soon as we put them beside the leading persons. Though partly modelled on the Marquis of Hertford, Steyne making love to Becky (supposing he ever did) would give the same impression of the half-alive trespassing on life as the monster with its coils and dials lurching towards the maiden in a horror film. And apart from the liveliness of its leads, *Vanity Fair* has, too, an astounding array of walk-on parts and extras – hordes of people, receding into the distance, and quite redundant to the novel, except that they destroy the feeling that it *is* just a novel, all fiercely making lifelike gestures, brandishing addresses and marriage certificates and genealogies and pets and reading matter and musical instruments and particulars of their weight, height and colouring. There are the endless ramifications of the Gaunt family, and the O'Dowds, with their Irish connections, and the Bute Crawleys, and poor Briggs, with her memories of a hectic young writing master, twenty four years back, and a lock of his yellow hair which she still cherishes in her desk upstairs; and Captain Macmurdo sitting up in bed in a silk nightcap reading *Bell's Life*; and the unfortunate Jim with his bulldog which almost eats Miss Crawley's Blenheim spaniel; and Becky's maid, Mademoiselle Fifine, who vacates Curzon Street together with four richly gilt Louis Quatorze candlesticks, a gold enamelled snuff box which had once belonged to Madame du Barri, and quantities of other loot, and who may or may not have subsequently kept a milliner's shop in the Rue de Helder at Paris under the name of Madame de Saint Amaranthe; and Steyne's man Monsieur Fiche, who is suspiciously attached to the interests of Steyne's mistress the Countess of Belladonna, *née* de Glandier, whose husband, the Count Paolo della Belladonna, is celebrated for his entomological collections and absent on a mission to the Emperor of Morocco; and Wagg, the celebrated wit; and Wenham, and Wenham's father, a small coal merchant in the North of England, and Mrs. Wenham, who was allegedly asked to supper with Lord Steyne and Becky on the fateful night, but was prevented by one of her headaches from getting into the novel at all; and Mrs. Mango of Mango, Plantain & Co., Crutched Friars, and the Pineries, Fulham, who has no right to be allowed in except that she shares the same doctor as Amelia, and who brings along with her her children Ralph Plantagenet and Gwendoline and Guinever Mango and her son's wife Lady Mary Mango; and wretched, beribboned

Horrocks flitting up the black oak stair at Queen's Crawley, and opening her hopeful account at the Mudbury Branch Savings Bank, and filching peaches from the Scots gardener's hothouses; and Molly the housemaid blubbering in the passage when little Rawdon goes away to school; and young Edward Dale of Dale, Spiggot and Dale of Threadneedle Street, who makes old Sedley weep with gratitude when he sends him some silver spoons from the Sedley sale, and who married Miss Louisa Cutts, daughter of Higham and Cutts, the corn-factors, in 1820, and now lives at Muswell Hill; and the Tutbury Pet; and old Tom Moody the huntsman, and his son Jack who weighs five stone and measures eight-and-forty inches; and – but there is no end to them, nor to the precise, gratuitous details about their fortunes and fancies that Thackeray loads onto them to make them look solid (details often more or less culinary, as we might expect, from Cuff's rum-shrub, and Sir Pitt's tripe and onions, and the Boggley Wallah snipe, to the Maraschino administered by Mrs. Raggles to Becky's cook, and the devilled fowls' legs and soda water that the young bloods breakfast off in Knightsbridge Barracks, and the cayenne pepper, pickles and guava jelly that arrive from Rawdon in Coventry Island, and the lozenges and tamarinds which Mr. Linton, in his affection for Amelia, extracts from the surgery drawers for little Georgy, compounding draughts so delectable that it is a luxury for the child to be ill). As Thackeray indulges himself among these swarming personages, breaking off to follow them to their homes or peer into their futures, he gives the impression that he is not so much inventing as exploring – tracing threads in an infinitely involved fabric of life that stretches away from him on all sides, any fibre of which he might quite easily and entertainingly have selected instead of the lives of Amelia and Rebecca and their friends. So often and so joyously does he digress that the digressions become almost more important than the story, and create the illusion that his book is as capacious as life itself.

Postscript

In the end, the emphasis should be on Thackeray's personality, for it is enduringly appealing, and permeates all his best work. It was a personality in which self-doubt was deeply ingrained. Were we to seek the source of this, we might consider, among other things, his mother's early desertion of him. To be banished from the maternal presence at the age of five, shortly after the death of one's father, and consigned to a remote, punitive and loveless environment, is not an experience calculated to enhance one's opinion of one's general amiability and worth. Social criticism, irony, and hauteur were not incompatible with Thackeray's self-doubt. On the contrary, they were a natural defence; besides, a clear perception of his own shortcomings helped to make him a more penetrating critic of other people's.

True, self-doubt had its disadvantages. We have seen that Thackeray, after the writing of *Vanity Fair*, deliberately set out to make his books more complaisant. This disastrous step could not have been taken had his need for approval not made him unduly susceptible to certain kinds of social pressure. But if self-doubt thus played its part in destroying him as a writer, it also saved him from dogmatism, because it was irreconcileable with the self-esteem on which dogmatism feeds. This is one of the factors that most markedly distinguish him from Dickens. It is also one for which he has been most rashly censured. Positive thinkers (like Carlyle) have accused him of not being able to think, without realizing that his scepticism showed him the arbitrariness of their creeds – those small little orthodoxies, as Orwell put it, that contend for our souls. Downright critics (like J. Y. T. Greig) have wished him more downright. Thackeray needed, Greig affirmed, 'to build himself up into a compacted and self-reliant personality'. But had he done so we might have had only another J. Y. T. Greig, not a Thackeray.

Even when his interests were most deeply concerned, Thackeray was not self-prizing. 'After all, Esmond was a prig', he admitted, typically, to Trollope when discussing the unpopularity of his favourite novel – 'then he laughed and changed the subject.' Buffoonery soon ousted melancholy in him – and *vice versa*: he was 'always trifling, and yet always serious'. And because he did not value himself overmuch, he was prodigal with his gifts: 'he laughed, and ate, and drank, and threw his pearls about with miraculous profusion' (Trollope, again).

Self-doubt helped to make him generous, as well as prodigal – as (to close with a last quotation from Trollope) this anecdote suggests:

I once heard a story of woe from a man who was the dear friend of both of us. The gentleman wanted a large sum of money instantly, – something under two thousand pounds, – had no natural friends who could provide it, but must go utterly to the wall without it. Pondering over this sad condition of things just revealed to me, I met Thackeray between the two mounted heroes at the Horse Guards, and told him the story. 'Do you mean to say that I am to find two thousand pounds?' he said, angrily, with some expletives. I explained that I had not even suggested the doing of anything, – only that we might discuss the matter. Then there came over his face a peculiar smile, and a wink in his eye, and he whispered his suggestion, as though half-ashamed of his meanness. 'I'll go half,' he said, 'if anybody will do the rest.' And he did go half, at a day or two's notice, though the gentleman was no more than simply a friend.

There could be few better memorials.

Index

Addison, Joseph, 21
Alison, Sir Archibald, 99
Allingham, William, 81
arms, women's, 46–8
Arnold, Matthew, 102
Artaud, Antonin, 122
Athenaeum, 93, 145
auction sales, 74–6

Balzac, Honoré de, 30
Bell, Robert, 175
Bentley's Miscellany, 15
Berghem, Nicolaas, 37
Betjeman, John, 74
Blackwood, John, 22
Blessington, Countess of (Marguerite Power), 18, 75
Bowes, John Bowes, 13
Brine, John Grant, 31
Brontë, Charlotte, 19, 21, 41
Brookfield, Mrs. William Henry (Jane Octavia Elton), 19, 47, 75, 80, 125, 183
Brougham, Henry Peter, Baron, 18
Broughton, Sir John Cam Hobhouse, Baron, 18
Browning, Mrs. Robert, 18, 146
Buller, Mrs. Charles, 73
buttons, 43–5
Byng, Frederick Gerald ('Poodle'), 18
Byron, George Gordon, Lord, 95, 167
Don Juan, 95, 98

Carlyle, Thomas, 19, 35, 37, 202

Carmichael-Smyth, Major Henry, 11, 12, 163–4
Carmichael-Smyth, Mrs. Henry (previously Mrs. Richmond Thackeray), 11, 12, 16, 19, 64, 106, 151
Castlereagh, Viscount (later fourth Marquess of Londonderry), 18, 25
Chadwick, Edwin, 153–4
Chapman, Edward, 25
Charterhouse School, 12, 21, 26–28, 164–5
Chesterfield, George Stanhope, Earl of, 19
Cimarosa, Domenico, 120
Claude of Lorraine (Claude Gelée), 38, 93
Cockerell, S. P., 128
Coke, Desmond Francis Talbot, 28
Congreve, William, 127, 157
Connolly, Cyril, 181
Conrad, Joseph, 146
Cornelius, Peter von, 94
Cornhill Magazine, 64
Coulon, M., 38
Courvoisier, François Benjamin, 49–50, 82
Cowper, Hon. Charles Spencer, 18
Cruikshank, George, 14, 55, 65, 99

Daumier, Honoré, 35
Delacroix, Ferdinand Victor Eugène, 98
Dicken, Charles Rowland, 28

204

Dickens, Charles, 18, 22, 25, 58, 65, 72, 96, 103, 129, 131, 135, 137, 164, 195–6, 200, 202
  American Notes, 25
  Oliver Twist, 15
  Pickwick Papers, 58
Didelot, Frédéric, 105
Don Quixote, 34
Dou, Gerard, 36
dressing-cases, 69
Dujardin, Carel, 37
Duvernay, Marie-Louise, 106

Eliot, T. S., 41, 46
  Four Quartets, 147
  Waste Land, The, 90
Elssler, Fanny, 104, 122
Engerman, S. L., 25

Faerie Queene, The, 43
Fay, Leontine, 13
ferronnières, 68
Fitzgerald, Edward, 13, 19, 34, 103, 115
flagellation, 28–9
Flaubert, Gustave, 96
  Madame Bovary, 20, 96, 139
  Sentimental Education, 126
Fogel, R. W., 25
Foreign Quarterly Review, 97, 100
Forster, E. M., 192
Forster, John, 18
Fraser, James, 16, 158
Fraser, John, 190
Fraser's Magazine, 15, 45, 49, 68, 156

Garrick Club, 22, 158
Gautier, Théophile, 104–5
Gavin, Dr. Hector, 154
Gleig, G. R., 189
Goethe, Johann Wolfgang von, 14, 119
  Sorrows of the Young Werther, The, 96
Goldsmith, Oliver, 20
gooseberry bushes, 60–1

Graham, Mary, 175
Granville, Granville George Leveson-Gower, Earl of, 19
Greig, J. Y. T., 202
Grimaldi, Joseph, 115

Hadath, John Edward Gunby, 28
Hamilton, William Alexander (styled Marquess of Douglas), 18
Hannay, James, 182
Hardy, Barbara, 63
Hayward, Abraham, 79
Hertford, Francis Charles Seymour-Conway, Marquess of, 200
Herwegh, Georg, 100
Household Words, 164–5
Howden, John Hobart Caradoc, Baron, 18
Hugo, Victor, 97
  Rhin, Le, 97

Irvine, J. W., 165

James, Henry, 45
Jerrold, Douglas, 19, 24
Johnson, Samuel, 20, 158
Jones, Chester, 81
Joyce, James, 51–2

Kock, Charles Paul de, 94

Lawrence, D. H., 141–2, 171
Leech, John, 19, 162
Lemon, Mark, 19, 20
Levinson, André, 105
Lewes, G. H., 179

MacDonald, John D., 190
Maginn, William, 14
Maignon, Louis, 104
Manet, Édouard, 45
Mann, Thomas, 63
Mars, Mlle (Anne Françoise Hippolyte Boutet), 13
Martineau, Harriet, 19
Marx, Karl, 100

Milnes, Richard Monckton, Baron, 79
Milton, John, 98
Molesworth, Lady, 18
Morning Chronicle, 15
Morton, Saville, 13
mothers-in-law, 137–8
Mozart, Wolfgang Amadeus, 120
Murray, John, 189
Mysteries of Udolpho, The, 34

New Monthly Magazine, 15, 81
Nijinsky, Vaslav, 107

Orwell, George (Eric Blair), 9, 150, 202
Overbeck, Johann Friedrich, 94

pantomime, 114–20, 124
Pauline, Mlle, 13, 18
Paxton, Joseph, 78
Peregrine Pickle, 157
Perrot, Jules-Joseph, 105, 107
Perry, Kate, 98
Poussin, Nicolas, 93
Procter, Bryan Waller, 60
Procter, Mrs. Bryan Waller, 126
Punch, 9, 15, 19, 23, 72, 81

Quarterly Review, 162

Racine, Jean, 97
Raine, Dr. Matthew, 28
Ray, Gordon N., 10
Redgrave, Richard, 36
Richards, Frank (Charles Harold St. John Hamilton), 28
Richardson, Samuel, 157
Rothschild, Lady Louisa de, 18
Rowlandson, Thomas, 157
Rubens, Peter Paul, 35, 37, 38, 40–1, 52–3, 66
Ruskin, John, 36
Russell, Dr. John, 12

Sand, George, 39
Schiller, Johann Christoph Friedrich von, 14, 119
Scott, Sir Walter, 99

Shakespeare, William, 97–8
  Hamlet, 97–8
  King Lear, 97
  Titus Andronicus, 43
Shawe, Merrick, 31
Shawe, Mrs. Matthew, 16, 68, 137, 139
Silver, Henry, 28
sirens, 88–9
Smith, Eliza, 32
Smith, Horace, 34
Sontag, Gertrude, 108, 110
Soulié, Frédéric, 24
Southwood-Smith, Thomas, 153
Soyer, Alexis, 80, 85
Spedding, James, 34
Stanfield, William Clarkson, 115
Stanley, Lady (Henrietta Dillon-Lee), 18
Steele, Sir Richard, 159
Stendhal (Henri Marie Beyle), 190
Sterne, Laurence, 157
Stewart, J. I. M., 188
Stone, Frank, 45, 83
Stowe, Harriet Beecher, 24
Strindberg, August, 140
Sutherland, J. A., 37
Swift, Jonathan, 21, 157

Taglioni, Marie, 13, 38, 66, 93, 103–8, 112
Tennyson, Alfred, 125
Thackeray, Anne Isabella, 16
Thackeray, Harriet Marian, 16
Thackeray, Jane, 16, 99, 135
Thackeray, Richmond Makepeace, 11
Thackeray, Mrs. William Makepeace (*née* Isabella Gethin Shawe), 16–17, 19, 51, 80, 85, 89
Thackeray, William Makepeace: Birth, 11; childhood and school-days, 11–13; undergraduate career, 13–14; loss of fortune, 15; marriage, 16; rise in society, 18–20; death, 78

Thackeray, William M.—*contd.*
Works:
Artists, The, 89, 173
'Ballad of Bouillabaisse, The', 80
Barry Lyndon, 15, 42, 44, 46, 60, 91, 124, 156, 157–8, 160
Bedford-Row Conspiracy, The, 35, 55
Beulah Spa, 51
Bob Robinson's First Love, 32, 61
Book of Snobs, The, 9, 15, 20, 23, 32, 44, 64–6, 70, 72–3, 80, 83, 126, 133–5, 156, 179
Captain Rook and Mr Pigeon, 71
Catherine, 15, 31, 44, 129
Caution to Travellers, A, 95
'Chronicle of the Drum, The', 99
Cox's Diary, 55, 67, 83, 108–9
Cruikshank's Gallery, 91
Curate's Walk, The, 51
Denis Duval, 54, 146–7
Dennis Haggarty's Wife, 68, 139–41
Dinner in the City, A, 81
Dr. Birch and His Young Friends, 27
English Humourists of the Eighteenth Century, The, 20, 22, 117, 127, 157
Exhibition Gossip, An, 98
Fatal Boots, The, 9, 30, 55
Fat Contributor Papers, The, 71
FitzBoodle Papers, The, 43, 46, 52, 71, 85, 119
Flore et Zéphyr, 105, 108
Four Georges, The, 22, 119, 124
Going to See a Man Hanged, 49–50
Great Hoggarty Diamond, The, 15, 16, 65, 83, 137
Heads of the People, 89
Henry Esmond, 9, 12, 20–1, 43, 45, 47, 50, 56, 70, 124, 145, 148, 154–61, 191
Hobson's Choice, 137
Interesting Event, An, 66

Irish Sketch-Book, The, 15, 16, 26–7, 37, 39, 47, 48, 70, 81, 166, 169–71, 175
Journey from Cornhill to Grand Cairo, Notes of a, 15, 117–18, 166–9, 175, 194
Kickleburys on the Rhine, The, 40, 42, 118–19, 137
Legend of the Rhine, A, 51
Little Dinner at Timmins's, A, 9, 55, 86, 137
Little Spitz, 83
Lovel the Widower, 22, 71, 89, 113–14, 141, 148
Meditations in Solitude, 61
Memorials of Gormandizing, 9, 10, 84
Men and Coats, 66
Men's Wives, 27, 39, 65, 82, 131
Miss Tickletoby's Lectures on English History, 29, 61
Mr. and Mrs. Frank Berry, 131
Mr. Brown's Letters to his Nephew, 23, 44, 48, 72
Mrs. Perkins's Ball, 42, 62
Newcomes, The, 14, 20, 21, 28, 32, 36, 38, 43–4, 46, 48, 50, 52, 56, 60, 62, 64, 66–7, 72, 76, 78–9, 83, 90–2, 100, 103, 107, 116–17, 126, 128, 131–132, 136, 138–9, 142–6, 161–5
Night's Pleasure, A, 26
On a Chalk Mark on the Door, 24
Our Street, 62, 128, 154
Paris Sketch-Book, The, 15, 39, 52, 82, 96, 105, 120–2, 141
Partie Fine, The, 65, 72, 94
Pendennis, 12, 16, 20, 21, 27–8, 31–2, 42–3, 45, 48, 50–2, 55–6, 58–62, 66–7, 71–2, 74, 85, 89–90, 98, 106–9, 113, 126, 135, 150–5
Philip, 22, 28–9, 31, 39, 43, 45–6, 51–2, 66–9, 76, 83, 101, 108, 128, 130, 137–8, 142–3, 146–7

Pictorial Rhapsody, A, 92
Picture Gossip, 72
Plan for a Prize Novel, A, 72
Professor, The, 15, 91
Ravenswing, The, 39, 48, 58, 65, 76, 83, 109–12, 133
Rebecca and Rowena, 61, 116, 120, 137
Rolandseck, 72
Rose and the Ring, The, 71, 91
Roundabout Papers, The, 39, 52–3, 89, 93, 108, 133, 148, 174
St. Philip's Day at Paris, A, 45
Second Funeral of Napoleon, The, 15, 23, 123–4
Shabby Genteel Story, A, 15, 26, 30–1, 40, 44, 55, 68, 83
Shrove Tuesday in Paris, 121
Strictures on Pictures, 82
Tremendous Adventures of Major Goliah Gahagan, The, 15, 71, 83, 91
Vanity Fair, 11, 12, 16, 17, 18, 20, 25–8, 32, 37, 39–41, 44, 50–1, 53–6, 59–65, 67, 69, 71–8, 86–9, 109–14, 116, 119–20, 125, 129, 136, 141, 143, 145, 150, 172–5, 177–202
Virginians, The, 9, 27, 29, 42, 46, 82, 89, 101, 109, 124, 133, 146, 157–8, 160–1, 191
Wolves and the Lamb, The, 113
Yellowplush Papers, The, 15, 29, 41, 44, 58, 61–2, 67, 137
Tillotson, Geoffrey, 10
Times, The, 15, 35
Tolstoy, Count Leo Nikolaevich, 97, 105, 109, 186, 189, 194
War and Peace, 177, 190–1
Town Talk, 22
trade-names, 71–2
Trollope, Anthony, 202–3
Turner, Joseph Mallord William, 36–7, 83
Twain, Mark (Samuel Langhorne Clemens), 166

vehicles, 69–71
Venables, George, 12–13
Veronese, Paul, 50
Vestris, Gaetano Appolino Baldassare, 105

Waldegrave, Countess, 18
Weimar, 14, 119–20
Weld, W. W., 25
Wells, H. G., 16
Woolf, Virginia, 84, 192

Yates, Edmund, 22, 158